Bc

PORT DEVELOPMENT IN THE UNITED STATES

Report prepared by the
Panel on Future Port Requirements of the United States
Maritime Transportation Research Board
Commission on Sociotechnical Systems
National Research Council

National Academy of Sciences
Washington, D.C.

1976

* * * * * *

This is a report of work supported by the Departments of Commerce, Defense, and Transportation under provisions of Contract N00014-75-C-0711 between the National Academy of Sciences and the Office of Naval Research.

* * * * * *

The National Research Council was established in 1916 by the National Academy of Sciences to associate the broad community of science and techno-logy with the Academy's purposes of furthering knowledge and of advising the federal government. The Council operates in accordance with general policies determined by the Academy by authority of its Congressional charter of 1863, which establishes the Academy as a private, non-profit, self-governing membership corporation. Administered jointly by the National Academy of Sciences, the National Academy of Engineering, and the Institute of Medicine (all three of which operate under the charter of the National Academy of Sciences), the Council is their principal agency for the conduct of their services to the government, the public, and the scientific and engineering communities.

International Standard Book Number 0-309-02448-X

Library of Congress Catalog Card Number 76-5180

Inquiries concerning this publication should be addressed to:
Executive Secretary
Maritime Transportation Research Board
National Research Council
2101 Constitution Avenue, N.W.
Washington, D. C. 20418

Available from
Printing and Publishing Office
National Academy of Sciences
2101 Constitution Avenue, N.W.
Washington, D. C. 20418

Printed in the United States of America

PANEL ON FUTURE PORT REQUIREMENTS

OF THE

UNITED STATES

Eric Schenker, *Chairman*
Professor of Economics
Senior Scientist, Center for
    Great Lakes Studies
Director of the Urban Research
    Center
The University of Wisconsin-Milwaukee

MEMBERS

Austin E. Brant, Jr.
Partner
Tippetts-Abbett-McCarthy-
    Stratton

R. H. Herman
Vice President-Logistics
Exxon Corporation

Harold M. Mayer
Professor of Geography and
    Associate Director
Center for Great Lakes Studies
University of Wisconsin

Stephen Moore
Professor, Department of
    Civil Engineering
Massachusetts Institute of
    Technology

J. Eldon Opheim
General Manager
Port of Seattle

Edward S. Reed
Executive Port Director
Port of New Orleans

Talmage E. Simpkins
Co-Director
Labor-Management Maritime
    Committee

John T. Starr, Jr.
Chairman, Department of
    Geography
University of Maryland
Baltimore County

LIAISON REPRESENTATIVES

R. Keith Adams
Acting Chief of Transpor-
    tation and Coastal Zone
    Branch
Department of the Army

Ernest T. Bauer*
Chief, Division of Ports
Office of Ports and Inter-
    modal Systems, Maritime
    Administration
Department of Commerce

---

*Deputy Director, Office of Deepwater Ports, Department
of Transportation (since August 15, 1975).

F. D. McGuire **
Deputy Assistant Commander
  for Facilities Planning
Naval Facilities Engineering
  Command
Department of the Navy

Peter Schumaier ***
Acting Chief, Economics &
  Special Projects Division
Office of Policy and Plans
  Development
Department of Transportation

William R. Riedel
Chairman, Ports & Waterways
  Planning Staff
U.S. Coast Guard Headquarters

* * * * * *

Leonard E. Bassil
Project Manager
Maritime Transportation
  Research Board

Virginia L. Allen
Staff Secretary
Maritime Transportation
  Research Board

* * * * * *

Panel members serve as individuals, contributing
their personal knowledge and judgment, and not as
representatives of any organization by which they
are employed or with which they may be associated.
Liaison representatives attend for their respective organizations to provide information or opinion
on issues under discussion, but have no vote on
conclusions and recommendations.

** Until July 1, 1975

*** Economic Policy Analyst, Office of Assistant Admini-
strator for Policy and Analysis, Federal Energy
Administration (since August 19, 1974).

iv

FOREWORD

This report is the culmination of a study conducted under the auspices of the Maritime Transportation Research Board of the National Academy of Sciences - National Research Council. The study was undertaken as part of a continuing program to provide advisory services to the federal government, aimed at improving the maritime transportation system of the United States. The study was made at the request of the MTRB's sponsors.

The question of future port requirements for the U.S. embraces a number of complex, interwoven issues, both institutional and technical, that affect private and public interests. Accordingly, an interdisciplinary panel was formed to examine the question. The areas of competence represented by the members of the Panel on Future Port Requirements are: transportation economics, port planning and operations, operations research, geography, civil engineering, marine environment, labor rate regulation, logistics, and federal policy. Dr. Eric Schenker, of the University of Wisconsin at Milwaukee, was selected as Chairman of the Panel. A three-man committee of the Board, comprising Howard Gauthier, Russell O'Neill, and C. R. Redlich, reviewed this report and accepted it for publication.

I extend my thanks to the Panel members and liaison representatives for their willingness to serve on the Panel and for their fine work. My thanks also go to the review committee and the Project Manager for their efforts on behalf of the Board.

Robert J. Pfeiffer, Chairman

January 1976
Washington, D.C.

PREFACE

The importance of foreign trade to the economic well-being of the United States has been brought forth dramatically to the American people over the last several years. The Soviet wheat sale; two devaluations of the dollar; shortages of steel, fertilizer, and other raw materials and finished products; and, of course, the oil embargo and price increases have created an interest in international economics that was formerly restricted to a relatively small number of specialists. The knowledge that the United States must export agricultural and manufactured products in order to pay for its imports has been coupled with an awareness that the nation is dependent on the rest of the world for a large proportion of the essential raw materials necessary to maintain a high standard of living. This keener understanding has underscored the role of maritime transportation and the importance of ports as vital links in the total transport system.

The ports of the United States have proved themselves capable of adjusting to the growth of the country's foreign and domestic trade. To cope with revolutionary changes in shipping technology, efficient new facilities have been built to handle the increased volume of cargo, operations have been improved and expanded, and new procedures have been created. However, as ports built new facilities, questions were raised regarding the need for large expenditures that might prove unprofitable in light of competition from other ports. At the same time, concern for the environment and coastal zone was growing, along with increased recognition of social programs, thus intensifying competition for scarce financial resources between ports and other public needs. At present, the effect of resource allocation, environmental concern, inflation, and federal legislation and regulation is an increase in the costs and decrease in the sources of funds of almost every port in the United States to the point where many may be unable to finance their expansion or improve their facilities.

The Panel on Future Port Requirements of the United States examined the patterns of growth and demand for ocean port services and identified issues and problems of national concern that result from port development and operations. The members reviewed the history of port development in the United States, the current status of the Nation's ports, and the environmental effects of port development and activities. We have attempted to place the problems and promise of ports in the United States in perspective and have recognized the necessity to develop a policy by which the nation's waterborne commerce will be moved efficiently, effectively, and economically. We have also recognized that environmental and economic considerations can and must be balanced for purposes of port development.

The Panel worked under the aegis of the Maritime Transportation Research Board as part of the Board's program to provide guidance toward improving the flow of waterborne commerce within the United States and between the nation and the rest of the world. Panel members served without compensation, as individuals contributing their personal knowledge and judgment, at the invitation of the National Academy of Sciences - National Research Council. Liaison representatives, on the other hand, are designated by their agencies, at the request of the National Research Council, to participate in panel discussions and to share information and the views of their respective organizations with the panel members. Liaison representatives do not have a vote during the panel's deliberations. Every member and liaison representative gave generously of his time, both in attendance at meetings and the writing of the report. Each is to be commended for his interest, commitment, and contribution to the panel's effort.

Eric Schenker

Eric Schenker, Chairman

January 1976
Washington, D.C.

viii

ACKNOWLEDGMENTS

The panel held 12 meetings, many of which were for fact-finding purposes. Eight ports were visited as the panel endeavored to determine directly the problems affecting the industry. We gratefully acknowledge the cooperation and assistance of the following individuals who made presentations and arranged port tours for the panel:

George Altvater
Port of Houston

Paul Amundsen
American Association of
    Port Authorities

Al Bienn
The Boeing Commercial
    Airplane Company

Michael Bunamo
The Port Authority of New
    York and New Jersey

Hazel Brown
Harry Lundeberg School of
    Seamanship

C. S. Devoy
Galveston Wharves

Robert Fletcher
Port of Seattle

Richard Gardner
Office of Coastal Zone
    Management
NOAA

Jerome Gilbert
The Port Authority of New
    York and New Jersey

Roger Gilman
The Port Authority of New
    York and New Jersey

David Glickman
The Port Authority of New
    York and New Jersey

Jerome Goldman
Friede and Goldman, Inc.

Henry Joffray
Port of New Orleans

Gene Jones
Galveston Wharves

Warren Lovejoy
The Port Authority of New
    York and New Jersey

Gene McCormack
Lykes Bros. Steamship
    Company

Hugh M. McLelland
Office of Sea Grant
NOAA

P. J. Mills
Superport Authority of the
    State of Louisiana

Clifford Muller
Port of Seattle

Frank Nolan
International Terminal
    Operating Company

Ben Nutter
Port of Oakland

Thomas Soules*
Port of Boston

Paul Osborne
The Boeing Commercial Airplane
  Airplane Company

Donald Taggart
Port of San Francisco

Pierre Reeh
Port of New Orleans

Frank Thrall
U.S. Coast Guard

John Savage
The Port Authority of New
  York and New Jersey

Arthur Yoshioka
Port of Seattle

    Also, we wish to give special credit to Benton
Goodenough of the Pacific Maritime Association for his
paper, "Technological Change in the West Coast Maritime
Industry," which he contributed to the panel.

*Now Director of the Port of San Francisco

CONTENTS

CHAPTER 1

INTRODUCTION

The Panel on Future Port Requirements of the United
States was formed by the Maritime Transportation Research
Board to examine the implications of technological change
and public policies on port functions such as planning,
development, and operations; to assess the impact of these
functions on ports, the localities in which they are
located, and those they serve; and to determine the interaction between port agencies and the federal government.
The panel sought to identify issues and problems of national concern resulting from port activities in order to
suggest ways of solving these problems and meeting future
port needs of the nation.

The panel has classified issues faced by U.S. ports
into four major categories: (a) decision-making on federal,
regional, state, and local levels; (b) measures of national,
regional, and local requirements; (c) institutional constraints; and (d) use of shorelines. Problems in these
areas come under the broad headings of finance, regulation,
legislation, manpower, and environment. The panel has
not established a formula by which the number, type, and
location of ports in the United States can be decided.
Rather, it has presented guidelines for determining port
investments, taking into consideration federal support
for port programs and activities.

The study has been conducted by the panel in three
parts:

    •••Major issues arising from current trends
       were identified and policy questions
       raised by these trends were specified.

···The present performance of commercial
functions by ports and the institutional
influences on ports were identified and
examined in terms of (a) the effects of
major internal variables such as labor
and commodity form and external forces
such as trade patterns, changing ship
technology, and the impact of competitive
modes of transport at work in the port
and its hinterland; (b) the federal
interest and role in ports; and (c) local,
state, and national needs related to port
development and operations.

···Future challenges resulting from the
interaction of forces influencing port
development were addressed and alternative
policy approaches were presented.

Background

In the late 1960s, containerization became a major
force in waterborne carriage of general cargo. The
technological problems of containerization had largely
been solved. However, the institutional problems caused
by the impact of containerization and the results of
technological change were unclear. Concern over the
implications of containerization grew as the maritime
industry and federal agencies were confronted with changing conditions, such as

···Alleged overbuilding of port facilities
for handling containers.

···Possible obsolescence of ports that did
not develop container-handling facilities.

···Increasing costs of maintaining and
dredging channels for ports, especially
for those smaller ports that might not
be economically viable.

···The role of the federal government in
coastal zone management, land-use planning,
and environmental programs that directly
affect port development.

...Reductions in work opportunities for
longshoremen as a result of greatly
increased productivity of containerized
cargo handling.

Other questions, directly concerned with the long-
held position that the ports were competitive and operated
in the spirit of free enterprise, were

...How many ports are needed in the United
States?

...What kinds of ports are needed--specialized
or multipurpose?

...Where should these ports be located?

...What is the division of responsibility
between the federal government and the
port industry?

...What is the relationship of port development to federal maritime policy in
general?

These issues disturbed the port industry and led
to a controversey between it, represented by the American
Association of Port Authorities (AAPA), and several
federal agencies. The central issue to this argument was
the question of the role of the federal government in port
planning and development. Several agencies had called
for comprehensive port studies on a national scale. The
AAPA opposed these studies because of a fear they would
lead to a National Port Plan and concomitant loss of local
control. No federal studies were undertaken, but the
questions raised by the dispute persist in the problems
caused by new technology. (For a review of the reports
that spurred the opposition of the port industry and
current AAPA attitudes, see Appendix A.)

Problems Affecting Ports

Ports in the United States are confronted with
problems of adapting to the world shipping revolution
caused by technological advances in maritime transportation. Containerization and the development of superships,
notably oil tankers or VLCCs (very large crude carriers),

have created a demand for services and facilities that
has placed a financial burden on ports.

Containerships of steadily increasing size and
speed affect general cargo trades and exert a demand for
new and more costly marine terminals and cargo-handling
facilities. Superships primarily affect the bulk cargo
trades, both dry and liquid; petroleum carriers of 500,000
deadweight tons and dry bulk ships now approaching 200,000
deadweight tons are evidence of the changes taking place.
The giant size of these new ships provides inherent cost
advantages through economies of scale. However, large
size also curtails flexibility on world trade routes.
These large ships pose problems for ports where their
draft exceeds existing channel depths. This is particularly
true of the VLCCs, which usually require more than 70 feet
of water under the keel—far more than any port in the
mainland United States can provide other than those in
Puget Sound. The new generation of ships influences port
channel depths, the development of high-value waterfront
land, and the construction of offshore berthing facilities.

Deepening and widening the channels, approaches,
and anchorages at all major ports in the United States
would be both physically impracticable and financially
prohibitive. Environmental considerations at large
population centers work against the deep-draft tanker,
new refining centers, ore smelters, and petrochemical
complexes. The ports of the nation face difficult choices
in terms of the environment, capital expenditures, and
national defense considerations.

Another problem related to technical progress in
the carriage and handling of general cargo is the compe-
titiveness among ports, which can bring duplication of
expensive facilities. In contrast to many foreign
countries, competition has always been a factor in the
United States port industry. Competition had led to the
introduction of new efficient cargo handling systems and
operational procedures and has given incentive for port
management to adapt to, and advance, technological progress.
Coincident with this progressive approach, however, are
large investments in land and money. These expenditures
might lead to wasteful competition that could result in
a dissipation of resources by ports as they attempt to
attract business.

The problem of competition is compounded because containerships are so expensive that economical operation precludes calls at numerous ports. To make the larger investment in containerships profitable, their potential for high productivity must be fully exploited. With a given load capacity, productivity of a ship can be increased by reducing voyage time. Voyage time is a function of speed at sea and time spent in port. Speed at sea is essentially a design function modified by such variables as sea-state, fuel costs, etc. Time spent in port can be reduced by making fewer port calls or by shorter turnaround time. The number of calls and turnaround time in port are not completely independent of one another because with fewer port calls, more cargo must be transferred at each stop. The additional cargo transfer may or may not require extra time in port, depending on the facilities available for moving it. Fewer port calls, therefore, will show the greatest net saving of time by eliminating additional sailing time, harbor transit and manuevering time, docking and undocking time, support activity to prepare for cargo handling, and readying for sea required for each additional port visit.

The trend, therefore, is to concentrate cargo and calls at a limited number of ports on a given coast. The question facing a port is whether to supply, at high cost, economical and efficient services to attract more traffic or to wait for a demand to develop. Generally the necessary investments are made in anticipation of the traffic. The potential for inefficient allocation of resources is great, but the prevailing view has been that competition is basic to the free enterprise system and has led to the strong port system in the United States.

A matter of major concern is the dredging and maintenance of adequate channels to handle traffic demands. The federal government, through its power to withhold or extend authorization and funding for channel projects, is capable of directly influencing port development and port use. Because funds are limited, there is an inherent tendency to promote a selective policy toward ports that appear to be economically successful, to the detriment of marginal ports. Implicit in this discussion is the two-fold question: Should a public policy for ports be established by the federal government that will determine the number, type, and location of ports in the United States, or should the principle of competition and independence from federal involvement and control be the guiding factor?

In addition to the delicate questions surrounding the allocation of resources, competition, and federal control, the ports in larger population centers are becoming increasingly involved with social considerations. Water pollution, recreational use of waterfront land, threats to wildlife and fisheries, redevelopment of waterside areas, rapid transit, freeway systems, and urban renewal all impinge on port development and demand attention. The conflicting demands may require new multistate or intrastate agencies to deal with jurisdictional, political, and financial problems of local, state, and national authority and responsibility.

Regional ports or new deep-draft offshore terminals also raise important jurisdictional, economic, and financial questions. If the ideal locations are remote and undeveloped, should new highway and utility systems and industrial complexes be designed to serve each new development? Will the expected transportation economies be nullified by costs for land acquisition, environmental controls, highways, and new utility systems?

The Port's Role in the Economy

The tonnage of waterborne exports and imports in U.S. foreign trade totalled more than 631 million long tons in 1973, as shown in Table 1. This was an increase of about 204 million tons from 1969, or a 48 per cent gain. Much of the gain can be attributed to the carriage of liquid and dry bulk commodities, but it must be noted that high-value general cargo commodities increased by 25 per cent from 1969 to 1973. The value of the cargo carried in the Nation's oceanborne trade is also significant. From 1969 to 1973 the total value of exports and imports doubled, from $41.9 billion to $84 billion, as shown in Table 2. The value of general cargo was $49.6 billion for 1973. The total value of all U.S. exports and imports for 1973 was approximately $140 billion.[1] Of this total, U.S. ports handled approximately 60 per cent. According to the Bureau of Census, the value of U.S. foreign trade in 1974 was approximately $199 billion; 60 per cent of the value of foreign commerce handled by ports is almost $120 billion. (The preliminary figures for 1974, shown in Table 2, show the waterborne foreign trade value to be $124 billion.)

---

[1] U.S. Department of Commerce, Bureau of Census, *Summary of U.S. Export and Import Merchandise Trade,* Jan. 1975.

TABLE 1 -- TONNAGE OF COMMERCIAL CARGO CARRIED IN U.S. OCEANBORNE FOREIGN TRADE
(In Thousands of Long Tons)

Year	Total Exports and Imports			Exports			Imports		
	Total	U.S. Flag	U.S. (percent)	Total Exports	U.S. Flag	U.S. (percent)	Total Imports	U.S. Flag	U.S. (percent)
1969	427,479	19,785	4.6	159,160	10,888	6.8	268,319	8,897	3.3
1970	473,246	25,230	5.3	193,557	12,366	6.4	279,689	12,864	4.6
1971	457,434	24,376	5.3	163,456	10,812	6.6	293,978	13,564	4.6
1972	513,566	23,764	4.6	185,103	11,110	6.0	327,463	12,654	3.9
1973	631,572	39,903	6.3	226,003	14,488	6.4	405,569	25,415	6.3
1974*	628,726	41,006	6.5	220,390	13,342	6.1	408,336	27,664	6.8
Liner Service									
1969	41,912	9,709	23.1	23,546	5,479	23.3	18,366	4,230	23.0
1970	50,387	11,817	23.5	29,234	6,905	23.6	21,153	4,912	23.2
1971	44,209	10,129	22.9	22,730	5,328	23.4	21,479	4,801	22.3
1972	44,641	9,798	21.9	22,855	5,340	23.4	21,786	4,458	20.5
1973	51,244	13,216	25.8	28,278	7,822	27.7	22,966	5,394	23.5
1974*	52,970	15,589	29.4	29,540	8,835	29.9	23,430	6,754	28.8
Non-Liner Service									
1969	212,036	4,589	2.2	120,693	3,927	3.3	91,343	662	0.7
1970	240,723	5,364	2.2	146,625	3,664	2.5	94,098	1,700	1.8
1971	220,741	4,792	2.1	126,027	3,905	3.0	94,714	887	0.9
1972	242,564	3,795	1.6	146,267	2,909	2.0	96,297	886	0.9
1973	281,910	4,535	1.6	178,249	3,084	1.7	103,661	1,451	1.4
1974*	281,518	4,909	1.7	171,088	2,158	1.3	110,430	2,751	2.5
Tanker Service									
1969	173,531	5,487	3.2	14,921	1,482	9.9	158,610	4,055	2.5
1970	182,136	8,049	4.4	17,698	1,797	10.2	164,438	6,252	3.8
1971	192,484	9,455	4.9	14,699	1,579	10.7	177,785	7,876	4.4
1972	226,361	10,171	4.5	16,981	2,861	16.8	209,380	7,310	3.5
1973	298,418	22,152	7.4	19,476	3,582	18.4	278,942	18,570	6.7
1974*	294,238	20,508	7.0	19,762	2,349	11.9	274,476	18,159	6.6

*Preliminary

SOURCE: Office of Subsidy Administration, Division of Trade Studies and Statistics, U.S. Maritime Administration

TABLE 2 -- VALUE OF COMMERCIAL CARGO CARRIED IN U.S. OCEANBORNE FOREIGN TRADE
(In Millions of Dollars Value)

Year	Total Exports and Imports			Exports			Imports		
	Total	U.S. Flag	U.S. (percent)	Total Exports	U.S. Flag	U.S. (percent)	Total Imports	U.S. Flag	U.S. (percent)
1969	41,877	8,067	19.3	19,972	4,277	21.4	21,905	3,790	17.3
1970	49,682	10,273	20.7	24,488	5,148	21.0	25,194	5,130	20.4
1971	50,425	9,886	19.6	22,653	4,485	19.7	27,772	5,401	19.4
1972	60,529	11,119	18.4	25,592	4,794	18.7	34,937	6,325	18.1
1973	84,006	15,900	18.9	39,922	7,171	18.0	44,084	8,729	19.8
1974*	124,237	22,058	17.8	55,947	10,154	18.1	68,290	11,904	17.4
Liner Service									
1969	27,216	7,448	27.4	13,496	3,813	28.3	13,720	3,635	26.5
1970	33,519	9,652	28.8	16,446	4,740	28.8	17,073	4,192	28.8
1971	32,399	9,203	28.4	14,858	4,061	27.3	17,541	5,142	29.3
1972	37,383	10,348	27.7	16,008	4,291	26.8	21,375	6,057	28.3
1973	49,640	14,425	29.1	22,220	6,458	29.1	27,420	7,967	29.1
1974*	63,687	19,474	30.6	30,910	9,317	30.1	32,777	10,157	31.0
Non-Liner Service									
1969	11,068	433	3.9	5,483	365	6.7	5,585	68	1.2
1970	12,162	401	3.3	6,805	302	4.4	5,357	99	1.8
1971	13,167	412	3.1	6,597	328	4.9	6,570	84	1.2
1972	17,397	417	2.4	8,268	310	3.7	9,129	107	1.2
1973	25,216	638	2.5	15,773	465	2.9	9,443	173	2.4
1974*	34,571	804	2.3	21,321	545	2.6	13,250	259	2.0
Tanker Service									
1969	3,593	186	5.2	993	99	10.0	2,600	87	3.3
1970	4,001	225	5.6	1,237	106	8.6	2,764	119	4.3
1971	4,859	271	5.5	1,198	96	8.0	3,661	175	4.7
1972	5,749	354	6.2	1,316	193	14.7	4,433	161	3.6
1973	9,150	837	9.1	1,929	248	12.9	7,221	589	8.2
1974*	25,979	1,780	6.9	3,716	292	7.9	22,263	1,488	6.7

*Preliminary

SOURCE: Office of Subsidy Administration, Division of Trade Studies and Statistics, U.S. Maritime Administration

In addition to being an important element in the nation's foreign trade, ports are significant contributors to the economies of the cities and regions in which they are located. According to a recent study by the Federal Maritime Administration, the port industry, in 1972, handled over 1.6 billion tons of cargo, generated over $30 billion in direct dollar income, provided jobs for over 1.2 million people, and contributed over $1.1 billion to the balance of payments account.[2]

To handle the huge tonnages involved in the country's waterborne commerce, the port industry has invested over $3.2 billion in facilities since 1966. The Maritime Administration, on the basis of a recent survey, estimates that U.S. port capital expenditures for the 5-year period from 1973 to 1977 will be approximately $1.5 billion.[3] Table 3 shows the cost distribution by type of facility. The magnitude of these investments in facilities under- lines the importance that states and localities place on port development. Fund raising will be difficult, given the growing competition for the use of public funds and alternative uses for waterfront property. In addition, stringent environmental constraints could delay the exe- cution of port plans and increase costs.

Port Issues

In this report, the Panel on Future Port Require- ments focuses on the specific topics of port planning and development and the role of the federal government in the process. It reviews the history of port development in the United States, describes the nature of the port in- dustry, and discusses the character of the responsibility for various aspects of port planning and development.

---

[2] U.S. Department of Commerce, Maritime Administration, *A Survey of Public Port Financing*, U.S. Government Printing Office, Washington, June 1974, p. 1.

[3] U.S. Department of Commerce, Maritime Administration, *North Atlantic Port Development Expenditure Survey*, U.S. Government Printing Office, Washington, March 1974, p. 8.

TABLE 3 -- PROPOSED NORTH AMERICAN PORT CAPITAL EXPENDITURES BY REGION AND FACILITY TYPE (1973-1977)

Region	Conventional General Cargo	% of Regional/ National Total	Specialized General Cargo (Container, RO/RO, Barge-ship)	% of Regional/ National Total	Liquid & Dry Bulk Cargo	% of Regional/ National Total	Total Regional/National	% of Grand Total
North Atlantic	$119,367,500	33%	$229,993,000	64%	$ 5,800,000	2%	$ 355,160,500	20%
South Atlantic	53,471,665	47%	55,086,665	48%	5,064,094	5%	113,622,424	7%
Gulf Coast	52,199,109	8%	45,786,233	8%	496,596,186	84%	594,581,528	34%
Pacific Coast	77,489,100	21%	219,096,600	60%	71,453,000	19%	368,038,700	21%
Alaska, Hawaii & Puerto Rico	22,323,000	62%	7,642,000	22%	5,741,000	16%	35,706,000	3%
U.S. Great Lakes	7,432,622	42%	4,066,666	24%	5,842,000	34%	17,341,288	2%
U.S. Total	332,282,996	23%	516,671,164	38%	590,496,280	39%	1,484,450,440	87%
Canada	36,038,000	16%	133,416,000	60%	51,050,000	24%	220,504,000	13%
Grand Total North America	368,320,996	21%	695,087,164	41%	641,546,280	38%	1,704,995,440	100%

SOURCE: A North American Port Development Expenditure Survey, Maritime Administration--U.S. Department of Commerce, March 1974

With regard to safety, the panel decided that this is an all-encompassing subject that would require a major study effort and was beyond the scope of the panel's charge. Many studies have been conducted and are ongoing relating to the carriage of hazardous cargoes, the environmental and safety aspects of oil carriage by supertankers, and communication and control of ship traffic in congested waters. This knowledge reinforced further the panel's decision not to consider the issue of safety in the study.

During its deliberations, the panel addressed the problems of the port industry in terms of the following policy issues:

1. Should there be concern for the scale and character of future ports in the United States nationally or regionally? A parallel issue is: Who should be concerned, and who would best be equipped to make the investigations that would throw light on the future requirements?

2. Should the present policy of "no policy" regarding financing, construction, and operating ports be continued? In other words, is it, or is it not, desirable to continue free competition among ports, with survival of the fittest? Should dredging continue as a federal activity? Would shippers and the general public benefit to the greatest extent by a national policy, with federal control or direction of attempting to balance the supply and demand of port facilities, or would it be better to continue the present competitive relations?

3. Since rate structures and practices largely determine the ports to be used, or, indeed, whether a movement will take place at all, should the inland components of intermodal movements be regulated in the same manner as domestic movements, and by the same agencies, or should some alternative policy be initiated? Or should there be no regulation of international intermodal movements?

4. In determining federal environmental
   policy regarding port development and
   port operation, how is the balance
   to be found between the economic and
   other benefits of ports on the one
   hand and the environmental constraints
   on the other?

5. In estimating future port requirements,
   one important set of variables is the
   short-run effects of decreased, or at
   least changed, labor requirements at
   the ports. To what extent, and how,
   should public agencies develop policies
   to cushion the effects of a labor
   surplus? Should this problem be subsumed in the general national policies
   of dealing with technological unemployment, or should the problem be separately
   identified and handled?

Discussion of these policy issues has resulted in
a series of recommendations that the panel anticipates
will assist port agencies, all levels of government, and
the general public in their attempts to solve problems
and meet future challenges facing the port system in the
United States. The intent of the study is to supply a
conceptual framework within which those parties concerned
with the port industry can determine their respective
roles in the planning, developing, and financing of port
facilities.

technical

CHAPTER II

TECHNOLOGICAL CHANGE AND PORT DEVELOPMENT

Since World War II, and especially in the past decade, maritime transportation technology has been changing at an unprecedented rate. Not since the replacement of sails by steam in the nineteenth century has shipping been subject to such a radical change. In liquid bulk transport, the supertanker has produced significant cost savings in economies of scale. In transport of dry bulk commodities, the increase in ship size and the consequent savings in transportation costs have been scarcely less spectacular. In the movement of general cargo, the technological revolution has been even greater with the widespread development of containerization, roll-on-roll-off (RoRo) ships, and barge-carrying ships such as LASH and Seabee. Complementing these revolutionary changes, land transportation of goods has also undergone significant technological change through the following:

- Creation of the Interstate Highway System and analogous systems in other countries;

- Development of long-distance trucking and pipelines;

- Growth of inland waterway transportation in the United States and Western Europe;

- Establishment of COFC (container on flatcar) and TOFC (trailer on flatcar), or "piggyback," to take advantage of scale economies in water and rail transportation over long distances and the flexibility of the truck; and

••Development of barge-carrying ships
combining inland water transportation
and ocean carriage.

These developments indicate the need for efficient
planning and operation at the interfaces between modes
to ensure the fast turnaround of ships, which produce no
economic return while they are loading and discharging.
As the efficiency and speed of movement between terminals
improves, the need for comparable efficiences in the
operation of terminals increases. No longer is it practical for general cargo liner vessels, for example, to spend
more than half of their lifetimes in port; the construction
and operation costs of ships are much too great to permit
extended idle time. The increasing tempo of economic
activity generally points to the necessity for minimizing
delays for goods in transit.

Technological changes in transportation, together
with large costs for the "hardware" of modern transportation systems and the need for effective utilization of
the transport plant and the labor force, dictate the
necessity for developing efficient ports. Evidence that
ports in the United States have adjusted to the changing
demands of modern transportation is apparent in the
functional, technological, and locational obsolescence of
many older and traditional ports. The organization and
operations of ports also are undergoing rapid change. Substantial expenditures have recently been made for channels
to accommodate large deep-draft ships and for waterfront
and back-up landward facilities for moving cargo to, from,
and within ports.

The rapid pace of technological change in transportation, the resultant shifts of traffic flows, and the
associated problems of the ports and their hinterlands
all point to the need for reexamination of the traditional
policies and practices of port development and operation
at national, regional, and local levels. Added to these
forces are the problems related to the environment, the
energy crisis, a new social awareness, and urban decay.
Ports cannot be planned, developed and operated independently of the regions on which they depend for traffic
and for which they serve as gateways. They also cannot
be considered independently of their relations to their
immediate vicinities because of their effects on employment
and the local economic base. In addition, demands for

land--particularly shore land, an increasingly scarce
resource--commonly involve the ports in competition with
other land uses.

The United States has never had a national port
plan, and no commercial port or group of ports has ever
been under complete control of the national government.
The port industry, historically, has been decentralized.
Individual ports compete with each other for the available
traffic. This competition reflects the American traditions
of free enterprise and local control. At the same time,
the ports of the united States have received from federal
agencies many benefits directly related to their development and operation. The navigable rivers and harbors,
with very few exceptions, are maintained and improved
under congressional authorization by the U.S. Army Corps
of Engineers. In no other nation is the improvement and
maintenance of navigable channels within harbors a central
concern of the national government while the building and
operation of terminal facilities remains a decentralized
local concern.

Railroads and Port Development

Before the opening of the West, American ports did
not compete with one another. Land transportation was
difficult and costly, while communication by water was
cheaper and more efficient. Consequently, the colonies
and later the Atlantic seaboard states relied on water
transportation not only for contact overseas but also for
exchanges with each other through coastwise shipping and
inland waterways. Since each of the coastal regions de-
pended on specialized production and exports for its
economic base, ports were essential. Each port developed
its own connections with the hinterland, first by road
and inland waterway, later by canals and railroads. Because of the difficulties of inland transportation, the
hinterlands of the various coastal ports rarely overlapped.

Following the American Revolution, the nation
turned its attention to the westward expansion of its
frontiers. At the same time its commercial ships traded
in every ocean. The Atlantic seaboard states, although
abandoning their territorial claims to the lands west of
the Appalachians, competed intensely for the trade of the
advancing frontier. Each New England port developed a
specialized commerce overseas. Boston, with its excellent
harbor, became the dominant New England port in the

region.[4] However, all New England ports, including Boston, were handicapped by their peripheral location in competing for the traffic of the territory outside of New England itself. Nevertheless, Boston sought to overcome this locational disadvantage by constructing railroads to the west; by 1835 it had a line to Worcester.

A few years later, the system pierced the barrier of the Berkshires, connecting with the railroads through the Mohawk Valley to the Great Lakes. The first regularly scheduled transatlantic steamship service, the Cunard line, started with Boston as the western terminal in 1840. By 1847 the route was extended to New York in order to tap the superior hinterland connections of that city.

New York rapidly became the leading port of the United States. Long before the coming of the transatlantic steamship services, it was served by regularly scheduled sailing ships. New York's excellent harbor, its location at the apex of the cotton triangle between the American South and northern Europe, its proximity to New England, and its location on the "water level" route inland via the Hudson and Mohawk River valleys to the Great Lakes and interior lowlands combined to favor the rapid growth of the Port of New York.[5] At first, New York's principal access route to its hinterland was the Hudson River. The Erie Canal, opened in 1825, provided an all-water route, although seasonal, between New York and the Great Lakes hinterland as well as to the developing area of upstate New York. However, when New York secured two all-rail connections to Lake Erie, passenger traffic and a substantial proportion of goods traffic shifted to the railroads. In the following year, New York and Chicago were connected by two all-rail routes.

The ports south and southwest of New York along the Atlantic seaboard had no water-level route nor could they develop an all-water route to the Western hinterland. Thus, they sought to compensate for their geographical handicaps by energetically developing their own transportation facilities across the Appalachians. Philadelphia entered the competition with New York in 1826, when the Pennsylvania

[4] Morison, Samuel Eliot, *The Maritime History of Massachusetts, 1838-1860*, Sentry edition, Houghton Mifflin Co., Boston, 1961, p. 421.

[5] Albion, Robert Greenhalgh, *The Rise of New York Port, 1815-1860*, Charles Scribner's Sons, New York, 1939, p. 485

legislature authorized a canal, later succeeded by a system of canals, inclined planes, and short railroads. This system, in turn, was converted into an all-rail route between Philadelphia and Pittsburgh. Meanwhile, Baltimore entered competition in 1827 by building the Baltimore and Ohio Railroad. It reached the Ohio River at Wheeling, West Virginia, in January 1853, and the line was eventually extended to Chicago and St. Louis.

More southerly ports also sought inland connections, not to the Midwest, but rather to the interior South. Richmond, for a while, was important, but its inland connection did not compensate for the inadequate channel in the James River when larger ocean-going ships became common. The dominant ports of the southern region became those of Hampton Roads, at the entrance of Chesapeake Bay, and Charleston, South Carolina. Hampton Roads became prominent when the Norfolk and Western, Chesapeake and Ohio, and the Virginia (since absorbed into the Norfolk and Western), the so-called Pocahontas railroads, reached the coalfields of southwestern Virginia and West Virginia. Charleston became the leading southeastern port with the opening of one of America's first railroads; the Charleston and Hamburg, now a part of the Southern system.

On the Gulf Coast, railroad penetration into the interior came somewhat later than on the Atlantic seaboard, primarily because the Mississippi River system furnished easy waterway transportation. The Civil War, however, interrupted North-South river traffic, and led to increasing importance of the railroads. New Orleans, on the Mississippi delta, dominated the North-South trade and was the major port for the Gulf of Mexico. However, with the decline of steamboat traffic on the rivers, New Orleans relied increasingly upon its railroad connections between St. Louis and Chicago. Other Gulf ports such as Tampa, Gulfport, Mobile, and Port Arthur, although without major inland waterway routes to the interior, were in large measure developed by particular railroads.

Railroad penetration from both the Atlantic and Gulf coasts into the overlapping Midwestern hinterland during the latter half of the nineteenth century brought all of the Atlantic and Gulf ports into competition. The ports competed with each other within the coastal ranges and between the two coasts. With increasing predominance of scheduled cargo-liner services in the ocean trades to these ports, shippers in the interior were offered competitive rates from both coasts. For decades, the ports sought to attract traffic by offering the maximum possible number of steamship services as well as by competing for rate advantages on the overland portions of the movements. The major ports on each coast had advantages which the "outports" sought to overcome by equalization of the combined rail-water rates between inland and overseas points through rail rate differentials. Thus, on the North Atlantic range, Philadelphia, Baltimore and Hampton Roads enjoyed rail rates to and from many Midwestern points which were 2 or 3 per cent below those rates applied through New York. Boston, to overcome its peripheral location, had inland rates on import and export traffic that were equal to those through New York.

With inland rates to and from the ports fixed, each of the railroads involved in international traffic sought to attract to the respective port or ports it served the maximum number and frequency of liner services, in order to compete effectively. To maximize their bulk commodity traffic, the railroads tried to attract unscheduled ships, or tramp services, to the ports they served. To accomplish these ends, each of the railroads sought to develop and operate its own port terminal facilities. They offered not only incentives of good and expeditious service through the terminals, but inducements such as free or low-cost berthage to ships that provided traffic to the railroad.

Thus, many of the major coastal ports had terminals which were railroad owned and railroad operated. In the Port of New York, such terminals were typically located west of the Hudson River; the railroads offered free lighterage service between such terminals and ocean-going vessels in other parts of the harbor. Many piers along the periphery of Manhattan and in Brooklyn were railroad piers, served by lighters and car-floats that connected with the terminals of the railroads on the west side of the harbor. The result was a plethora of terminals, with much cross-hauling within the port district, and proliferation of competitive piers on the waterfronts.

World War I demonstrated the inefficiency of such an arrangement, with cargoes backed up on the railroads far into the continental interior awaiting passage through the ports. Eventually the federal government had to assume control of the railroads. Subsequently, the Port of New

York Authority (now the Port Authority of New York and
New Jersey) was created by interstate compact between the
states of New York and New Jersey to develop a more
rational internal pattern of port development and operation.[6]
At other major ports, the railroads also sought competitive
advantages by operating waterfront terminals. The situation was described by a noted authority on ports in the
1920s:

> With the exception of New York, port
> development in the United States has
> been of one railroad, by one railroad,
> to serve one railroad. The waterfront,
> the railroad pier, and even the line
> of ships berthing at the pier have all
> come to be considered by the railroad
> as a part of its own private system....
> When the rate structure solidified...
> the only competition left between the
> railroads was the competition at the
> terminals. The effect of this compe-
> tition at the terminals for maritime
> freight has been to disrupt American
> ports into as many disconnected sec-
> tions as there are railroad terminals
> at the port. The result has been
> disastrous to American port development.[7]

Many relics of that era survive today, principally
in the form of finger piers and slips. This configuration
was designed to provide maximum contact between the water
areas and the land so that the ships could be accommodated,
while the railroad yards were located nearby. Congestion
of vehicular traffic on the marginal roads and on the
streets leading to the waterfront, as well as at the land-

---

[6] New York, New Jersey Port and Harbor Development Com-
mission, *Joint Report with Comprehensive Plan and
Recommendations*, New York, 1920, p. 495, also: Bird,
Frederick L., *A Study of the Port of New York Authority*,
Dun & Bradstreet, Inc., New York, 1948, p. 191.

[7] MacElwee, Roy S., *Port Development*, McGraw-Hill Book
Co., New York, 1926, p. 273.

ward ends of the piers, was excessive. Expansion of
back-up areas was commonly inhibited because the port
terminals were built in an era when much of the traffic
originated and terminated in the commercial and industrial
establishments near the cores of the cities. Horse-drawn
drays were limited in operating distance between local
origin and destination points and piers. Commonly, waterfront marginal streets also had railroad tracks, causing
intolerable confusion between street traffic and railroad
switching. Transfer of cargoes between ship and shore,
between pier and warehouse, and between ships and railroad cars and drays, was labor-intensive. The basic
methods of cargo transfer had not significantly changed
since ancient times.

Mechanization of Cargo Handling

Large-scale mechanization of cargo handling began
a generation or two ago. Bulk commodities characterized
by continuous flow could be handled by gravity, suction,
conveyor belts, tubes, and other devices. The result
was that many cargoes formerly handled as discrete items
were increasingly handled in bulk. Petroleum, originally
handled in drums, started moving in tankers by the beginning of the twentieth century. Grain and other commodities,
formerly handled in bags, increasingly were transferred
and shipped in bulk. It was not until the 1940s, however,
that sugar became a bulk cargo rather than a general
cargo. In short, scale economies derived from treating
a standardized commodity as a continuous flow were applied
to an ever-expanding list of cargoes.

Mechanization of general cargo sought to reproduce
economies of scale, achieved earlier in bulk cargo handling,
by creating a continuous flow of identical or nearly
identical packages that could be handled as a unit. The
first step, which was widespread during World War II, was
to stack boxes and other items on wooden or metal plat-
forms, or "pallets," move them by forklift vehicles, and
transfer them between ship and shore as units rather than
as individual items. The transfer of cargo, however, was
still labor-intensive; and turnaround, or in-port time, for
a general cargo liner was typically 10 days or more. Some
cargo, especially in the coastwise trades that survived
World War II, was handled horizontally through side
is, hand trucks, and tractors. These
ere labor-intensive and slow.

technical

Changes Affecting Ports

Since World War II, many changes have been made
in the basic physical and operational patterns of port
facilities and their locations, rendering most of the
general cargo piers obsolete in both location and design
and creating demands for new facilities and new locations.
At the same time, new forms of port organization and
management have become necessary. These trends were
evident even before the advent of the supertanker, the
containership, the RoRo vessel, and the barge-carrying
ship.

The character and location of port facilities were
also changed by the rapid growth of local and intercity
motor trucking, the expansion of express highway systems,
the development of TOFC and COFC railroad services,
initiation of the unit-train for movement of bulk commodities, and the growth of pipelines for bulk liquid
transportation. Along with these developments, the changing physical structure of the cities was also a force
shaping port requirements.

Ports, especially commercial and diversified ports,
create a multiplier effect. They set in motion a chain
of economic activities that, in turn, creates demands for
additional employment and additional land areas for port-
dependent commercial and industrial establishments. These
demands create further needs for land for residential,
recreational, and service uses needed by the population
deriving its support from port-based activities. Many
commercial, manufacturing, and warehousing activities
require extensive land areas for easy access by rail and
truck and, in some instances, by air as well. They also
need uninterrupted land areas for straight-line production
and for single-story buildings capable of carrying heavy
floor loads. Many such businesses have moved to outlying
locations on the urban periphery and to the suburbs.
Heavy industries also require extensive land areas for
expansion, areas generally not available in the central
parts of cities. Thus, the old general-cargo pier
areas along the downtown waterfronts and the commercial
and industrial activities that constitute the origins
and destinations of the port's cargo, have separated.
Furthermore, movements originating and terminating beyond
the metropolitan areas of the ports can be handled much
more effectively on the landward side if the warehouses,
transit sheds, classification yards, intercity truck

facilities, and highway approaches are located in areas peripheral to the cities, where land is less expensive and more readily available for development.

As the locations of the port terminals became obsolete, new waterfront and landward areas for terminals and associated facilities had to be absorbed closer to the urban periphery. Generally, new ports tend to be located seaward of the older clusters, partly because of the deeper channels required by the larger ships and partly to reduce transit time between the terminals and open water. Where water intervened between the older cities and the port hinterlands, new terminal areas tended to develop on the landward sides of the port areas. For example, port activity has moved to the New Jersey side of the New York port district and to Oakland on the landward side of San Francisco Bay. Meanwhile, the older terminal areas, centrally located with respect to the cities, deteriorated. Later, some of them became prime prospects for large-scale urban renewal. In a few instances, such areas remained under the jurisdiction of the public port authorities, which could derive substantial revenues from the sale or lease of the valuable waterfront land no longer required for port purposes.

Containerization

Within less than a decade, the container has revolutionized transportation of general cargo on virtually all of the world's major ocean routes. Intense competition among ports for available and prospective cargoes has forced the ports to provide, if they expect to be successful, highly efficient services, frequent and regular seaward and landward schedules, and fast turnaround for vessels and cargoes. The tremendous increase in capacity and speed of containerships represents a significant increase in prospective cargo flow through the port. The need for increased capacity has resulted in a demand for more land adjacent to the port terminals, for mechanization of the terminals themselves, for better landward connections by rail and highway, for deeper, wider, and straighter approach channels, and for marginal wharves to replace centrally located but obsolete finger piers in some ports. Furthermore, to justify large investments in channels, land, sophisticated and expensive cargo handling equipment, and the ships themselves, it became necessary to concentrate traffic in relatively few but highly efficient ports. As a result, load centers (ports of great capacity) are now developing. Because of their efficiency, these load centers can attract traffic from ever-widening hinterlands and from less competitive ports on the same and other coasts.

To concentrate cargoes at the high-capacity load centers, the "mini-bridge" has developed. Traffic to and from hinterland origins and destinations is transported overland, or in a few instances by coastal feeder vessel services, to the load centers, even though other ports may be closer. Some mini-bridge movements may be transcontinental, with traffic between the Pacific Coast and Europe handled through Gulf or Atlantic Coast ports. Transpacific traffic originating along the Atlantic seaboard and on the Gulf Coast is transhipped at Pacific Coast ports rather than moved by all-water routes through the Panama Canal. The ultimate is the "landbridge," which is the transcontinental movement of cargoes that neither originate nor terminate in North America but are transported overland by railroads or trucks between Atlantic and Pacific Coast ports. In many instances, overall transit times by mini-bridge or landbridge are comparable with the all-water routes via the Panama Canal or around Africa and prospectively through a restored Suez Canal. Costs to the shipper are competitive.

The mini-bridge service has come under sharp attack from the International Longshoremen's Association and port management on the East and Gulf Coasts. Charges have been brought before the Federal Maritime Commission (FMC) stating that the diversion of "naturally tributary" cargo does serious financial damage to ports that have invested hundreds of millions of dollars in cargo-handling facilities. It is also claimed that the mini-bridge has been devised as a technique to evade the container rules of the ILA and is a threat to labor stability. On the other hand, those who are benefitting from the mini-bridge service argue that ports should not be allowed to use regulatory channels to force steamship companies to provide direct service deemed less economical or efficient than overland transshipment. As of the end of 1975 the FMC continued to accept mini-bridge tariffs while investigating this controversial rail-water system.

In terms of scale economies, the containerships have their landward counterparts in container trains, unit trains, and semitrailer and "double bottom" trucks operating on express highways. In a few cases, the land bridge and mini-bridge include air links across the continent ("sea-air"), with at least one instance of a joint tariff involving a transpacific steamship line and a domestic airline.

Containerships represent investments that must be amortized at the rate of many thousands of dollars per day. As a result, containerships cannot economically serve ports that do not offer very substantial volumes of cargo and that do not permit rapid turnaround. Consequently, some of the most important routes are served by a limited number of ports; in some instances only one at each end. Philadelphia on the Atlantic Coast and Portland on the Pacific Coast have had a substantial proportion of their general cargo traffic diverted because their location is unfavorable for rapid turnaround of containerships and because they are located in the shadow of larger nearby ports that have been able to attract the preponderant volumes of traffic. New York and Baltimore have taken much of Philadelphia's traffic and Seattle has done the same to Portland. Smaller ports, such as Sacramento, California, have container services by all-water routes in which feeder vessels transport the containers to the load centers.

An important example of the effects of containerization on a trade route is the decline of general cargo movements between Great Lakes ports and overseas. Much of the cargo is carried overland to the major coastal ports in the United States and Canada, which are connected with the Great Lakes region by numerous railroads and express highways over which containerized loads can be quickly transported. One foreign-flag operator has a feeder service between Montreal and the Great Lakes with small all-container vessels on time-charter. That service has been moderately successful, but it has been able to capture only a limited share of the total available cargo for the Great Lakes-overseas trade in competition with overland services. Inevitably, the St. Lawrence Seaway will continue to be primarily a waterway for transportation of bulk commodities, but in the bulk trades, a decreasing proportion of the world's oceangoing bulk vessels are

physically or economically capable of transiting the
Seaway into the Great Lakes.[8]

The rapid move to containerization of cargo had
made a high proportion of conventional break-bulk ships,
carrying miscellaneous general-cargo as discrete items,
obsolete. Since containerships are much faster, turn
around in port much more quickly, and are substantially
larger than the break-bulk vessels, one containership may
effectively replace four or five conventional vessels.
Relatively new break-bulk ships, including some not more
than 5 years old, have been laid up or scrapped. Others
have been converted into containerships for service until
the operators can replace them with vessels designed for
container traffic.

Replacement of smaller conventional break-bulk
ships by containerships has produced notable effects on
the physical patterns of the ports they serve, changing
the emphasis from providing docks to that of providing
upland areas for marshalling containers. The advantages
of high speed and large capacity would be largely lost if
turnaround time in port were not very much less than for
break-bulk ships. Fewer ships that spend less time in
port need less contact area between water and land in the
ports, since the need to accommodate large numbers of

---

[8] In April 1975 the Maritime Administration initiated a
Great Lakes-Overseas Marine Transportation Market
assessment study to determine the possibility of re-
vitalizing general cargo services from Great Lakes
ports. The study will attempt to define the potential
for general cargo traffic movements and develop a
marketing strategy and operational plan to attract
U.S.-flag operators to the service. In addition, three
33,000 DWT container/bulk carriers of a design compatible with the competitive and physical environment
of the St. Lawrence Seaway have been proposed to
serve the Great Lakes-European trade, contingent on
both construction and operating differential subsidies
from the Maritime Administration.

ships at berth is reduced. Additionally, many of the older berths used by conventional ships have been idled, leading to a greater concentration of cargo moving across the wharves. Thus, the amount of cargo passing through the container terminals in any given period of time is several hundred per cent greater than formerly. The result is a greatly increased need for land adjacent to the berths. A typical berth for a containership, involving from 700 to 900 lineal feet of wharf, requires at least 20 to 30 acres of contiguous level land for the sorting and handling of containers, while ideal conditions might call for as many as 50 acres per berth. Obviously, these extensive tracts of land are not generally available adjacent to the waterfronts in or near the central parts of port cities. Even if they were available, it would not be desirable to develop them for port terminal uses, because the industrial establishments that generate the local traffic have tended to locate on the urban periphery and beyond, as have the classification yards, freight forwarders, and other activities. Also, there are many more intensive uses for the scarce centrally located land areas adjacent to the waterfronts.

Port Labor

The relocation of general cargo terminals from central to peripheral locations, frequently across harbors and often into other municipalities, has caused an imbalance between the available port labor force and the requirements of the new facilities. On a larger scale, the development of load center ports has increased labor surpluses in the declining and redundant port areas while shortages occur in some of the ports and port areas experiencing rapid growth of container traffic. If port labor is casual, hired on a day-to-day basis, acute unemployment results in some areas. However, if the labor force is guaranteed an annual wage, both employers and employees make efforts to shift the labor force as conditions demand. In some ports. seniority and other rules and regulations have tended to inhibit the flexibility of labor demanded by changing patterns of traffic flow. On the Pacific coast, a long step toward solution of this problem was taken when labor and management agreed to flexible provisions to facilitate transfer of longshoremen, accompanied by seniority and fringe benefits, between areas of individual ports as well as among ports. With appropriate "phasing down" of the port labor force through attrition, early retirement, and inducements for reducing the work force through sharing between management and the unions of the economic benefits of containerization, the remaining port labor force can be utilized more effectively.

Despite containerization, there is still a need for some labor to handle conventional break-bulk general cargo. Certain trade routes, serving overseas regions where inland transportation is relatively undeveloped or where there is a need to create employment through labor-intensive rather than capital-intensive operations, as in some developing countries, may continue to be served by break-bulk ships for some time. Although a few break-bulk ships are constructed each year, such trade routes employ relatively few new ships. Some port officials have called attention to the need to retain in major ports as well as some smaller ports a capacity to handle break-bulk cargoes by conventional methods. Furthermore, military requirements for handling cargoes in regions lacking container facilities suggest a need for retaining a capability to handle break-bulk cargoes at ports of the United States.

Other Forms of Unitized Cargo Ships

Paralleling the rapid growth of containerization is the development of ships to carry other forms of unitized cargo, most notable roll-on-roll-off (RoRo) and barge-carrying ships. Although neither type is as numerous as the containerships, each has introduced new sets of port requirements and prospects.

The Roll-On-Roll-Off (RoRo) Ship

The RoRo vessel is one into which trucks, heavy machinery, military vehicles, and other equipment are loaded and discharged on their own wheels, either under their own power or with the aid of tractors. In most instances, a RoRo ship in commercial service handles primarily motor trucks and semitrailers (usually called a trailership). Some ships combine RoRo and container capabilities. The RoRo vessel is the cargo-carrying counterpart of the familiar harbor ferryboat where automobiles and trucks are driven aboard by means of connecting bridges or ramps. The oceangoing RoRo is typically loaded and discharged through stern ramps and sometimes via side ports. In recent years, a high proportion of the passenger vessels that have been added to the world's merchant fleets have been ferries, combining RoRo for automobiles and trucks with extensive passenger accommodations. Some of

these alternate between short sea ferry services and
seasonal cruise services. RoRo vessels reduce the time
in port for loading and discharge of cargo and, at the
same time, reduce or eliminate the need for expensive
shoreside cranes and other specialized cargo-handling
equipment. However, they generally require extensive
staging areas at or near the terminals for vehicles awaiting loading. Also, like containerships, they require
adequate approach roads to the waterfront terminals that
do not conflict with other land traffic and maximum insula-
tion from incompatible land uses.

LASH and SeaBee Ships

Intermodal transportation involving both ocean and
inland waterway movement is facilitated by the recently
developed barge-carrying, or "kangaroo" ships, in which
loaded barges are carried aboard oceangoing ships. The
two basic types are the LASH (lighter aboard ship), into
which the barges are lifted by large cranes mounted at the
ship's stern, and the SeaBee, which loads by floating barges
onto elevators in the ship's stern and lifting them aboard.
All of the present barge-carrying ships also have extensive container-carrying capability, thus making them quite
versatile.

With the barge-carrying ships, inland ports along
the river systems--the Mississippi system in North America
and the extensive waterways of Western Europe, for example--
are provided with break-bulk, or non-unitized, cargo service directly overseas. Up to now, however, the principal
advantage of the barge-carrying ship has been that it need
not be tied up in port while the individual cargo items
are transferred. The barges provide access to the multitude of terminals along the waterfronts of the ports, including terminals where water depths are insufficient to
accommodate the deep-draft oceangoing ships.

Dry Bulk Transportation

Although the changes in ships and ports engaged in
transportation of dry bulk commodities have not been as
prominent as those involving general cargo, the impact on
ports has also been significant. Bulk commodities are
distinguished from general cargo in that the former can be
handled as continuous flow by gravity, conveyor belts,
suction, and other devices. As a result, large tonnages
can be handled with very little port labor. However,

mechanized bulk cargo handling requires heavy investment in terminal facilities and often in land areas for stock-piling. A high proportion of bulk movements are directly to and from waterfront industries. Thus, much of the traffic is handled over private facilities and does not pass through the port.

A typical bulk movement is handled by unscheduled or "tramp" ships or in fleets owned directly or indirectly by the shipper. The "general trader" ships, adaptable for a variety of tramp trades and commodities, although still significant, are rapidly being supplanted by highly specialized ships designed for the transportation of individual commodities. Some commodities, such as sugar, which formerly were packaged and handled as general cargo, are now typically moved as bulk cargoes with consequent economies of scale both aboard the vessels and at the ports. However, the practice of using some bulk commodities as "bottoming cargoes" to round out excess capacity of the scheduled cargo liners is still significant to some ports as a means of attracting liner services. The liners can thus depend on a cargo from the bulk stockpiles when the general-cargo offerings are light.

With the appearance of the large "dry bulker," with greater draft than the "general tanker," channel deepening has become, in some cases, a prerequisite for a port to retain and increase its traffic. Some ports, unable to justify deeper channels, have lost bulk traffic. However, containerships and most dry bulk ships have access to virtually all major ports of the United States through existing channel approaches. The greatest pressure to deepen channels is exerted by large tankers responding to the nation's liquid bulk traffic demand.

Tankers

The rapidly increasing worldwide demand for oil and the heavy reliance, especially in Europe, on the Middle East as a source of petroleum fuel have combined to produce a sharp rise in the size of the world's tanker fleet and in the size of individual tankers. Also, closing of the Suez Canal with subsequent increased voyage lengths accentuated the economies of larger tankers and led to the development of the VLCC. The result is a demand for channels and terminals beyond the potential of most existing ports.

The world's tanker fleet has increased from 11.6 million gross tons in 1939, representing 16.9 per cent of the world tonnage of oceangoing merchant ships to 115.4 million gross tons, or 39.8 per cent of the world merchant ship tonnage in 1973.[9] At the same time, larger tankers were being constructed in each successive year. The typical tanker of the World War II period was 16,000 deadweight tons (commonly called a T-2 tanker). By 1966, a tanker of over 200,000 deadweight tons had been placed in service. Two years later, tankers exceeding 300,000 deadweight tons had been built, and in 1973 two tankers exceeded 400,000 deadweight tons, with ships of more than 500,000 tons on order and million-tonners under design. (It must be noted that the worldwide economic slowdown that began in 1974 has led to a reduction in oil usage and a concomitant over supply of tanker tonnage. Many tanker orders have been cancelled and a substantial amount of carrying capacity has been removed from the market, thus placing in doubt any future plans for tanker construction.)

As in the case of dry bulk, the petroleum terminals, both crude and product, are almost entirely privately owned and operated. Consequently, public port facilities are not generally a consideration. However, providing channels with adequate depth for the large tankers involves a complex of public policy issues. Traditionally, the federal government has assumed responsibility for construction and maintenance of waterways and harbors, with few exceptions, in contrast to terminal facilities, which are matters of local government and private responsibilities. Except for ports on Puget Sound and for Long Beach, there are no ports in the mainland United States capable of handling even a moderate-sized supertanker. Most of the larger ports have channel depths of 35 to 50 feet, whereas the supertankers have drafts of between 60 and 100 feet. Consequently, the United States is not served by supertankers, which represent the lowest cost method of long distance petroleum transport.

Despite a declared policy of national self-sufficiency in energy, it is evident that for some time there will be a continuation of large petroleum imports to the

---

[9] *Lloyd's Register of Shipping,* Annual Report 1973, London, 1974, p. 101.

United States. Therefore, the construction of adequate
facilities for tankers becomes an issue of national importance. Complicating the issue is public consciousness
of the hazards to the environment of tanker operations.
Many people have been alarmed by the prospects of oil
spills resulting from collisions and groundings of tankers
and of possible aesthetic deterioration caused by operation
of terminals and refineries.

It is clear that providing adequate channel depths
for containerships, dry bulk carriers, and RoRo and
barge-carrying ships is not as much of a problem as that
of providing access for the supertankers now in existence.[10]
Offshore terminals have been suggested as a solution to the
problem of handling supertankers and their cargoes. Such
terminals could be artificial islands in deep water on
the continental shelves, with or without associated refinery and storage facilities. Perhaps "monobuoy" or
single-point mooring (SPM) terminals are more feasible.
The tanker ties to the monobuoy, is free to swing with
winds and currents, and discharges its cargo through a
connection with a submarine pipeline to storage and refining facilities, which may be on the coast or inland.

A policy for offshore terminals was established in
December 1974 when the Deepwater Port Act became law. That
law authorizes the Department of Transportation to license
and regulate any deepwater ports in waters beyond the
3-mile limit. Adjacent coastal states (those that will be
connected to the facility by pipeline or would be located
within 15 miles of the off-shore port) will be able to veto
any proposal found inconsistent with its coastal zone plans.

In addition to crude oil tankers, other liquid bulk
carriers have also created important considerations for
future port requirements. Specialized chemical tankers of
great variety and liquified gas tankers (LNG, liquified
natural gas, and LPG, liquified petroleum gas) raise new
problems. LPG and LNG are transported under extremely low
temperatures. Cryogenic tankers to carry these products
are among the most sophisticated and expensive of all

---

[10] American Association of Port Authorities, Committee on
Ship Channels and Harbors, *Merchant Vessel Size in the
United States Offshore Trades by the Year 2000*, American
Association of Port Authorities, Washington, 1969.

ship types. To meet the future energy requirements of the United States, rapid expansion of the world's fleet of LNG and LPG tankers, including a number under United States registry, has started. The hazards of LNG transportation are not completely known, and much resistance to the presence of such vessels in United States ports has been expressed.

Offshore terminals that allow the large tankers to moor far from the coasts may reduce the dangers from collisions, strandings, and explosions, particularly if the terminals are connected with shoreside and inland installations by submarine pipeline. Were smaller ships to be employed, either directly from overseas or as lighters connecting shoreside and offshore terminals, the large number of moving vessels could, it is held, increase the probability of accidents. However, the issue of offshore terminals, although of great importance, is peripheral to the principal concern of this report, since the facilities would be highly specialized. It is of concern, however, in relation to the effects that such terminals may have on existing and prospective ports.

N.P.A

CHAPTER III

INSTITUTIONAL ASPECTS OF PORT DEVELOPMENT

Ports have developed competitively throughout our
national history, largely with private capital and under
private control. More recently there has been an increasing trend toward control and operation of the terminal
facilities by local public bodies, mainly states and municipalities, or bodies created by them. Harbors, on the
other hand, continue to be under public control or operation by the federal government; whether the nation should
continue to improve and control the navigable waterways
is not the issue.

A major institutional issue, and perhaps the most
complex and troublesome one, is the extent to which port
planning should be done on a regional or national basis.
Subsumed within that question is the need for comprehensive
studies of port requirements. The American Association of
Port Authorities, representing the public port industry,
has traditionally held that ports are competitive, that
competition is in the public interest, and that any prospect of nationwide research on port requirements, whether
conducted by the federal government or not, could lead to
national port planning.

Arguments for the study of the port requirements
of the United States are strong. The hinterlands of the
individual ports are no longer mutually exclusive but
overlap, so that extensive areas of the United States are
served by more than one port, commonly by several ports
or even ranges of ports on different coasts. A shipper
in the Midwest has a choice of ports, generally at competitive rates, on the Atlantic, Gulf, and Pacific Coasts.
He can also ship from a Great Lakes port through the
St. Lawrence Seaway. Within each coastal range a number

of ports are in competition, although in recent years the development of load centers has resulted in the by-passing of some traditional ports by mini-bridge and other means.

The federal interest in ports is complex. Navigable channels are a federal responsibility, and many millions of dollars are spent each year in the discharge of that responsibility. Several questions bear on this subject: To what extent are such expenditures justified in enabling a potentially obsolete port to remain in competition? Will there be sufficient traffic for many such ports in view of the trend toward concentration? Are expenditures for channel construction and maintenance discriminatory?

One argument against national determination of port requirements is that each port has unique attributes. New Orleans, for example, has an easily accessible and extensive natural hinterland in the Mississippi basin but poor natural site conditions, with silting and flooding requiring constant dredging. Seattle has just the opposite an excellent natural site, with deep water close to shore, but a hinterland that is a long distance away and on the opposite side of one or more mountain barriers. Therefore, it can be argued, if one port receives a subsidy through expensive channel dredging, to overcome its physical disadvantage, the other should receive a similar subsidy applied to inland rates to overcome its locational disadvantage.

Each port body and private interest involved in port development and operation, it is argued, should take its own risks and should make its decisions on the basis of the knowledge that it generates or that is made available to it. This is a neutral argument, for it does not preclude national or regional port studies; results could be interpreted by each port as it wishes. The argument against centralization of port studies is based on the fear that such studies would lead to national port planning and eventually to federal control. This would reduce the freedom of action of those ports with inherent disadvantages that are willing to apply local initiative and investment in return for the benefits of the multiplier effect on the local and regional economy. Free enterprise is an American tradition, and most people in the port industry feel it should be maintained through local initiative. Further, opponents of central planning feel there is no certainty that national port planning will lead to an improvement in the nation's port industry, particularly when economic, political, and social conditions are changing so rapidly, both internationally and domestically. Development of a national port plan could remove some of the flexibility ports now have to adjust to varying conditions.

Completely local or regional determination of port investment could result in excessive unused capacity if each port competes for the same traffic. Some unused capacity may be beneficial, desirable or undesirable. There are strong arguments for unused capacity. One is that it provides a choice for the shipper, ship operator, and land carrier. Ports would compete on a cost basis and on their ability to give good service. Competition, with the better ports ultimately getting the most traffic, is held by many to be a desirable condition, even at the expense of investment in facilities used at less than capacity. A second argument in favor of unused capacity is that provision must be made for handling of seasonal, cyclical, or unanticipated traffic peaks. It is obviously impossible to provide for all peaks, but even though cargo berths may be unused for substantial periods, this does not mean they are not needed. A high load factor-- ratio of use to available capacity--may divert traffic from a port or may produce intolerable delays during peak periods. The effect of changing traffic patterns may well be permanent. They could, however, result in sub- stantial investments by individual ports that would not be justified by the traffic that could be diverted from other ports.

Ownership and Control

Throughout much of the nineteenth century and in the early twentieth century, the navigable waterways and harbors were, as they continue to be, a federal responsi- bility. Port facilities have traditionally been a private or local responsibility. In virtually no other major maritime nation is there the dichotomy between federal responsibility for channels and local responsibility for ports that exists in the United States and that underscores the current controversy over the prospective role of the federal government in port development. In most other countries the separation of responsibility for harbor and terminal facilities either does not exist or is not as clearly defined as in the United States. Typically, a foreign port authority, whether national or local, is concerned with both harbor and terminals. Significantly, there is no evidence that ports in other countries where such complete control exists have developed any more efficiently than those in the United States.

Since the turn of the century, port facilities (as distinguished from the harbors and channels) in the United States have come increasingly under public, non-federal, control. Until that time, the shore facilities were owned and operated by railroads, by terminal companies organized for the purpose, and by industries that generated the port traffic. Most United States port terminal areas were complexes of diverse ownership with little, if any, coordination among the various terminal owners and operators. The railroads were highly competitive, and in many ports railroad-owned and controlled waterfront terminals were dominant. In some instances the railroads individually or jointly owned and operated waterfront belt lines for transfer of goods within the respective port areas. Where bodies of water constituted barriers between terminal the railroads developed lighterage services for goods and ferries for passengers, as in New York Harbor and San Francisco Bay.

As ports grew, such arrangements became unsatisfactory and were commonly chaotic. Following the port congestion of World War I, the Port of New York Authority (now the Port Authority of New York and New Jersey) was organized to simplify the transfer and movement of port-related cargo and passenger traffic within the metropolitan port district. It was the first public interstate port agency, established by bistate compact and approved by the U.S. Congress. The Port of New York Authority, however, was not the first port authority under public auspices. The concept of the special-purpose governmental authority had been conceived and placed into operation several decades earlier. One of the first was the Sanitary District of Chicago, which was established in 1889 and dealt with water resources including ports.

During recent decades the special-purpose port authority has become increasingly common. In many instances, the definition of "port" has been stretched to include many ancillary and some unrelated activities. Port authorities, in addition to operating port terminals and port-oriented railroad switching facilities, may operate airports, transit lines, convention and exhibition halls, bridges, tunnels, and office buildings. Besides being an instrument with special competence for development, operation, and promotion of a port, the port authority, as a special-purpose public body, is often regarded as a device to circumvent state-imposed debt limits that may prevent municipalities from issuing bonds to finance public improvements.

In some ports, the development of the public authority concept has not been accompanied by unification of the port's facilities. Some ports still have a multiplicity of public agencies, each concerned with some terminals or some portion of the port, whereas other ports have most or all of their facilities and operations under unified control. The public port authority may be regulatory, or it may be an operating agency. It may operate facilities it owns, or it may lease the operation to private contractors who, in turn, may be land or water carriers, stevedoring companies, or other types of organization. Most major ports in the United States consist of combinations of controlling organizations, although the trend has been moving from private owners to public control. Increasingly, ownership of the waterfront terminal areas, if not the facilities themselves, has become public. In a few instances, notably Houston, Texas, and Stockton, California, the public port authorities also administer the principal channels.

The public authorities, of which there were only four at the beginning of the twentieth century in the United States, have proliferated rapidly; most major ports are now administered and many are owned by such bodies. In some cases, as in South Carolina, Massachusetts, and Virginia, the authority is a special-purpose state agency that controls all ports of the state, even though there may continue to be private terminals within the port areas. In Maryland the port authority is a part of the State Department of Transportation. Some port authorities, such as New York, Philadelphia, and St. Louis, are bi-state organizations.

Usually, the port agency is an autonomous or semi-autonomous public body, having some of the powers that the states normally grant to municipalities. For some ports, such as Seattle and Cleveland, the port authority is county-wide. In many ports, the authority is municipal, even though the waterfront lands may involve more than a single municipality.

Port Economics

In the United States, the harbors may be freely used by anyone with suitable ships, whereas it is customary in many foreign ports to charge "port dues" for the use of the harbors. The terminals, whether public or privately owned and controlled, may be leased to individual steamship companies on an exclusive or preferential basis, or they may be common-user berths. Many private terminals are operated exclusively by the railroads or industries that control them and are thus restricted to the interests of the terminal owner. Pilotage and other services may or may not be performed by the port organizations; separate user charges are assessed for such services. Except for the trend toward public control of terminal facilities, it is difficult to generalize on the nature of port ownership and operation.

The underlying basis for the trend toward public port development and operation is the public benefit. A public agency can ensure that all prospective users able to benefit from the port facilities have access to them on equitable terms and can bear the high costs of capital financing. Port facilities rarely produce sufficient income to amortize increasingly large investments; they commonly do not even cover the out-of-pocket costs. Many of the benefits and some of the costs are "external" and benefit the community as a whole. Therefore, the community is justified in assuming some of the port costs in return for tangible and intangible benefits.

Ports produce a "multiplier" effect in the form of employment and income to the port community, however the community is defined.[11] The geographic spread of the multiplier effect may be essentially local, confined to the city or metropolitan area of smaller ports, or may be more widespread, extending to a nationwide hinterland in the case of major ports. With the growth of load centers, hinterlands involve substantial portions of the United States, if not the entire nation.

---

[11] Schenker, Eric, *The Port of Milwaukee: An Economic Review*, The University of Wisconsin Press, Madison, 1967.

The huge investments required for a port to remain competitive are beyond the capabilities of most local governments. The creation of port authorities with power to incur long-term debt has helped overcome the economic barrier to adequate port development. The public receives benefits from industry attracted to the port region and from lower transportation costs. Thus, jobs directly related to the port operation and in port-oriented industrial and commercial activities are created.

It is very difficult to isolate the job opportunities and the investment in industrial and commercial development that can be directly attributed to a given port, but the economic impact of a major port is very large and extensive. More than a decade ago, it was estimated that over 200,000 people were directly employed in activities at the Port of New York. These included steamship companies, railroads, truckers, air carriers, warehouseman, stevedoring contractors, freight forwarders, tugboat operators, and others.[12] The indirect employment is impossible to estimate, since the effects of a port's ability in attracting and holding industry and commerce are subsumed in the entire regional economy.

The Port of Baltimore, which handles substantial traffic in both bulk and general cargo, generated $626 million of direct economic benefit in 1966 and created primary employment for over 62,000 people.[13] In Seattle, in 1969, the port generated 39,000 jobs, $322 million in payrolls, and over $1 billion in business activity in King County, Washington. It was estimated that a ton of seaborne cargo at the Port of Seattle generated $110 in gross payrolls. The study that drew these conclusions about Seattle stated that:

12 Chinitz, Benjamin, *Freight and the Metropolis*, Harvard University Press, 1960, p. 2.

13 Hille, Stanley J., and Suelflow, James E., *The Economic Impact of the Port of Baltimore on Maryland*, University of Maryland, Department of Business Administration, College Park, June 1969.

King County residents in 1969
supported the Port of Seattle with
$8,186,000 in tax levies. The
39,087 commerce-oriented job
holders and the maritime commerce-
oriented private enterprises paid
in excess of $39,000,000 in state
and local taxes. Thus, apart from
generating substantial local employment, the harbor was a source
of net fiscal revenue to the State,
County and City.[14]

Port Governance

There are no "federal" or "national" ports in the
United States. Ports are governed by non-federal institutions such as state and local governments and, in some
instances, by private enterprise. Their powers and jurisdiction range statewide or are limited to a defined portion
of a municipal waterfront, from facility development to
construction and operation, and from exclusively maritime
facility development to a wide range of industrial and
transportation interests.

Ports may play varied roles in their respective
regions. One port may be responding to a specific facility
need in a limited hinterland while another may be providing
transshipment facilities for regions well beyond its normal
hinterland or other facilities not directly related to
maritime industry (such as airports and rapid transit
passenger systems). In most cases, institutional differences derive from these varying roles.

Although response to shipping needs is clearly
at the non-federal level, the federal government does
serve in a regulatory position. It has promulgated federal
rules and regulations for safety standards, pollution
control, navigation control, tariffs, customs, etc. It has
also given limited funding assistance. However, the state
and local governments are the "prime movers" as port
developers.

---

[14] *Seattle Maritime Commerce and Its Impact on the
Economy of King County*, Port of Seattle Commission,
1971.

All ports in the nation can be generally subdivided into two governmental types--local and state. (Some private, usually specialized, facilities that may be large enough to qualify as a port are exceptions.) A major variable is the amount of territory within the port's jurisdiction. The typical state port authority includes an entire state, often under a Department of Transportation, and is responsible for locating port sites and developing port facilities within the state. Local ports may be controlled by a municipality, county, or special district. They provide facilities in response to localized developments that arise within the shipping industry. In many cases, however, a locally controlled port effectively serves statewide or even broad regional interests. (The U.S. Midwest, for example, is served by ports on all four coasts--Great Lakes, Atlantic, Gulf and Pacific.)

Local port organizations may encompass several countries, or they may be departments within a city government, although often governed by a separate harbor commission. The Port Authority of New York and New Jersey is an example whereby two states have made a reciprocal legislative compact to create a separate, bistate authority with jurisdiction over one physical port embracing parts of two states. The Port of Seattle is an example of an independent municipality whose port boundary coincides with that of a large county, King County, Washington. The city of Portland, Oregon, is similar except that its port boundary includes three counties. Most California port organizations are separate harbor commissions under city government. East Coast ports generally are under state jurisdictions.

Governing bodies of ports also vary. Some consist of appointed commissioners from a municipality whereas others are composed of elected commissioners. The degree of autonomy is clearly greater when a port is a special-purpose district, which may have independent taxing power, instead of a departmental unit within a city or county. State organizations also vary in the extent of local control they exercise. In some states several physically distinct ports have consolidated into a larger port body, as in Virginia and South Carolina. In other cases, ports are under a State Department of Transportation, which has authority for all transportation within a state, as in Maine, Maryland, and Hawaii.

Regional Port Planning Studies

The growth of statewide transportation and land-use planning makes it increasingly apparent that port interests can be served best by becoming involved in the planning process from the very start. An important factor bringing ports together in cooperative port planning is the awareness that competition is not limited to that between neighboring ports, but rather has expanded to include competition between regions, states, and seaboards. Another important consideration is the recognition that participation in the planning process will ensure that port development programs will not be imposed but will reflect the interests of the ports, consistent with the public interest. Evidence of this attitude exists on the West Coast, where ports have joined to prepare regional and state port systems studies.

The ports in the San Francisco Bay region, for example, have reactivated the Northern California Ports and Terminal Bureau (NORCAL) to cooperate with the Metropolitan Transportation Commission (MTC), which is required to develop a port and surface access system for the Bay Area. The MTC is developing the Bay Area plan for a comprehensive state transportation plan. NORCAL (not including Sacramento and Stockton) has prepared a seaport system study that has been submitted to the Maritime Administration for funding, and is currently under way. In addition, the California ports have joined through the California Association of Port Authorities (CAPA) to develop a maritime plan for the state plan.

The Washington Public Ports Association and the Port of Porland, with the U.S. Maritime Administration, have cooperated in conducting a comprehensive analysis of the requirements and capabilities of the region's ports. The report, entitled *Port Systems Study for the Public Ports of Washington State and Portland, Oregon,* was issued in March 1975.[15] According to the report, the purpose of the study is to

> ...predict what may happen to waterborne
> commerce in the future, to assess
> changes in techniques or capabilities

[15] The Aerospace Corporation, *Port System Study for the Public Ports of Washington State and Portland, Oregon,* Seattle, March 1975.

by which the ports could accommodate
future demands, and to recommend port
improvements. These inprovements are
identified on an aggregated regionwide
or subregional basis. Thus, the study
provides a basis for future cooperative
port development without restricting
the flexibility or capability of individual ports of the region to respond
to changing market demands. From this
perspective, it can be seen that this
study is not an end in itself. Rather,
it should be considered a base from
which groups of ports, or individual
ports, may continue their developmental
process in a cooperative and coordinated
manner. Furthermore, it should be
revised periodically as required to
reflect the evolving regional character
and the changing needs of waterborne
transportation.

The study's primary objective is to

...develop a sound planning base on which
future policy decisions may be made
relative to the development and use of
public port facilities in the State of
Washington and Portland. However, as
a result of its comprehensive nature,
the study serves three additional important purposes:

  ° The study indicates the roles of
    public ports in Washington State
    and Portland for handling domestic
    and foreign shipping needs to
    the year 2000.

  ° The study identifies regional
    port development and financial
    requirements.

  ° The study suggests and in fact
    is the first product of a process
    for cooperative port planning
    and development action.

The study highlights the importance of new organizational approaches to port actions and identifies the appropriate roles for collective action. The report states

> Coordination of individual port actions
> in the future is the element necessary
> to ensure mutually supportive port deve-
> lopments. To effect such coordination,
> individual port authorities of the
> region need a mechanism for making re-
> gional port policy decisions and for
> guiding future developments of the
> region's ports. The study concludes
> that authority for such a mechanism
> exists within the Washington Public
> Ports Association. Currently, the
> Association membership includes the
> ports under study (except for the Port
> of Portland). It remains only to
> establish within its framework the
> means of carrying out a systematic
> and cooperative port development pro-
> gram. For these reasons the study
> recommends the establishment of a
> Cooperative Port Development Committee
> within the Association.

In addition, the study recommends that consideration be given to the inclusion within the committee of Oregon ports along the Columbia River. Their participation in the committee activities would help to ensure effective utilization and development of regional port resources.

The recommended Port Development Committee, as stated in the report, would review construction projects for cargo handling facilities, "thereby increasing the effective utilization of limited land and water resources and public funds." Also, it is expected that the review process would "facilitate the organization of consortia of ports to take advantage of opportunities which might be larger than the available resources of any one port."

The significance of the Port System Study, separate from its findings, is that the effort was a comprehensive analysis of regional port requirements conducted by competing ports. Both the Washington State-Portland and NORCAL studies are joint efforts with the Maritime

Administration, which has taken the position of favoring regional cooperation on port planning matters, with emphasis on industry initiative and participation.[16] This appears likely to be the trend of the future.

Environmental Effects

Ports, by their very nature, interact extensively and unavoidably with physical, chemical, biological, and social systems. Port operations, such as loading, unloading, and storage of cargoes, require a multitude of physical facilities that interface with land, air, water, and social environments. Port activities focus on the coastal zone, which not only is one of the most productive and complex biological systems of the earth but also supports intense social systems. Interactions between ports and coastal environments raise problems of water, air, and land quality and cultural, aesthetic, historical, and other social issues. In addition, ports attract a myriad of other human activities that also affect the environment.

During the past several years, attention has focused on the potential environmental effects of deepwater ports, especially for handling oil supertankers. Provisions of the National Environmental Policy Act of 1969 (NEPA), the 1972 amendments to the Water Pollution Control Act, and the Coastal Zone Management Act of 1972 require proposals for all future port developments to include careful and extensive evaluation of potential environmental effects. If recent experience with environmental issues involving utilities and other industries is indicative, the rate of port development in the future may be substantially affected by environmental considerations.

Environmental problems associated with ports arise from two sources: facilities, which permanently alter the environment, and operations, which may result in temporary or permanent effects caused by cargo spillage, waste discharges, and vessel movement. The effect depends on the particular facility under consideration and the condition of the environment on which changes are imposed. For example, dredging may have significant environmental effects in one case but may not even be required in another

---

[16] U.S. Department of Commerce, Maritime Administration, *Ports of the Pacific,* Conference on Maritime Administration's Role in Port Development, Transcript of Proceedings, San Francisco, July 2, 1974.

case, or the sediment and sediment transport characteristi
may be such that dredging does not significantly add to
natural disturbances. The following discussion considers
the general nature of port-related environmental effects
in four categories:

> •••Harbor and channel development and
> maintenance for ship operation,
>
> •••Berthing and land-side terminal
> facilities for handling and storage
> of cargo,
>
> •••Ship operation activities, and
>
> •••Offshore terminals and related facilities
> such as pipelines.

Identification of alterations of the environment
do not imply either net detrimental or beneficial impacts.
Final evaluation of any physical or chemical change depend
on translating such changes into ecological and social
effects. Ecological considerations include effects on
species populations and biological communities and their
values. Social effects include cultural, aesthetic, and
historical considerations. The decision-making process
must balance economic and environmental considerations.

Harbor and Channel Development

The primary problems associated with harbor and
channel development arise from maintenance dredging and
spoils disposal. However, construction of structures such
as breakwaters, jetties, dikes, and locks have side effects
that cause concern. Potential effects of dredging include
changes in water and groundwater quality, alteration of
water circulation patterns, and disruption of benthic
(marine bottom) habitats and resident organisms.

Water Quality

Changes in water quality may be caused by
increased turbidity, changes in salinity, and increased
heavy metal concentrations or other chemical changes in-
duced by disturbance of bottom sediments. Changes in
turbidity are temporary if the dredging activity is short-
lived. However, continuing maintenance dredging may result
in essentially permanent increases in turbidity. The most

significant effects of increased turbidity are reduction
of light penetration, causing a potential decrease in
local photosynthetic production, and interference with
the feeding apparatus of filter-feeding species such as
commercially important shellfish.

Salinity intrusion patterns may change due to
circulation pattern changes and from effects on freshwater
aquifers, threatened by reduction in nearshore substrata
overlying aquifers. The mixing of esturarial saline waters
and fresh groundwater alters the quality of both. In
addition, resuspension of botton sediments may result in
release of heavy metals and other toxic substances or in
an increase in organic matter. Reduced water quality may
significantly affect a wide range of local populations.

Patterns of Circulation

Significant changes in water circulation
patterns include changes in flushing rates, velocity
fields, and scouring and erosion. In some cases, increased
flushing rates and tidal mixing may increase biological
activity and reduce local concentrations of pollutants.
The lack of generalized models of estaurine circulation
make predictions extremely uncertain.

Dredging Effects

Changes in marine habitats and effects on
associated species result from both direct removal of
dredged material and redeposition of bottom sediment
suspended during dredging. Direct loss of organisms and
substrata is a temporary effect if the dredging activity
is temporary and substrata texture is not altered by
removing material. Permanent dredging activities or dredging to bedrock result in corresponding permanent changes
within the dredged area. Resettlement of suspended
materials poses potentially widespread and long-term
biological effects. Currents may carry suspended sediments long distances from the area of dredging. Deposition
may cover productive bottom areas and prevent settlement
and recolonization by certain species. The texture of
coarse-grained sediments or hard substrata may become
permanently altered.

Dredging Spoils

Intentional deposition of the bulk of dredge spoils is an extreme case of redeposition. In addition to the alteration of bottom layers, dredge spoils may be deposited on land sites, destroying the landforms as they exist and creating new landforms. In some cases, such changes may be beneficial; in others, detrimental. There may often be a conflict between preservation of nearshore wetlands and creation of areas suitable for urban and industrial development.

Structures

Provision of harbor and channel areas suitable for vessel manuevering may require auxiliary structures, including breakwaters, jetties, dikes, and locks. The principal intent of such structures is to alter directly the environment by changing the circulation and flow patterns. Alterations of scouring and shoaling characteristics, as well as changes in water quality, especially salinity, may be associated with changed flow patterns. Breakwaters and similar structures also create additional habitats for assemblages of marine organisms associated with the particular type of substrata provided. However, organisms formerly associated with the area of the structur are destroyed. In addition, structures such as dams may prevent migrations of anadromous species such as salmon and other organisms that spawn in areas of lower salinity. In addition to environmental changes that may have ecological consequences, construction of various facilities may also have social implications. Aesthetic and cultural issues associated with visual impacts and provisions of recreational sites may introduce additional conflicts that require resolution.

Berthing and Terminal Facilities

Terminal facilities pose a land-use problem affecting social systems as well as natural environments. The effect depends on several factors, including the cargo handled and the extent and type of handling--processing, storage, transfer, etc. In addition, significant impacts may be associated with discharges from processing facilities into both air and water. Several of the problems associated with the integration of port activities with other urban land uses have been summarized by the Army Corps of Engineers:

Of major concern in shore facility problems is the need for space and structures for storage of large quantities of bulk commodities. Oil will require large tanks, taking of considerable space, and altering the nearby landscape's visual character. Some of the dry bulks (especially grain and phosphate) have to be protected from the weather to maintain their value. Other bulks can be stored outside, but they will still require large areas to accommodate enough volume to satisfy requirements matching the use of superships. Even when the berthing and loading/unloading are located offshore, there is generally the need for onshore storage. The only exception to this is in the development of offshore islands with storage capacity.

If the site is an existing port, there will still be a need for expanded storage. In fact, finding the space may be a significant problem in a heavily developed area. It could well mean the displacement of other land uses and will have to be evaluated on an individual basis. The kind of impact on a new area will be different. The site will probably be selected so that space is not the problem. The visual aspects may be very significant. Also, where large surfaces must be paved or otherwise covered, there may be a significant alteration in the behavior of precipitation runoff from these surfaces. This must be taken into account during the design phase of development. In new development, there is also the opportunity to select sites which cause a minimum of environmental intrusion by avoiding ecologically sensitive areas and by placing structures back from the immediate shoreline.

A final element in the analysis of
shore facilities is the development
of processing facilities and other
industry associated with the bulk
commodities. This can have a more
significant environmental impact than
any other component of a port system
over a long period of time. Processing
facilities themselves frequently use
large land areas; generate waste products that add to air and water pollution and solid waste disposal problems;
create significant intrusion on the
visual environment; place demands upon
local water supplies; and, if successful,
create employment that will tend to
increase area population and demand
for housing and services such as roads,
sewers and schools. If the area of
the new port is already heavily developed,
such new growth can create congestion
that places severe burdens on existing
utilities and services. Developments in
new areas can take these problems into
account through proper site selection,
design and planning. But there is no
automatic guarantee that it will happen.
In fact, it is likely not to happen in
a satisfactory way unless effort is put
into this aspect of any new port during
the planning and design phase of development and is followed by the implementation of enforceable controls.[17]

Successful development of port facilities will
depend on the extent to which these land uses are made
consistent with the emerging character of the urban area
of which they are a part. Social effects such as neigh-
borhood disruption by truck traffic and displacement of
recreational facilities are as important as potential
effects on natural systems.

[17] Department of Army, Corps of Engineers, *U.S. Deepwater
Port Study: The Environmental and Ecological Aspects
of Deepwater Ports*, Institute of Water Resources, IWR
Report No. 72-8, v. IV of V, Aug. 1972, pp. 23-24.

There is a potential for environmental improvement
from construction of landside facilities. Expansion of
facilities in existing ports may lead to renovation of
undesirable waterfront areas, installation of modern and
effective effluent and emission controls, and general
improvement of the environment.

Ship Movement and Operation

Ships may affect the environment from their physical
presence and movement and from discharges and spillages
during operations and cargo handling. A large, deep draft
ship in confined channels may cause unusual currents,
turbulence, and surface waves. If currents are strong
enough to induce erosion and suspension of sediments, some
problems similar to those associated with dredging, such
as increased turbidity, may occur. More likely to be
important are the effects on other vessels, especially
small recreational craft, and on facilities such as wharves
and docks.

Intentional discharge of pollutants from ships is
diminished by new regulations that require effective on-
board treatment or use of onshore treatment facilities.
However, accidental spills of cargo or fuel during cargo
transfer or from collisions and groundings may result in
significant environmental effects, depending on the location
and nature of the material spilled. Use of very large
crude carriers has focused attention on oil spills. Experience has demonstrated that oil spills occurring near
shore may cause significant ecological damage, the duration
of which is debatable. Problems associated with other
bulk commodities have recently been evaluated by the Army
Corps of Engineers with the following conclusion:

> The major environmental impacts in
> the storage and handling of dry bulk
> commodities are associated with land
> use, aesthetics, and dust generated
> during operations. The latter can
> be extensively curtailed and controlled
> by existing technology, and the
> significance of the former two will
> depend primarily upon the other uses
> of the area. In general, the environ-
> mental impacts of the dry bulk commo-
> dities themselves are not significant.[18]

---

[18] *Ibid*, p. 63.

Offshore Facilities

Offshore facilities may affect the environment due to the structure itself or its physical links with the shore. The effect will vary with the structure. Mono-buoys, or single point mooring buoys (SPM) have little or no environmental effect. Man-made islands, however, may alter water circulation patterns and cause major shifts in benthic communities. In most open water areas the effects are not likely to be extensive but they cannot be ignored. Although areas of shellfish and other bottom species may be disrupted, offshore structures are likely to provide additional shelter and feeding for many marine species, especially finfish. In some localities, offshore installations may not be feasible because of frequent rough seas.

Pipelines, trestles, or other cargo transfer methods between the offshore facility and the shore may also affect the environment. Structures above water create visual changes that have aesthetic implications. The effects of pipeline construction are generally only tempo-rary until the bottom materials readjust to their pre-pipe-line configuration. However, in intertidal areas such as salt marshes, careful evaluation of impacts must be made because trenches may cause permanent damage.

Evaluation of Ecological Impact

Environmental change associated with port develop-ment must be translated into implications for change in biological populations and communities. Some method must then be adopted for evaluating these biological changes and their social, cultural, aesthetic, and historical consequences. These consequences must then be calculated with the economic costs and weighed against benefits associated with the proposed facility. Prediction of ecologic shifts in populations and communities is uncertain and difficult. Ecological systems are defined by immense numbers of variables complexly related by many partially known or unknown linkages. The dynamics of marine communities remain largely unknown and virtually unpredic-table. Knowledge of the processes by which populations and communities recover from major perturbations depends on the life histories and environmental requirements of the involved species. For most marine organisms, such information is not available and cannot be obtained with-out several years of comprehensive field and laboratory study.

The lack of understanding of ecological systems should not be used either as an excuse to undertake major developments with no environmental input or to prevent needed development. Each proposal must be assessed for its environmental impact, identifying sources of uncertainty and indicating needs for data and research. In any case, where significant ecological changes of unknown direction are possible, alternatives should be evaluated for their flexibility to permit future adjustments and to minimize irreversible actions. Activities threatening unique resources such as endangered species and historical sites should be carefully noted.

The decision to reject or accept any or all alternatives remains a social and political one. An objectively presented statement of the potential effects and a clear statement of the uncertainties involved in the predictions will allow the decision to be based as much as possible on the realities of the situation and its alternatives than on emotion. The attachment of values to particular changes must be part of the actual decision to undertake any proposed activity. A clear distinction should be made between assessing environmental vulnerability and the decision to select among alternative courses of action. The desirability or undesirability of a particular change depends on a value system that includes the interests of diverse groups.

Legal Considerations and the Environment

Five federal laws related to port development and their environmental effects are

- •••The Water Resources Planning Act of 1967 (WRPA);

- •••The National Environmental Policy Act of 1969 (NEPA);

- •••The Coastal Zone Management Act of 1972 (CZMA);

- •••The 1972 Amendments to the Water Pollution Control Act (WPCA);and

- •••The Marine Protection, Research and Sanctuaries Act of 1972.

Other federal and state environmental legislation may also affect port development, but the foregoing provide

the dominant federal legal considerations. Offshore
facilities pose special situations that may involve international jurisdiction.

The Water Resources Planning Act of 1967

The Water Resources Planning Act of 1967 (WRPA)
affects port development through the Water Resources
Council's "Principles and Standards for Planning Water and
Related Land Resources."[19] The Principles provide the
basis for federal participation with other organizations
in planning federally assisted programs for water and
related resources.

The Principles require an approach to planning
that recognizes the distinct objectives of national economic development and environmental quality. Each alternative plan must account for all beneficial and adverse
effects on these two objectives, measured in monetary and
nonmonetary terms. The Principles recognize that priorities
and preferences of those affected may vary and that full
agreement on trade-offs between objectives may not always
exist.

The most immediate and obvious effect of these
Principles and Standards on port development is on the
activities of the Corps of Engineers, especially dredging.
All Corps of Engineers projects must comply with the
Water Resources Council Principles and Standards. However,
because the Principles only became effective in 1973, their
implications for port development remain to be seen. In
theory, the framework for planning future federally assisted port development is established in the Principles.

The National Environmental Policy Act of 1969 (NEPA)

The National Environmental Policy Act of 1969 requires the preparation of environmental impact statements
for any federally financed actions significantly affecting
the quality of the environment. Council on Environment
Quality Guidelines for preparation of impact statements
require consideration of several points, including the
following:

> •••Indirect as well as direct impacts on
> the environment;

---

[19] *Federal Register*, V. 38, No. 174, Monday, Sept. 10, 1973,
pp. 24778-24869.

•••Alternatives to the proposed action;

•••Unavoidable adverse effects;

•••Relationships between local short-term uses of man's environment and the maintenance and enhancement of long-term productivity; and

•••Any irreversible and irretrievable commitment of resources.

The preparation of environmental impact statements typically requires significant cost and manpower. Personnel requirements are also changing, according to Van Lopik and Stone:

> Before 1969 the major consideration in port development involved engineering and economic feasibility of a project. Both of these factors are closely inter-related, but the end result was a cost/benefit determination of some type. If costs exceeded benefits, port development plans were usually halted. Exceptions occurred in the cases of military or other types of subsidized operations where cost was not a fundamental consideration. Environmental planning was nonexistent and commitments of natural resources (e.g., land or water areas, air and water quality) were usually made without the benefit of adequate environmental assessment. Growth of existing ports was, and in many cases probably still is, justified by pointing out the growth of competing ports.

> The National Environmental Policy Act (NEPA) of 1969 [1] changed this situation by requiring that environmental feasibility be judged along with engineering and economic feasibility, providing federal monies were involved in some way. Port authorities and industry now need to seriously consider employing environmentalists as members of their design and planning sections. Engineers or other

present employees are not easily
"retreaded" for these positions.
Port authorities and industrial
companies are also considering the
appointment of environmentally-
oriented outside directors to their
boards. Environmental data needs and
potential impacts must be identified
in the early stages of planning and
design. Although some courts and
governmental agencies are hesitant to
halt major projects of significant
economic benefit on the basis of
potential environmental impact of
"external" costs, this cannot be relied
on to assure that proposed activities
will be carried out.[20]

The Coastal Zone Management Act of 1972 (CZMA)

The primary purposes of the Coastal Zone Management
Act of 1972 (CZMA) are

···To preserve, protect, develop and improve
coastal resources;

···To assist States in developing coastal
zone management programs; and

···To encourage close cooperation among
federal, state, regional and local agencies,
and the public, particularly regarding
coastal zone environmental problems.

The CZMA affects port development in several ways.
First, management programs (Sec. 305) that may be developed
by coastal states must include (a) an identification of
the boundaries of the coastal zone subject to the manage-

---

[20] Schenker, E., and Brockel, H.C., Eds. "Environmental
Planning for Future Port Development," *Port Planning
and Development,* Proceedings of Conference on Port
Planning and Development as Related to Problems of
U.S. Ports and U.S. Coastal Environment, Milwaukee,
Nov. 27-30, 1973, Cornell Maritime Press, Cambridge,
Md., 1974, pp. 156-157.

ment program; (b) a definition of permissible land and
water uses within the coastal zone; (c) an inventory and
designation of areas of particular concern within the
coastal zone; and (d) broad guidelines on priority of uses
in particular areas, including specifically those uses of
lowest priority. Clearly, all of the aspects of a management program will affect port development.

Second, prior to granting approval of a management
program by a coastal state, adequate consideration of the
national interest involved in the siting of facilities
other than local in nature must be shown (Sec. 306(c)(8)).
Virtually all port development is other than local in nature
and therefore falls under this section of the act. Furthermore, it must be demonstrated that local land and water
use regulations within the coastal zone do not unreasonably
restrict or exclude land and water uses of regional benefit
(Sec. 306(e)(2)).

A third aspect of the importance of the CZMA to
port development is the provision for interagency coordination and cooperation (Sec.307). In particular, states
are given authority to certify that activities requiring
a federal agency license or permit comply with the state's
management program. If a state does not grant such
certification, the license or permit cannot be issued unless approved by the Secretary of Commerce.

Because development of programs under the CZMA is
just beginning, the full impact of the act on port development is unclear. However, in states adopting plans,
there is little doubt that ports will be affected. A
significant feature of emerging plans will be the regional
consideration of all environmental matters. In addition,
more systematic treatment will be given to urban and
industrial developments that evolve from port development,
thereby providing a mechanism for balancing economic and
environmental considerations and improving regional planning.

Boyer has discussed the problems that must be considered in port planning:

> With the emphasis placed by the federal
> coastal zone law on long-term planning
> and management of invaluable and irre-
> placeable coastal resources, present

practices of ports relative to land
for expansion must be compatible
with a regional plan considering
alternate uses. Where ports are in
close proximity to large urban areas,
port engineers will have to accept
the fact that their work area will
have to be shared in some measure with
recreational interests. In large
cities individuals tend not to recognize
the direct connection between their
personal welfare and the commerce of
the port area. In fact, there is a
highly vocal minority who are against
"progress" in the form of industry
and commerce. With the increasing
public emphasis on leisure, recreation,
and aesthetics, as the cities grow
larger there is an increasing demand
to utilize the waterfront for recreation.
The tremendous upsurge in pleasure craft
not only makes demands for waterfront
space but causes conflict with the
increasing size of commercial ships
in narrow channels. At the same time
there is a great change going on in the
shipping industry requiring major
changes in port development.[21]

The Water Pollution Control Act (WPCA)

The Water Pollution Control Act (WPCA) is the basis
for regulating waste discharges into water bodies and for
maintaining ambient water quality. The 1972 Amendments
to the Act provide that effluent standards for waste discharge must be established by the Environmental Protection
Administration (EPA) for various industries. Each industry
will have limits for pollutant discharges. The limits on

---

[21] Schenker, E., and Brockel, H.C., Eds. "A Discussion of
Environmental Problems Looming Ahead," *Port Planning
and Development,* Proceedings of Conference on Port
Planning and Development as Related to Problems of U.S.
Ports and U.S. Coastal Environment, Milwaukee, Nov. 27-30
1973, Cornell Maritime Press, Cambridge, Md., 1974,
p. 198.

concentrations and total weight of pollutants discharged
from a particular source are specified by a discharge
permit, which must be obtained from the EPA. Upon meeting
certain qualifications, states may be authorized by the
EAP to issue discharge permits.

Numerous port-related activities clearly come under
the discharge permit program, including dredge spoil disposal. There is a need for standards that reflect local
conditions and background levels of various water quality
contaminants.

The Marine Protection, Research and Sanctuaries Act of 1972

The Marine Protection, Research and Sanctuaries Act
of 1972 (Section 103 of the Act is commonly referred to as
the Ocean Dumping Act) regulates the dumping of all types
of materials into ocean waters. Regulated dumping of
spoils is prompted by the emphasis on preservation of marine
life. Allocation of shoreline for housing, airports, free-
ways, and recreational facilities makes it difficult for
ports to utilize available waterfront properties for improvements and expansion. Water quality control standards
established in many states affect future dredging of
channels as well as the disposal of spoils.

The Marine Protection, Research and Sanctuaries Act
of 1972 strictly limits dumping into ocean waters of any
material that would adversely affect human health, welfare,
amenities of the marine environment, ecological systems,
or economic potentialities. Since no discharge of oil
or oily wastes, including ballast, is to be permitted, it
will be incumbent on the ports to provide shoreside recep-
tion facilities for oil and other waste substances.

Balancing Environmental and Economic Considerations in Port Development *Coul.*

Future port development plans must include considerations of the environment as well as economic factors.
However, finding workable solutions that respect the inte-
grity of coastal ecosystems, are economically viable, and
provide the greatest social benefit will be a difficult
task. Specific regional needs and attitudes will also
influence the effort. The problem is to determine port
development policy alternatives that will allow balancing
environmental and economic factors.

Port development is only one of many demands on the
diverse resources of the coastal zone. Many states have
limited shoreland management programs, such as wetlands
protection and site location regulation, that affect port
operations and development. However, the overlapping of
interests in the coastal zone has stimulated an increasing
concern for establishing comprehensive coastal zone management programs. Any examination of port development policy
alternatives for balancing environmental and economic
considerations must be conducted in the context of overall
coastal management.

Economic Considerations

Environmental management is an economic problem.
In addition to land, labor, and capital, the coastal zone
provides wealth in the form of direct and indirect services,
such as waste receptor and life-sustaining, amenity, and
material supply services.[22] Maintaining and enhancing the
value of the coastal zone require that environmental
resources be included in allocation and development decisions. Environmental quality problems often arise from
misallocation of environmental resources among their alternative uses. If a value can be assigned to environmental
resources that will be appropriately weighed by all those
who make decisions affecting the use of the coastal zone,
then resources will be efficiently allocated.

To suggest policy alternatives, the characteristics
of coastal zone resources must be examined to see why
they are misallocated in the present market system. Im-
proper pricing is the principal cause of failure of the
market to equitably allocate environmental resources.[23]
Lack of well-defined ownership, i.e., the common property
nature of environmental resources, leads to a breakdown
in pricing mechanisms. Property rights in the coastal zone
are often poorly defined. For example, a port authority's
decision to purchase and convert marshlands into port-related facilities may affect many individuals who derive
important values associated with the fish, wildlife and

---

[22] Freeman, A.M., et al., *The Economics of Environmental
Policy*, John Wiley & Sons, New York, 1973.

[23] Freeman, *op. cit.*

and outdoor amenities of the marshland. There is no effective market mechanism for including these third party values in land prices. As a result, there is no economic incentive to allocate these resources to their best use, which might be other than development.

Two conditions must be met for proper pricing; First, it must be possible to exclude non-buyers from resource use and, Second, prices must reflect the value to society of lost opportunities when resources are applied to a particular use. When prices do not exist for products such as clean water, resources will be allocated to other products, even though more valued, but misrepresented, uses exist.

Products subject to market failure are often referred to as public goods. A public good is a product or any entity whose use by one person does not preclude similar use by another. Likewise it is impossible to exclude any member of the community from benefiting from the provision of the good. Since the availability of a good is largely dependent on the ability of the producer to collect revenues from users, private producers will not provide adequate supplies of goods that have an element of publicness. Many services derived from the coastal resources have elements of public good. There is no incentive for any one firm or individual to invest in the reduction of pollution in coastal waters since all will benefit equally whether or not they provide funds. To ensure proper production and allocation of public goods, public or governmental action is needed.

The key problem appears to be one of valuing. If an equitable determination of the true values of resources can be made, then the real costs and benefits of alternative choices can be computed, and the market system becomes an effective decision-making mechanism. The validity of this logic lies in the assumption that true costs are reflected in market prices--an assumption that is not now valid for many environmental resources, such as the coastal zone. The multi-objective planning approach required by the Water Resources Council Principles and Standards and the management programs of the CZMA reflect a recognition of the inadequacy of the market system to allocate environmental resources.

Although many attempts have been made to quantify the value of environmental resources, so far there has been no successful approach. The inability to specify acceptable costs for environmental resources may be an inherent characteristic of the problem. Samuels summarizes the dilemma in the following words:

> Costs are no less relative and arti-
> factual than the ecological alterna-
> tives chosen by social institutions
> such as market and government...All
> discussions of ecosystem policy must
> come to grips with the problem of
> costs....[24]

Furthermore, Manheim et al. point out that "individuals have different priorities and values and that "any attempt to quantify these values to obtain well-defined social goals is not only possibly an impossible task but also unnecessary."[25] In addition, such attempts (cost/benefit analysis) obscure the real differences that exist and "...hide the issues--Who gains? Who loses?--instead of bringing them out....[26]

Political Considerations

In addition to economic problems due to market failures, there are political barriers to environmental trade-offs. Most important are two interacting forces:

1. Jurisdictional spillover: i.e., coastal land uses and environmental problems that overlap political boundaries such as towns and states, and

---

[24] Samuels, W.J., "Ecosystem Policy and the Problem of Power," Environmental Affairs, Vol. II, No. 3, 1972, pp. 580-596.

[25] Manheim, M.L., et al., Community Values in Highway Location and Design, M.I.T. Urban Systems Laboratory Report No. 71-5, Dec. 1971.

[26] Ibid. p. 18.

2. Localized political decision-making:
   i.e., decisions on the environment or
   allocation of resources that may affect
   an entire region but that are made by
   local government bodies.

The problems of jurisdictional spillover would be
virtually nonexistent if localized decision-making bodies
were to include the costs and benefits that accrue to all
who are affected by a particular activity.[27]

Technological Change and the Port Labor Force

Rapid advances in the technology of maritime transportation, connecting inland transportation, and goods
handling at the ports, combined with geographic shifts of
waterborne commerce, have led to increased productivity
and have created massive changes in the demand for port
labor. Many economic, social, and human problems result
from the generally decreased demand. The changing labor
requirements of ports and the concomitant changes in labor
practices constitute major challenges to virtually all
ports of the United States.

In those ports that have undertaken large investments in capital equipment to implement new technology,
the problem of labor force adjustment is most important.
For these ports there are three possibilities for the
future. Certainly the most desirable from the point of
view of both the port employer and the employee is the
possibility that the new investments will attract enough
new traffic to require a port labor force at least as
large as the present force. This would be possible if
the increase in productivity resulting from new cargo
handling methods is balanced by the rise in traffic. The
second possibility is that traffic through the port will
increase enough to make the investment profitable, but
not enough to offset increased productivity, so that the
labor force must be reduced. Finally, it is possible that
port traffic may not increase at all, may increase insuffi-
ciently to justify the new facilities, or will decline.

---

[27] Duscik, D.W. (ed.), *Power, Pollution and Public Policy*,
M.I.T. Press, 1971.

The attraction of traffic to large ports may affect even those ports that make no investment in new facilities. In regions in which the attraction of a single large port becomes very strong, all competing ports may face the necessity of reducing their labor force.

Regardless of traffic volume, there is need for some type of change in the relationship between port employers and their employees. In the case of a fast-growing, highly mechanized port, there is, at the very least, a need for retraining of some waterfront workers. There may be a need for a continuing reassessment of the employer-employee relationship to enable the port to make new investments required to keep it current. These concerns also apply to the successful mechanized port facing a redundancy of labor, but such a port also has the problem of reducing the port's labor force.

The problems surrounding port management and labor translate into needs that public agencies must consider, such as

···The need for port employers and employees to reach agreement with respect to the introduction of new methods of cargo handling;

···The need for retraining employees to fill new positions;

···The need to find new positions for workers displaced by the new technology or for workers refused entry into the market when the work force is being reduced;

···The need for large-scale retraining and reemployment of workers displaced by the losses in traffic or closure of small ports.

The Impact of Technological Change on the Labor Force

One of the early impacts of automation in cargo handling was on the West Coast, with the total conversion of raw sugar movement from Hawaii to California from bags to bulk. Prior to the conversion, unloading of 10,000 tons of bagged sugar involved 6,650 man hours and 80 men; handling the same amount of cargo in bulk involved 1,000 man hours and 8 men. The increase in productivity was over 600 per cent.

With the prospective decrease in labor requirements, longshoremen decided to negotiate with ship operators and port managements in order to reach mutual accommodation to the new technical developments.

The Mechanization and Modernization Agreement, entered into by the International Longshoremen's and Warehousemen's Union (ILWU) on the Pacific Coast on October 18, 1960, gave employers freedom to introduce efficient labor-saving devices and to change work rules. In return, union members were compensated for job displacements and early retirements through a tonnage assessment. This agreement was renewed and broadened in 1966 and is considered the pioneer arrangement to harmonize jobs, workers, and mechanization in ports.

The reduction of the labor force at ports that accompanied containerization and other technological change is shown in Table 3. The table shows the number of Class A and Class B longshoremen registered at Pacific Coast ports in 1960, the first year of declining registration, and in 1972. In 12 years the number of longshoremen was reduced by 20 per cent, tonnage more than doubled, and man-hours decreased by 35 per cent. Much of the increased efficiency was due to containerization. In 1969, the first year for which the Pacific Maritime Association's Research Department separately identified container tonnage, 6.96 million tons moved in containers. During 1972, only three years later, the volume of container traffic almost doubled to 12.23 million tons, and this despite 35 days of strike.

The total hours worked in 1972 by A and B longshoremen and casuals was 15,866,209. That figure divided by 11,013 (total A and B registered work force) equals just over 1,441 hours per man, per year for the registered men, or 36 weeks of work per man. The difference between that figure and 48 weeks of work is to be partially made up by the pay guarantee plan.

In February 1975 the ILWU leadership negotiated a new 2-year contract with the Pacific Maritime Association covering 12,000 longshoremen in 35 locals. The straight-time rate would go to $6.50 an hour for the first 6 hours of basic 8-hour day, with the last 2 hours at an overtime rate of time and a half, or $9.75 an hour. In July 1976 the basic pay rate would go to $7.52 an hour.

TABLE 3

REGISTERED WORK FORCE, TONNAGE, AND MANHOURS, PACIFIC COAST PORTS

Year	Total A & B Registered Work Force[a]	Total Weighted Tonnage[b]	Man-hours
1960	13,941	19,877,926	21,945,523[c]
1972	11,013	40,689,409	14,413,528[d]

a. Exclusing clerks and walking bosses/foremen.

b. Total weighted tonnage = 1/5 total dry bulk + total general cargo.

c. Excludes 1,811,859 casual hours

d. Excludes 1,452,681 casual hours

Source: Research Department, Pacific Maritime Association

The Pay Guarantee Plan, originally conceived as a protection against mechanization, is considered a cushion against depression, according to the ILWU. Class A longshoremen would be guaranteed $12,168 annually, or $234 a week. In July of 1976 the guarantee would be $14,040 annually, or $270 weekly. The PMA would increase its contribution to a total of $19.5 million for the 2-year life of the contract. The employers pledged no layoffs (deregistration) for the life of the contract, and the union agreed to tighten procedures so more men would be available for weekend work. The new pay guarantee plan differs from the old in that it covers Class A men for 52 weeks, for a 40-hour week, rather than guaranteeing, for Class A men, 36 hours at a straight-time rate for a maximum of 48 weeks.[28]

Parallel measures for change have occurred on the East and Gulf Coasts, with employers seeking increased and improved manpower utilization and longshoremen pressing for job security. In 1959, the International Longshoremen's Association (ILA) in New York developed an agreement providing for royalties for each container that was loaded or unloaded (stuffed or stripped) away from the piers and hance did not involve members of the union. At the same time, work on containers of nonemployer association members was guaranteed to the ILA.

In 1964, on the East and Gulf Coasts, the ILA reached its first major agreement involving jobs and mechanization. It centered on the Port of New York, where pressure from mechanization and labor-saving efforts was greatest. The ILA agreed to reduce gang sizes, close registers, and ease work rules. In return, employers agreed to guarantee 1,600 hours of work a year to longshoremen, virtually ending casual employment and initiating a port-wide seniority system. The 1959 royalty agreement on containers was continued through this period. In 1966 container traffic

---

28 The pact was vetoed on the first vote by a large local, although two-thirds of the total coastwide membership favored the agreement. Attempts to over-ride the veto by a needed two-thirds majority on the second vote failed by a narrow margin--66.2 percent in favor versus 33.8 percent opposed. The refusal of the membership to approve the contract necessitated new negotiations for a contract to be effective July 1, 1975.

through the Port of New York amounted to 3 per cent of
all cargo. By 1968, it had risen to 12 per cent, and the
contract settlement that year included a 2,080-hour
guarantee and a new container clause. The ILA had made
containerization a top negotiating target and won the right
to stuff or strip all containers originating from or
destined to points within 50 miles of their ports as long
as they were not fully loaded and moving from a single
shipper or consignee (door to door).

The port of New York provides a prime example of the
impact of containerization on the longshore workforce. In
1968, approximately 40 million man-hours were worked by
ILA members; in 1975 the number is approximately 20 million
man-hours, or 50 per cent less. General cargo tonnage in
1973 was approximately 16 million tons, of which more than
half was containerized. At the same time the number of
longshoremen decreased from 23,000 in 1968 to almost
13,000 by February 1975, of which about 1,000 are surplus.

The 1974 ILA agreement was the first one reached
without a strike since the end of World War II. According
to the ILA, its basic proposition is that "any work that
has to do with containerization, with the loading and
unloading of a vessel, or with shipping waterborne cargo,
should not be subcontracted to anybody else but should be
solely performed by the ILA." To reach this goal, the
ILA and the various employers are cooperating to ensure
that ILA labor consolidates small shipments into containers
within the 50-mile radius. Violations of the new rules
can subject employers to a $1,000 fine. The new 3-year
agreement also includes an increase in the basic hourly
raise to $8.00 an hour by October 1976.[29]

The Labor Department estimates that containerization
and work rule changes saved employers on the West Coast,
and ultimately all consumers, about $1 billion from 1960
to 1970. The East Coast recorded a comparable $400 million
savings from 1965 to 1971, according to the same estimate.
The full extent of containerization has not been realized
yet. Employment in ports on both coasts is substantially

---

[29] These comments on the Port of New York are taken from
papers by Anthony Scotto and John J. Farrell presented
at the 15th Annual Conference of the Containerization
Institute, Oct. 1974.

less than it was following World War II. There is
virtually no prospect of any increase in port employment
in the future.

Labor and management responded quickly to the need
for mutual adjustment to the changing methods of general
cargo handling at United States ports. The American
experience rather closely parallels that of several other
leading maritime nations. So far, the adjustments have
been largely successful. However, much remains to be done
for management and labor to share equitably in the economic
advantages of increased efficiency.

Mutual involvement in the difficult problems caused
by new technology has marked a new labor-management relationship. Cooperation and coordination has given both
sides new insights into each other's problems. This
surely will mean more successful negotiations in the future
than might result from federal compulsory arbitration
legislation to settle disputes without work stoppages.

Requirements of Labor and Management

Until recently, the history of dockwork has been
essentially a history of casual employment, even though
the "shape-up" system did provide some steady longshore
gangs. As registration rolls for dockworkers were established, as guaranteed wages and pension and welfare benefits
were negotiated, and as large capital investments for new
equipment became necessary, the number of port employers
who could supply substantial work was reduced. Consequently, the relative powers of longshoremen's unions and
stevedores' and employers' groups increased. The present
situation is roughly that of the familiar case of bilateral
monopoly, in which two powerful monopolies must deal with
each other. Port workers facing advancing technology are
loathe to relinquish their guarantees on gang size and
labor intensive methods for fear that their jobs will be
imperiled. Nevertheless, unless the dockworkers permit
the introduction of enough equipment to keep the port
competitive they are in danger of losing their jobs as
traffic at the port decreases.

For their part, employers wish to gain maximum
profits from new investment, but unless they are willing
to bargain with labor, they will find themselves unable to
operate that port. The position is indeterminate, and the
final outcome is dependent on the relative bargaining abi-
lities of the two sides.

Public agencies must do all that is possible to facilitate negotiations. They must ensure that bargaining is done in good faith by both groups. They must stand ready to enforce laws protecting the rest of society and the economic and physical welfare of the region. Agreements are a compromise between labor and management. In general, the parties agree that labor will not insist on excessive hiring and restrictive working practices designed to ensure employment of unneeded longshoremen. In response to this concession, management agrees to share, with labor, profits from the investments to provide wage security.

There is another important area yet to be removed from contention, involving not only port management and labor but also non-port labor. The container, for domestic and international shipping, has made it possible for cargo to be packed at the point of origin and unpacked at the final destination without intermediate loading and unloading. Whereas dockworkers formerly worked directly with all cargo, they now receive an increasing number of full containers (door to door shipments). The question of who has the right to pack these containers is a thorny one, involving the teamsters and longshoremen's unions as well as port management and shippers.

New technology has created a need for retraining workers for new skills. Since this is a desirable goal for both the employer and the worker, there seems to be little reason for public entry into this matter, except perhaps in the area of general education classes designed to increase the educational level of the overall population. Certainly such programs would be helpful to dockworkers. Programs to retrain workers for jobs in the port should be the concern of those directly involved.

CHAPTER IV

DATA REQUIREMENTS FOR EVALUATION
OF PORT DEVELOPMENT

Detailed and accurate port information is necessary for formulation of policies, effective physical planning, day-to-day regulation and administration, financial auditing and programming, and public relations. To accomplish these tasks an inventory should be maintained of all the physical facilities and equipment currently at or serving the port, and records of performance should be kept. Ship arrival patterns, length of time in port, sizes and types of vessel, cargo loading rates, and similar data must be tabulated to establish the port's activity and efficiency in handling waterborne cargo.

Trends in types and volumes of cargo moving through the port should be closely monitored and worldwide developments in vessel design, handling techniques, containerization, etc., should be continuously reviewed. Analysis of such trends, markets, and supply sources forms the basis for the port's short and long-range tonnage forecasts. An appraisal of available historical and forecast information indicates significant deficiencies. The following discussion shows how useful data might be assembled and organized, treats some of the data and forecasts that are available, and comments on the methodology and techniques of forecasting.

Movement of Commodities

Aggregated cargo types of the most significant commodities and tonnages for 1972 are summarized in Table 4. U.S. totals of foreign waterborne traffic, including the Great Lakes, are given in Table 5 to illustrate the volume of trade for various commodities. Tonnages by

commodity groups are shown for 1965 and 1972. Only
commodities for which the 1972 tonnage equaled 1 per cent
of the 1972 total tonnage in either the export or import
trades are listed.

TABLE 4 -- 1972 FOREIGN WATERBORNE TRAFFIC [a]

COMMODITY	TONNAGE (short tons in millions)	PER CENT of TOTAL FOREIGN TRADE
Liquid Bulk		
Crude Petroleum	143.9	23
Petroleum Products	110.1	17
Dry Bulk		
Grains and products	78.2	12
Coal	65.9	10
Iron ores	40.6	6
Logs and woodchips	18.2	3
Aluminum ores	16.4	3
Phosphate rock	12.9	2
Iron and steel scrap	6.4	1
General Cargo		
Break bulk	67.0	11
Container	31.0	5
TOTAL	590.6	93

[a] Includes imports and exports

Data in both tables, except for the breakdown of
general cargo, are taken from *Waterborne Commerce of the
United States*, an annual publication prepared by the U.S.
Army Corps of Engineers.[29] The volume of general cargo
traffic and the separation between breakbulk and containerized cargo are from preliminary data prepared by the
Maritime Administration, the only agency presently collecting data on containerization. Moreover, some of the bulk
commodities may have moved as general cargo.

[29] U.S. Corps of Engineers, *Waterborne Commerce of the
United States, 1972*, Part 5, National Summaries, 1973.

TABLE 5 -- FOREIGN TRAFFIC: 1965 and 1972
(short tons in millions)

COMMODITY	1965 IMPORTS	1965 EXPORTS	1972 IMPORTS	1972 EXPORTS
APPAREL AND OTHER FINISHED TEXTILES	0.1	-	0.3	-
BASIC TEXTILES	1.1	0.3	1.2	0.3
CHEMICALS AND ALLIED PRODUCTS	2.8	9.2	7.9	17.3
COAL	-	50.1	-	55.9
CRUDE PETROLEUM	73.4	0.1	143.5	0.4
PETROLEUM PRODUCTS				
Kerosene	0.2	-	8.9	-
Distillate fuel oil	0.8	0.6	17.6	0.1
Residual fuel oil	56.8	2.4	76.8	2.1
Other	11.6	4.0	1.4	3.2
ELECTRICAL MACHINERY, EQUIPMENT AND SUPPLIES	0.2	0.3	0.9	0.4
FABRICATED METAL PRODUCTS	0.9	0.4	1.5	0.3
FARM PRODUCTS				
Grains	0.5	51.8	0.7	69.5
Others	4.6	1.9	4.5	1.9
FOOD AND KINDRED PRODUCTS				
Grain Products	0.4	5.4	0.4	7.6
Other	8.2	4.6	12.2	4.9
FOREST PRODUCTS	0.8	0.1	0.9	-
FRESH FISH & OTHER MARINE PRODUCTS	0.3	-	0.7	-
FURNITURE AND FIXTURES	0.1	-	0.2	-
INSTRUMENTS, PHOTOGRAPHICS AND OPTICAL GOODS, WATCHES, AND CLOCKS	-	-	0.1	0.1
LEATHER AND LEATHER PRODUCTS	0.2	-	0.3	-

TABLE 5 (CONT'D)

COMMODITY	1965 IMPORTS	1965 EXPORTS	1972 IMPORTS	1972 EXPORTS
LUMBER AND WOOD PRODUCTS				
Logs and woodchips	0.2	3.7	1.0	17.2
Other	4.7	1.4	6.3	1.9
MACHINERY	0.3	1.3	1.1	1.4
METALLIC ORES				
Iron ore	49.3	7.8	38.3	2.3
Aluminum ores	15.0	0.1	16.4	-
Other	5.0	0.1	3.4	1.1
MISCELLANEOUS MANUFACTURED PRODUCTS	0.4	0.1	0.5	0.1
NONMETALLIC MINERALS				
Limestone	0.6	1.1	7.8	1.5
Phosphate rock	0.1	6.2	-	12.9
Other	12.4	5.6	9.8	6.5
PRIMARY METAL PRODUCTS				
Coke	-	2.4	2.5	7.5
Iron and steel	10.7	2.2	17.1	2.3
Other	1.1	0.7	1.2	0.5
PRINTED MATTER	-	0.1	0.1	0.1
PULP, PAPER AND ALLIED PRODUCTS	4.0	3.0	3.2	4.8
RUBBER AND MISC. PLASTICS	0.1	0.1	0.4	0.1
SPECIAL AND MISCELLANEOUS SHIPMENTS	-	0.4	0.1	0.3
TOBACCO MANUFACTURES	-	-	-	0.1
TRANSPORTATION EQUIPMENT	0.7	0.8	2.7	0.7
WASTE AND SCRAP MATERIALS				
Iron and steel scrap	0.2	4.7	0.3	6.1
Other	0.2	0.4	0.1	0.6
TOTAL ALL COMMODITIES	269.8	173.9	397.6	232.4

Source: Part 5, National Summaries, *Waterborne Commerce of the U.S.*, Department of the Army, Corps of Engineers.

Factors Affecting Cargo Routing

Study of one port at a time does not adequately consider the effects of competition among ports. Port tributary areas often include extensive competitive zones that are serviceable equally well through competing ports. Thus, the tributary areas of various ports, as defined in separate studies, will generally overlap. Since any of several ports can capture tonnages to or from that area by exerting extra effort and offering inducements, forecasts must be careful not to "double count" such traffic.

Competitive factors that can influence the selection among ports for routing include the following:

···Quality and frequency of ship service;

···Quality and frequency of connecting land transportation;

···Efficiency of transfer facilities at the port;

···Availability at the port of services associated with shipping, such as steamship agencies, customs brokers, banks, and freight forwarders;

···Steamship rates;

···Port charges and regulations; and

···Rates by connecting land transportation.

Also to be considered is the current tendency toward specialization, which makes different ports better suited for certain types of cargo. Some ports have become identified with a particular movement, such as coal, oil, grain, or containers; at such ports a conflicting type of movement is likely to be slighted. The tendency for a specialized port to collect its special commodity movement from an unusually large tributary area results in certain economies of scale beneficial to all concerned. The trend toward port specialization must be recognized when attempting to predict future cargo routings.

A trend toward concentration of waterborne commerce through fewer but larger ports has come with specialization. This usually produces economies in ship operation, port handling, and connecting inland transportation but may also involve longer overland hauls to or from the port, presumably offset by the savings attained through concentration (load-centering).

In forecasting commerce through a particular port, recognition must be given to the possible inroads that can be made by competing modes. Air cargo can successfully compete with ocean freight in the transfer of high- and even medium-value commodities, especially perishables. Coastwise shipping and ocean and lake-wise movements between contiguous states or countries must contend with the overland competition of railroads and trucking lines. Thus, both changing patterns of shipping and changing costs of transportation must be studied carefully in evaluating a particular port's competitive position prior to forecasting traffic that may be expected to transit that port. Additionally, worldwide economic conditions must be considered when preparing a forecast. Economic changes can occur within a relatively short period of time and will be reflected in international supply and demand of goods and raw materials. Current U.S. and foreign policies should also be evaluated as to their effect on international commerce and shipping.

Cargo Movement Forecasts

Several studies of future U.S. trade volumes have been completed. These studies include details for numerous commodities, although there are no regional breakdowns. In addition to these studies, there is a wealth of data on the world's oceanborne shipping economics and vessel requirements compiled by foreign research organizations. Appendix B contains forecasts from existing studies for the following selected commodities: aluminum ores, crude petroleum, general cargo, grains, iron and steel scrap, iron ore, petroleum products, and phosphate rock. The studies cited are:

> *Oceanborne Shipping: Demand and Technology Forecast,* by Litton Systems, Inc., June 1968.

> *Forecast of U.S. Oceanborne Foreign Trade in Dry Bulk Commodities,* by Booz-Allen Applied Research, Inc., March 1969.

*Projection of Principal U.S. Dry Bulk
Commodity Seaborne Imports and Exports
for 1975 and 1995,* by Stanford Research
Institute, February 1969.

*U.S. Deepwater Port Study Commodity Studies
and Projections,* by Robert R. Nathan
Associates, August 1972.

*Forecast of World Trade in Containerizable
Commodities; 1975 and 1980,* by Manalytics,
Inc., June 1971.

Offshore Terminal System Concepts, by Soros
Associates, Inc., September 1972.

For illustration, summary forecast data for bituminous coal are given in the following figures and tables.
Total U.S. forecast data for bituminous coal seaborne
exports are summarized in Figure 1. All studies that
were utilized contain forecasts for total seaborne movements of export bituminous coal except for the Nathan
Study, which pertains to bituminous coking coal only. In
addition, the Litton study and the Nathan study excluded
exports to Canada whereas such exports were included in
the other studies. An illustration of a further possible
forecast for U.S. regions by foreign destinations is
shown in Figure 2. Such data are limited, but are necessary for the determination of port requirements. Projections for hinterland movements are not available.

Tables 6 through 9 present additional origin and
destination data for coal and are illustrative of the
types of data that are usually available from various
sources.

Forecast Methodology

Many levels of sophistication have been used to
forecast cargo movements at a given port, ranging from
the simple extrapolation of past experience to a commodity-
by-commodity analysis utilizing economic models. Different
approaches to forecasting volumes of waterborne commerce
include the following:

•••Adopting, or possibly adapting, an existing
forecast;

••• Projecting experience during a representative historical period as a straight line;

••• Using global (national) forecasts by others and projecting trends in relationships of local to global commerce;

••• Considering the supply or reserve at the commodity source;

••• Relating commerce volumes to measures of the economy (GNP, industrial, production, income levels, etc.) in principal market areas;

••• Delineating the port's tributary area on the basis of inland transportation costs, and examining trends in the area's economy;

••• Applying regional input-output methods of analysis to commodity movements;

••• Interviewing or canvassing by a representative number of shippers and consignees to learn their expectations or intentions for the future; and

••• Separately analyzing individual commodities or commodity groups with respect to reserves, production outlook, market areas, demand-related economic measures, competition, and trends in transportation changes and techniques.

Obviously, there has been little standardization of methods for forecasting port traffic. Although uniformity of method seems desirable, it is largely unattainable because of the wide variations in physical and economic characteristics and in traffic patterns among ports. Individual study probably will continue to prevail in port commerce forecasting, although refinement of techniques should continue.

Forecasting Techniques

Examples of some of the techniques used in forecasting waterborne commerce are furnished by several recent studies. Most of the data required in these analyses and forecasts were readily obtainable from

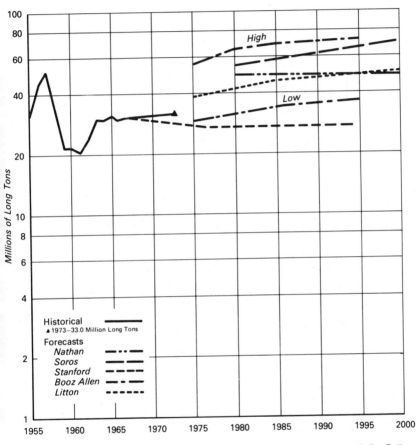

Historical data from Bureau of Census as quoted in "Projection of Principal U. S. Dry Bulk Commodity Seaborne Imports and Exports for 1975 and 1995", Stanford Research Institute

FIGURE 1

Forecasts of Bituminous Coal Seaborne Exports

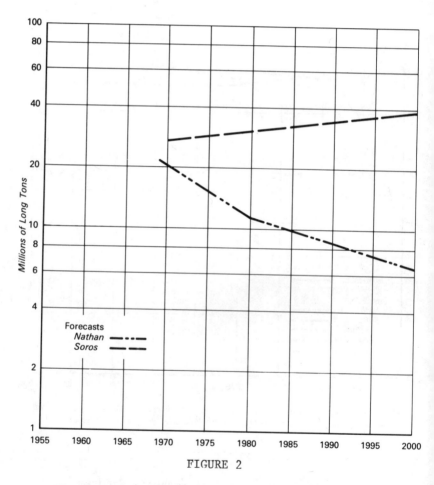

FIGURE 2

Forecasts of Bituminous Coal Seaborne Exports
from U.S. North America Area to Japan

TABLE 6

BITUMINOUS COAL-OCEANBORNE EXPORTS
(Thousands of Short Tons)

Foreign Destinations	Philadelphia	Baltimore	Hampton Roads	Mobile*	New Orleans	Los Angeles	Totals
				1970			
Western Europe	200	1,610	15,390	300	–	–	17,500
Mediterranean	–	240	4,280	–	–	–	4,520
Japan	50	2,600	24,680	700	190	265	28,485
E.C. of S. America	–	200	2,380	–	–	–	2,580
W.C. of S. America	–	40	220	–	–	–	260
Total	250	4,690	46,950	1,000	190	265	53,345
				1980			
Western Europe	280	1,850	17,350	900	–	–	20,380
Mediterranean	–	280	4,840	–	–	–	5,120
Japan	70	3,000	27,860	2,100	1,000	350	34,380
E.C. of S. America	–	230	2,700	–	–	–	2,930
W.C. of S. America	–	50	250	–	–	–	300
Total	350	5,400	53,000	3,000	1,000	350	63,100
				2000			
Western Europe	320	2,200	21,500	2,400	–	–	26,440
Mediterranean	–	330	6,000	–	–	–	6,330
Japan	80	3,600	34,570	5,600	1,600	500	45,950
E.C. of S. America	–	280	3,320	–	–	–	3,600
W.C. of S. America	–	70	310	–	–	–	380
Total	400	6,500	65,700	8,000	1,600	500	82,700

*Alabama State Docks Dept.; Forecast
Based Upon New Mine Development for Export

Source: 1970 Data: Coal Export Association, Association of American Railroads & Alabama State Docks Dept.
as quoted in "Offshore Terminal System Concepts," by Soros Associates, Inc., Table I-8

TABLE 7

U.S. OVERSEAS COKING COAL EXPORTS, 1980 and
2000: EXPORTING DISTRICTS; EXPORTING PORTS; OVERSEAS
DESTINATIONS (Millions of short tons)*

U.S. OVERSEAS EXPORTS	1980	2000
Exporting Districts		
Districts 1, 3 and 6[a/]	1.7	0.6
Districts 7 and 8 (Va. and W.Va.)	51.6	52.1
Alabama[b/]	1.1	0.6
All others[c/]	0.6	0.6
Exporting Ports		
Hampton Roads	51.6	52.1
Baltimore	1.7	0.6
Mobile/Pascagoula	1.1	0.6
Texas-Louisiana ports	0.6	0.6
Overseas Destinations		
South America:		
Zone 3	0.6	0.9
Zone 4	4.9	6.8
Total	5.5	7.7
OECD Europe:		
Zone 5	20.2	21.1
Zone 6	13.5	14.1
Zone 7	0.6	1.7
Total	34.3	36.9
Other Europe:		
Zone 7	0.6	0.6
Zone 8	0.6	0.7
Total	1.2	1.3
Japan:		
Zone 15	14.0	8.0
Overseas Total	55.0	53.7

Note: Overseas exports do not include exports to Canada, which go by lake and rai

a/ It is assumed that all District 1, 3, and 6 coal is destined for Northern Euro
b/ It is assumed that all Arkansas coal is destined for Japan.
c/ It is assumed that Alabama coal is divided equally between Japan and Northern
  Europe.
* Converted from Metric Tons

Source: *U.S. Deepwater Port Study Commodity Studies and Projections*, by Robert R.
  Nathan Assoc., Table 27, p. 398.

TABLE 8

TRADE FORECAST OF
U. S. OCEANBORNE COAL EXPORTS
(Millions of Long Tons)

	1970	1975	1980	1985	1990	1995
	41.22	55.31	66.03	71.29	72.51	77.10
Total Oceanborne Exports	31.78	41.16	47.79	51.21	52.51	55.08
	26.27	30.69	33.97	34.94	35.24	35.68

Countries of Destination	Medium Forecast Destinations					
ECSC (excluding Italy)	7.05	6.50	5.99	4.43	3.50	3.73
Italy	4.57	4.83	5.20	5.69	5.98	6.28
Other European Countries	3.50	3.57	3.57	3.52	3.36	3.53
Japan	13.38	22.01	27.82	31.99	33.68	35.26
South America	1.88	2.44	3.11	3.33	3.68	3.86
All Other	1.40	1.81	2.10	2.25	2.31	2.42

Source: Forecast of U.S. Oceanborne Foreign Trade in Dry Bulk Commodities by Booz-Allen Applied Research, Inc., Table 29 p. 123/124

TABLE 9

BITUMINOUS COAL SEABORNE EXPORTS:
PROJECTIONS FOR 1975 AND 1995
BY DESTINATION
(Millions of Long Tons)

Destination	1975	1995
Western Europe	20	19
Japan	8	6
Other	—	2
Total	28	27

Source: Projection of Principal U. S. Dry Bulk Commodity Seaborne Imports and Exports for 1975 and 1995 Stanford Research Institute, Table II, p. 42

published sources (e.g., "Economic Report of the President and "General Report of U.S. Foreign Trade"). Certain key information is reported sporadically (e.g., "1970 Origin-Destination Study of Foreign Trade," and "U.S. Census of Domestic Transportation"), and other data can be obtained only from special studies.

U.S. Deepwater Port Study

Prepared in 1972 by Robert R. Nathan Associates for the Institute for Water Resources, the 5-volume U.S. Deepwater Port Study report was the result of one of the most exhaustive recent studies of its kind. Volume II presents the commodity studies and projections as well as the underlying forecasts on economic aggregates.[30] All forecasts were carried to the year 2000.

Principal projections were the U.S. population and gross national product. The population estimates were taken directly from intermediate projections (Series C) prepared by the Bureau of Census.[31] The population distribution by state was projected to 1980 on the basis of estimates made by the National Planning Association, and the trends in distribution were extrapolated for succeeding years.[32]

The GNP projections were based on forecasts of three variables: employment, productivity, and hours worked per week. Employment was projected by using and extrapolating forecasts of participation rates by age groups made to 1985 by the Bureau of Labor Statistics and adjusting for institutional population and for the armed forces.[33] Productivity was projected at historical long-

---

[30] Robert R. Nathan Associates, *U.S. Deepwater Port Study Commodity Studies and Projections*, Aug. 1972.

[31] U.S. Department of Commerce, Bureau of the Census, *Current Population Report*, Series P-25, No. 442, March 20, 1970, and No. 448, Aug. 6, 1970.

[32] National Planning Association for Economic Projections, *State Economic and Demographic Projections to 1975 and 1980*, Regional Economic Projection Series, Report 70-R-1, April 1970.

[33] U.S. Department of Labor, Bureau of Labor Statistics, Special Report 119, Nov. 1970.

term growth rates. A declining number of hours per work
week was projected at a decreasing rate of decline based
on experience between 1948 and 1968.[34] The resulting
GNP projections were compared with those prepared by the
National Planning Association,[35] the Office of Business
Economics,[36] and the Economic Research Service of the
Department of Agriculture.[37]

The components of the GNP also were forecast to
2000, based on extrapolation of trends that had been projected to 1980 by the National Planning Association[38]
from a 1968 base.[39] Finally, the gross product originating
in each state was projected in three principal sectors to
the year 2000 using and extrapolating distributions forecast to 1975 by the National Planning Association.[40]

Other economic projections that were made as a
basis for forecasting commerce included population and
GNP in each of the European countries, Japan, and Canada.
Population figures were based on historical data of the

---

[34] Al-Smarrie and Scott, *Revised National Economic Projections to 1980*, National Economic Projections Series,
Report 71-N-2, National Planning Association, Nov. 1971.

[35] *Ibid.*

[36] U.S. Department of Commerce, Office of Business
Economics, 1971.

[37] U.S. Department of Agriculture, Economic Research
Service, *Discussion Materials: Informal Projections*,
Oct. 1970.

[38] Al-Smarrie and Scott, *An Economic Model for Long Range
Projections of the United States Economy*, National
Economic Projections Series, Report 71-N-1, National
Planning Association, 1971.

[39] U.S. Office of the President, *Economic Report of the
President*, U.S. Government Printing Office, Washington,
1971.

[40] National Planning Association, Center for Economic
Projections, *Economic Projections to 1980: Growth
Patterns for the Coming Decade*, National Economic
Projection Series, Report 70-N-1, March 1970; and *State
Projections to 1975; A Quantitative Analysis of Economic
and Demographic Changes*, Regional Economic Projection
Series, Oct. 1965.

Organisation for Economic Co-operation and Development [41] and on forecasts by the United Nations.[42] GNP to 1980 was adapted from forecasts by the OECD[43] and projected to 2000 at growth rates indicated by local levels of GNP per capita, with some judgment modifications.

Commerce analyses and forecasts were made in considerable detail for the following categories of bulk commodities: crude petroleum and petroleum products, iron ore, bauxite and alumina, coal, grains, soybeans and meal, and phosphate rock. Each of the studies used pertinent industry reports and reviewed the related technological elements in considerable detail. For example, United States and regional future demands on oil resources were taken and extrapolated from National Petroleum Council forecasts,[44] with consideration of estimates by the Secretary of Interior.[45] In forecasting iron ore movements, steel output and metallic input by furnace type were projected after evaluating the current trends in technology. The analyses and forecasts for the other commodities were equally complex reviews of trends in demand and technology and of projections based on relevant factors, including comparisons with other studies where available. Allocations to regions and to individual ports are less well documented.

---

[41] Organisation for Economic Co-operation and Development, *Labor Force Statistics 1957-68*, 1970.

[42] United Nations, Population Division, *World Population Prospects 1965-1985, As Assessed in 1968*, Working Paper No. 30, 1969; and *World Population Prospects, 1965-2000, As Assessed in 1968*, Working Paper No. 37, 1971.

[43] Organization for Economic Co-operation and Development, *The Growth of Output 1960 to 1980*, Dec. 1970.

[44] National Petroleum Council, *U.S. Energy Outlook: An Initial Appraisal 1971-85*, Interim Report Prepared by the Council's Committee on U.S. Energy Outlook, Washington, 1971.

[45] U.S. Congress. Senate, Statement by Secretary of Interior Before Committee on Interior and Insular Affairs, June 1971.

Forecast of Foreign Trade in Dry Bulk Commodities

Forecasts of foreign trade in various dry bulk commodities were prepared in 1969 by both Booz-Allen Applied Research and Stanford Research Institute (SRI) for the Maritime Administration.[46,47] Eight export and six import commodity classifications were investigated, with high, low, and "best estimate" projections of tonnages made for each to 1995. The approach used to prepare the forecasts was as follows:

•••Selection of significant commodities based primarily on recent average annual tonnage, commodity value, route distance, and strategic importance.

•••Assembly of both historical trade flow statistics and historical and projected economic indices.

•••Interviews with commodity experts.

•••Analysis of economic, technological, and commercial factors that strongly affect the volume, origins, and destinations of dry bulk movements.

•••Development of special forecasting techniques incorporating both historical trends of commodity movements and projections of production and consumption.

•••Development of a best estimate and a high-low range of forecast trade flows; country-to-country movements were projected.

---

[46] Booz-Allen Applied Research, Inc., *Forecast of U.S. Oceanborne Foreign Trade in Dry Bulk Commodities*, prepared for U.S. Department of Commerce, Maritime Administration, March 1969.

[47] Stanford Research Institute, *Projections of Principal U.S. Dry Bulk Commodity Seaborne Imports and Exports for 1975 and 1995*, prepared for U.S. Department of Commerce, Maritime Administration, Feb. 1969.

Regional Deepwater Port Facilities Studies

The Army Corps of Engineers conducted three separate studies of the needs for deepwater port facilities on the Atlantic,[48] Gulf,[49] and Pacific Coast.[50] All three reports were issued in June 1973 and were concerned largely with facilities for oil tankers. Forecasts of petroleum demand and supply were taken from the various current studies and reports on the subject, particularly the Nathan report, previously described. In addition, the Atlantic Coast report briefly treated the requirements for deepwater iron ore and coal facilities. Iron ore demand was related to GNP while coal export projections were taken from the Nathan report.

Foreign Trade Model of the Port Authority of New York and New Jersey

An econometric model has been developed by the Port Authority of New York and New Jersey to forecast commerce at the port through 1990. First, total U.S. foreign trade was forecast on the basis of foreign purchasing power for exports and of U.S. purchasing power for imports (U.S. purchasing power is defined in terms of the U.S. GNP and the ratio of the U.S. price level to the foreign area price level. Foreign area purchasing power is defined in terms of the foreign area GNP and the ratio of the foreign area price level to the U.S. price level). Future growth in purchasing power was projected in both cases in relation to the corresponding GNPs. Low and high tonnage projections, differentiating between general and bulk cargo but without further commodity breakdown, were derived for 1980 and 1990.

---

[48] U.S. Army Corps of Engineers, Philadelphia District, North Atlantic Division, *Interim Report: Atlantic Coast Deep Water Port Facilities Study*, June 1973.

[49] *Idem*, Lower Mississippi Valley Division, *Report of Gulf Coast Deep Water Port Facilities*, 13 vols., Vicksburg, June 1973.

[50] *Idem*, South Pacific and North Pacific Division, *West Coast Deepwater Port Facilities Study: Summary Report*, June 1973.

Second, New York's share of the total U.S. trade was projected on the basis of industrial activities and personal income in the port's hinterland, the relative dominance of foreign trading partners by geographic location, and the relative growth rates of commodities that are the specialty of the New York port. Low and high forecasts for New York to 1990 again were split between exports and imports within general and bulk categories.

Finally, an ocean-air modal split of general cargo through the port was forecast, based mainly on trends experienced in air penetration and in transportation rates in relation to shipment value. These general cargo forecasts were split in the same manner as the preceding.

Required Data

To evaluate the effects of technological changes and consequent shifts in the hinterland-port relationship for many commodities, it is highly desirable to have historical and forecast data to trace the trade routes of waterborne imports, exports, and coastwise movements of major commodities from source to destination. Data on exports, for example, would show the volume of a given commodity that originates in a particular U.S. hinterland, moves through a specific port range, and terminates in a certain foreign destination. To fulfill this format, data would necessarily include the following:

•••Commodity flows for all significant movements;

•••Trade routes indicating foreign origins and destinations, by commodities and countries;

•••Volumes of trade by significant commodities at U.S. ports, aggregated by regions; and

•••U.S. hinterland origins and destinations by significant commodities and volumes.

Commodity Groups

The various commodities moving through U.S. ports might be consolidated into major groups, such as

1. <u>Liquid bulk</u>--crude petroleum, petroleum products, liquified gas, and other.

2. <u>Dry bulk</u>--coal, grains, iron ore, aluminum ores, logs and woodchips, phosphate rock, and iron and steel scrap (sometimes classified as general cargo).

3. <u>General Cargo</u>--break-bulk, container, automobiles, iron and steel products (other than scrap), and wood products (packaged lumber, logs newsprint, plywood).

Trade Routes

Information on the domestic and foreign origins and destinations of significant commodities is necessary for analysis of selected commodity flows. Tonnages and the length of voyage between specific ports are also important in estimating the number and size of ships required for the various trades. Census data identify the foreign countries of origin and destination. For purposes of analysis these countries should be aggregated into the following regions: Canada, Caribbean, South America East Coast, South America West Coast, Western Europe, Mediterranean, Eastern Europe, West Africa, Middle East and East Africa, Far East, and Australia and New Zealand.

Port Ranges

Statistics on the volume of trade through various port ranges or customs districts are essential for analysis of port requirements. These coastal regions should be separated into logical ranges to or through which foreign trade and coastwise traffic flows. The following ranges are suggested, based on logical splits between interport competition: North Atlantic Coast, South Atlantic Coast, Gulf Coast, South Pacific Coast, North Pacific Coast, Great Lakes, Puerto Rico, Hawaii, Alaska, and American Samoa.

Hinterlands and Inland Routes

To relate the inland portions of traffic flows to the seaborne portions, the United States could be divided into the following inland regions: Northeast, Mid-Atlantic, Southeast, North Central, South Central, Southwest, and Northwest. Data on movements by mode to interior areas are difficult to obtain. In addition, importers and exporters frequently do not have complete knowledge of interior origins or destinations.

Suggested Data Format

For optimum usefulness, tonnages between foreign origins or destinations and United States ports of entry or exit should be shown in a matrix format. Iron ore has been chosen as an example. Table 10 shows the overall relationship between foreign areas and U.S. port ranges.

For maximum usefulness the matrix must be expanded to include the hinterland destinations, as shown in Table 11. Coastwise traffic should be included, but because there are no coastwise movements of iron ore, this traffic is not noted in Table 11.

Accumulation of historical data and preparation of forecasts in a detailed matrix format would allow informed and intelligent consideration of port development and inland transportation questions.

Availability of Historical Data

Numerous federal and nonfederal organizations compile and disseminate data on foreign and domestic waterborne commerce in a variety of formats. Federal agencies include the U.S. Army Corps of Engineers, Bureau of the Census, Maritime Administration, Department of Transportation, Bureau of Customs, and Interstate Commerce Commission. Since 1945 the federal program of collection and publication of waterborne commerce data has been coordinated by the Office of Management and Budget (and its predecessor agency) with the objective of producing the most useful data at the least cost.

Of the federal agencies, the Bureau of Customs, the Bureau of Census, and the Corps of Engineers are the major collectors and compilers. A brief description of the program of several agencies follows.

Bureau of Customs

The Bureau of Customs, Department of the Treasury, is the federal agency responsible for administering the tariff laws of the United States. Importers and exporters are required to file with customs officials information on waterborne trades. The data include statistics on modes, countries of origin and destination, quantities, values, and commodity classifications.

TABLE 10 -- IRON ORE IMPORTS: 1972

Origin	North Atlantic	South Atlantic	Port Range of Entry Gulf Coast	South Pacific	North Pacific	Great Lakes	Total
Canada	4.4	-	0.5	-	0.2	15.2	20.3
South America:							
East Coast	9.7	0.1	3.6	-	-	-	13.4
West Coast	1.0	-	0.7	-	0.1	-	1.8
Western Europe	0.1	0.2	-	-	-	-	0.3
West Africa	3.1	-	-	-	-	0.1	3.2
Far East	0.1	-	-	-	-	-	0.1
Australia	0.3	-	0.5	-	-	-	0.8
Total	18.7	0.3	5.3	-	0.3	15.3	39.9

Source: U.S. Bureau of Mines
Department of Commerce

-93-

TABLE 11 -- IRON ORE IMPORTS: 1972

Port Range/Origin	North East	Mid Atlantic	Hinterland Destinations South East	North Central	South Central	South West	North West	Total
North Atlantic								
Canada	-	*	-	*	-	-	-	4.4
South America								
East Coast	-	*	-	*	-	-	-	9.7
West Coast	-	*	-	*	-	-	-	1.0
West Europe	-	*	-	*	-	-	-	0.1
West Africa	-	*	-	*	-	-	-	3.1
Far East	-	*	-	*	-	-	-	0.1
Australia	-	*	-	*	-	-	-	0.3
TOTAL	-	*	-	*	-	-	-	18.7
South Atlantic								
South America								
East Coast	-	-	0.1	-	-	-	-	0.1
West Coast	-	-	0.2	-	-	-	-	0.2
Western Europe	-	-	0.3	-	-	-	-	0.3
TOTAL	-	-	0.3	-	-	-	-	0.3
Gulf Coast								
Canada	-	-	*	*	*	-	-	0.5
South America								
East Coast	-	-	*	*	*	-	-	3.6
West Coast	-	-	*	*	*	-	-	0.7
West Africa	-	-	*	*	*	-	-	-
Oceania	-	-	*	*	*	-	-	0.5
TOTAL	-	-	*	*	*	-	-	5.3
North Pacific								
Canada	-	-	-	-	-	-	0.2	0.2
South America								
West Coast	-	-	-	-	-	-	0.1	0.1
TOTAL	-	-	-	-	-	-	0.3	0.3

TABLE 11 (CONT'D)

Port Range/Origin	Hinterland Destinations							
	North East	Mid Atlantic	South East	North Central	South Central	South West	North West	Total
Great Lakes								
Canada	-	*	-	*				15.2
West Africa	-	*	-	*				0.1
TOTAL	-	*	-	*	-	-	-	15.3
GRAND TOTAL								39.9

* Not Available

Copies of the various customs forms and documents
are transmitted to the Bureau of the Census, which compiles the data under authority of the laws that make the
Secretary of Commerce responsible for dissemination of
trade information.

Bureau of Census

The foreign trade statistics program conducted by
the Bureau of the Census involves compilation and dissemination of data relating to imports and exports. These
statistics serve the needs of both government and non-
government users. The program includes a variety of data
presented in many different formats as reports, machine
tabulations, and computer tapes. The information is
compiled from import entries and export declarations that
importers and shippers are required to file with the
Bureau of Customs. These data include valuation, country
and area of origin and destination, vessels, and ports.
Some of the more important data are contained in monthly
vessel entrance and clearance reports. They include such
information as type of service (liner, tanker, tramp),
rig (motor, tug, barge, scow), customs district and port,
vessel manifest, vessel name, flag, ballast or cargo,
country and subdivision (or U.S. port of origin and
destination), cargo type (bulk or general cargo), and
vessel draft.

Army Corps of Engineers

The Army Corps of Engineers, which is responsible
for the improvement and maintenance of the navigable
waters of the United States in accordance with numerous
River and Harbor Acts, is authorized to collect data on
vessels, passengers, and cargoes moving on the waterways.
Waterborne commerce data are collected by the Corps and
published annually in a 5-part report entitled *Waterborne
Commerce of the United States*. These publications present
data on the movements of commodities and vessels at ports
and harbors and on inland and coastal waterways of the
United States, Puerto Rico, and the Virgin Islands. Data
on foreign commerce are supplied to the Corps by the
Bureau of the Census. Data on domestic commerce collected
by the Corps are primarily designed to meet its administrative requirements. The corps also provides data for
other government agencies, commercial and shipping firms,
and others interested in transportation. Generally, the
data compiled for domestic and foreign commerce include a

4-digit commodity listing of the import, coastwise, and internal traffic. Data are also included concerning the number and types of vessels calling and departing at each U.S. port.

Maritime Administration

The Maritime Administration administers programs authorized by various shipping statutes relating to ship-building, cargo promotion, and port development. These include operating-differential and construction-differential subsidy programs, ship mortgage insurance, vessel exchange, cargo preference, research, maintenance of reserve fleets, and other government aids to merchant shipping. To administer these programs, the Maritime Administration collects and compiles a variety of data on ships, bulk and general cargo tonnages (break-bulk and intermodal), individual port tonnages, and cargo values.

Interstate Commerce Commission

The Interstate Commerce Commission has jurisdiction over the operations, services, and rates of the domestic common and contract carriers by water, with respect to their operations on the high seas, the Great Lakes, and the inland waterways. The commission compiles annual data on the ton-miles of commodities transported by these regulated carriers.

Inadequacy of Current Data

Foreign and domestic waterborne commerce data collection programs currently conducted by the various federal agencies are generally not sufficient for assessing future port requirements, capacities, and related activities. There is a lack of cargo data to link the ocean legs of the import and export movements with the domestic or hinterland movements. Such data have been collected in the past for particular years on a one-time basis, but no attempts have been made to collect the data regularly.

The Bureau of Census made a special survey in September 1972 for general cargo. The survey, jointly sponsored by the Department of Transportation and the Army Corps of Engineers, collected information on the domestic origins and destinations of cargo moving in foreign trade by sea and by air. This had last been done in 1956. In-formation collected on the domestic movement included major modes of transportation between significant points, the distance, volume, and value. In addition, it included U.S. points designated for each state and the production and market areas. This information has been collected, processed, and stored on magnetic tape and is readily available. The report, entitled *Domestic and International Transportation of U.S. Foreign Trade: 1970*, notes that the data can be used to determine relationships between ports and foreign areas and to estimate and analyze selected general cargo flows through specific customs districts or ports by designated foreign trade routes. A similar survey is being planned for bulk commodities and will be entitled *Bulk Commodity Origin-Destination Study: 1973*. The report is sponsored by the Department of Transportation and the Army Corps of Engineers and is being prepared by the Bureau of the Census.

The Center for Great Lakes Studies at the University of Wisconsin-Milwaukee has analyzed a subset of the data contained in the public-use tapes of the 1972 report and found several shortcomings, notably in the data sampling technique. The report, *Analysis of International Great Lakes Shipping and Hinterland*, Special Report No. 23, states that "The sampling procedure employed to develop the data base was biased in a manner that prohibits valid inference for the sample to the population for any characteristics other than aggregate weight for ocean vessel shipments or aggregate value for air shipments." According to the Center's report, the sampling technique used for the 1972 report should not be repeated but rather "should be reconstructed to be perfectly random with each shipment having the same probability of selection."

The report also discusses the procedure for creating the Public-Use Tapes, stating that the number of errors found implies that an inadequate file-editing procedure was used, leading to a conclusion that "there are enough inconsistencies in the information provided for expanding the sample weight and sample value to estimated universe values to render these items untrustworthy." In addition, the report notes that there is an inconsistency and incompatibility of port and commodity codes used by the Bureau of the Census and the Corps of Engineers that does not allow direct comparisons.

The Center for Great Lakes Studies report draws the following conclusion about the 1972 Bureau of Census report:

> Supporters of this recent data collection effort (of the Bureau of the Census) foresaw a variety of uses including import market determination, domestic modal split analysis and specification of various hinterland characteristics. The uniqueness of this data source has already led to its use in the formulation of transportation related policies as well as in important decisions in both the public and private sectors such as investment in facilities. This widespread use has served to stimulate the effort that has been devoted to the preparation of this document. (Special Report #23.) Unfortunately, our analysis of these important applications, including that reported herein, is not completely valid.

Recommended Forecasting Procedures

In port planning it is desirable to make at least two estimates: first, a fairly short-range estimate for 5 to 10 years in order to determine immediate needs and, second, a longer range estimate for 15 to 25 years to establish the scope of future construction. At least 3 years will probably be needed to arrange financing and design and construct a new facility. After this, several years will be required for the new transportation patterns to be established. Frequently, a guide to a useful date for estimating completion will be the expected staging of some other corollary activity related to the port or waterway, such as construction of a connecting highway.

Forecasting the cargo potential for a port is an arduous task that requires access to data, familiarity with methodology, and knowledge of international trade. A good forecast is more than the sum of its individual parts. Forecasting is more of an art than a science.

The steps necessary to carry out a forecasting study, the data needs, and the analytical effort required are described in the following. The details may differ from port to port, but this outline and description provides a checklist for port planners.

Data Collection

The following types of basic information, necessary for the projection of potential port commerce, should be obtained through interviews with appropriate agencies, review of related previous studies, surveys, and questionnairs.

Traffic of the Port and Competing Ports

All available statistics should be gathered for the past 5 to 10 years on tonnages of commodity groups handled through the subject port and the competing ports. If possible, container cargo should be shown separately. Also, principal areas of origin and destination should be identified. Types of vessels generally used for each commodity should be determined.

Transportation Network Serving Ports

An inventory should be made of railway, highway, waterway, and airline transportation facilities directly or indirectly linking the port area and the competing ports with the inland regions. Maps should be prepared showing these routes and intermodal connections as well as any improvements in the transportation system either under construction or definitely planned. The maps permit tracing flows of port commerce to and from the hinterland, both at present and in the future.

Freight Rates and Port Changes

The selection of ports for cargo routing is based on the cost of transportation between the hinterland and the ports. Rail, highway, waterway, and air freight rates for the principal commodities to and from ports should be obtained from the carriers or organizations controlling cargo routings. Isodopane (equal rate contour) maps should be prepared for the port and its competitors.

Port handling charges are another factor influencing the routing of shipments. Schedules of port charges against the cargo (wharfage) and against the ships (dockage) should be obtained from the subject port and from competing ports.

Ocean Shipping Services

Current schedules of vessels calling at the subject port and competing ports should be collected, to show frequency of service to and from foreign and coastal ports. Shipping rates via those services should also be obtained from principal commodity classifications.

Competing Port Facilities

Descriptions should be prepared of facilities at competing ports. The tabulations should include the number of ship berths for each type of bulk and specialized cargo as well as for general cargo. All special storage and handling facilities and services should be noted. The survey should include a determination of plans for expansion or improvement of facilities and services at the competing ports.

Economic Factors Influencing Port Commerce

Statistics should be collected for the port hinterland on economic factors affecting potential port commerce. Such factors include, but are not necessarily limited to, the following: population (number, distribution characteristics); levels of income; agricultural production; mining; forestry; power output, industry (production, value added, employment).

Data Analysis

The collected data should be analyzed in the following ways to provide a basis for estimating future commerce and port requirements:

Boundaries of Present Tributary Area

Tabulations of areas of inland origin and destination for the principal commodities handled at the port should be prepared. These data would serve as the basis for a generalized map of the hinterland region served by the port.

Definition of Potential Tributary Area

Inland and ocean freight rates and port charges for each of the principal commodities considered potential to the port should be studied. The inland locations at which the total transportation cost would be equal through the subject port and through each competing port could then be determined. Such locations would define the boundaries of a tributary area, within which routing the subject port theoretically should be less costly than routing through other ports.

The region immediately surrounding the tributary area, where the total costs would be approximately the same for routing through the subject port or through other ports, could be considered as a competitive tributary area. It is a zone in which the development of commerce through the subject port could be substantial but would depend on attractions other than transportation costs alone, such as the type and frequency of ship services, adequacy of port facilities and services, and promotion.

Maps should be prepared showing the captive and competitive tributary areas for each of the principal commodity classifications. It is likely that the areas for different types of commodities will not be identical.

Trends in Commodity Shipments

The tonnages of principal commodities handled at the port and at competing ports should be analyzed to determine historical growth trends and possible shifts between ports. A pattern of imports, exports, and coastwise shipments that could serve as a basis for projecting future commerce flow would emerge. Where appropriate, average annual rates of growth should be computed.

Trends in Production and Consumption

An attempt should be made to correlate trends in waterborne commerce with economic measurements obtained for the tributary areas or overseas market areas. For example, trends in annual soybean and soybean product shipments should bear a relationship to trends in the annual production of soybeans or to economic conditions in overseas markets. Similarly, growth of receipts of consumer products at the ports could be associated with increases in population and income levels. Evaluations should also be made of foreign markets for exports.

Trends in Ship Sizes and Types

Developments in the size and type of ships serving ports in the region should be reviewed in relation to types of commodities usually carried. Maximum draft, length, capacity, average load, and special features should be analyzed to determine trends that might affect a port's capability to receive new ships. In particular, the use of bulk carriers, container vessels, and other types should be studied for any possible effect on port commerce projections and terminal design.

Projections of Potential Commerce

Based on the review and analyses of available information, various forecasts must be made for use in planning port development. Annual import, export, and coastwise tonnages of principal commodity types to be shipped through a port should be projected in considerable detail for the first 5 to 10 years, and in an aggregated form in 5-year intervals for the following ten or fifteen years. Commodities should be grouped according to their susceptibility to transport by ship type. Cargo to be carried aboard break-bulk ships should be subdivided according to handling requirements at the port, showing separately such special-handling general cargo as lumber, newsprint, heavy lift cargo, and vehicles.

The compilation and evaluation of necessary data for developing forecasts of port requirements and plans for future port expansion demands large and highly trained staffs devoted exclusively to research and development. The large costs involved would preclude most ports from conducting such research on an individual basis. The federal government could assist the port industry by taking the leading role in research and data collection and making its findings and the data available to all ports, preferably through a single agency. This would eventually lead to uniform guidelines for data collection and would eliminate the inconsistencies and lack of comparability that currently exist because of the variety of federal agencies currently collecting and preparing traffic and cargo. A special port industry committee, with representation from all transportation modes, could be established to advise the government of port data needs and could also assist ports in forecasting procedures.

A forecast is a function of the operating assumptions; in effect it is "valid" under one set of competitive factors. Forecasts should be made for several sets of competitive factors and even then should be subjected to sensitivity tests. Similarly, if we assumed a handling cost of X dollars per ton, we could ask what the forecast would be if handling costs were incrementally increased by $(X + \Delta X)$ dollars per ton. Lastly, we must note that forecasts (and some subportions of the forecasts) must stand the test of reasonableness. Analysis should not preclude the exercise of judgment.

CHAPTER V

ISSUES AFFECTING PORT DEVELOPMENT

The principal variables affecting the future growth
of ports are technological developments, port capacity,
regulation and rates, port financing, and environmental
and economic conflicts.

Technological Developments

Nearly all major technological developments in the
maritime industry in recent years have been directed toward
specialization. Ships are now designed for specific commodity movements, often over specific trade routes. Containerships are replacing older conventional or break-bulk ships
on many routes, while unitized loading (including palle-
tization) is replacing hand stowage on modern break-bulk
carriers, with obvious increases in efficiency. Even
general cargo ships are increasingly carrying containers
as part of their stowage. RoRo ships allow for more rapid
loading and discharging of certain containerized cargo.
LASH and SeaBee developments permit time and cost reductions
at downstream interchange points. In certain instances,
goods that had traditionally moved as break-bulk (e.g.,
sugar) are now handled exclusively in bulk.

Both high labor costs and the relatively small
growth in labor productivity in industrial nations are
responsible for these technological innovations. The
appearance of containerization with high costs for specialized ships, new container handling equipment, and new
terminals naturally results in the development of major
container ports or load centers--one or two ports in each
port range serving as the major terminal centers for most
container cargo of the region. Large, fast container
ships call only at these load centers. Cargo for other
parts of the region (including other ports) moves by smaller

feeder ship, barge, rail, or truck. Load centering produce economies of scale in port and terminal operations and in vessel utilization. Container vessels are expensive, and in-port time reduces the total annual volume of cargo they can handle. Container terminals are similarly expensive, and berths, cranes, and other equipment must have frequent use to be economically practicable. Technological development, specialization, and the resultant load-centering will continue and must be recognized in planning ports.

In less industrialized nations, fears are expressed that they may be forced to adopt containerization, even in the absence of a transportation infrastructure, in order to take advantage of technological developments. The full potential of container services is only attained when the regions at both ends of the route have reasonably well-developed internal transportation systems to serve complementary and balanced commerce. Those developing nations that have excessive unemployment and a shortage of foreign exchange are better served by a labor-intensive system than by a capital-intensive system.

Economies of scale for the movement of crude petroleum have resulted in the development of tankers too large to be accommodated in most ports in the United States The need for transshipping facilities has prompted the current interest in offshore terminals.

The federal government and private industry have studied alternative types and potential locations of offshore terminals. In most cases, projected offshore deepwater terminals should not adversely affect existing ports. Rather, there is likely to be increased activity in existing ports in support of the operations of such deepwater port facilities.

Port Capacity

Although the capacity of any single element of a port may be expressed as an absolute number, such as containers loaded per hour by a crane or vessel transits per hour through a channel, the aggregate capacity of a port cannot be so simply described. A number of physical constraints and operating policies directly affect the capacity of a port. In addition to these constraints and policies, port capacity is also affected by the demand imposed on the port, both in terms of the volume of each type of cargo the port is expected to accommodate and the time within which this volume must be handled. The capacity of a port must be determined with proper allowances for peak demands even though in off-peak periods much of the capacity is unused.

It would be possible, of course, to design a port facility so that its capacity would be fully utilized at all times. Under this situation, variations in demand would have to be accommodated by delaying ships, forcing them to wait at anchorage until vessels that arrived previously had been serviced. Also, cargo awaiting ships would be delayed or would be routed through a competing port. Although this approach to port operations would maximize the cargo handled at a port for a given set of facilities, an economic analysis incorporating both vessel cost and port facility costs would show that such an extreme case of port operations would represent a highly uneconomic use of resources. Conversely, designing a port so that vessels are never forced to wait also represents an uneconomic use of resources. As for any service operation, the least total cost is obtained by minimizing the sum of the costs of service facility construction and operation and the costs of ship and cargo delays. This results in a level of service at which vessels are infrequently forced to wait during peak periods.

Determination of such an economic optimum point requires a complex and detailed analysis of each port. While queuing theory and other concepts can be employed for the study of individual facilities or elements in a port, the interconnections among these facilities and elements are so complex that a sophisticated time-oriented simulation procedure may be necessary to determine fully the effects of modifications in facilities or changes in operating practices on vessel delays. Evaluating the economic costs of ship delays combined with capital and operating costs of physical facilities requires simulations using as inputs varying numbers of berths, entrance channel configurations, storage capacities, and operating policies and procedures. Such analyses to determine the economic balance for a port are, of course, costly and time consuming, especially in the larger and more complex ports.

No analyses of the capacity of individual ports or any detailed analyses of the existence of overcapacity at various ports or for the nation as a whole have been made in this report. On the basis of judgment and experience, however, it is concluded that under the competitive free market economy of the United States, and with recognition of the need to provide for short-term growth, there is no critical excess of port facilities in the nation. Ther are, at some ports, facilities that are not in use or are used for only limited periods each year. Many of these facilities are, however, obsolete in terms of current cargo-handling methods, and they would be inefficient and uneconomic to operate. That such facilities exist but are unused to their fullest extent is not an indication of overcapacity but rather is a reflection of the realities of economics in the competitive port industry of the Unite States. Requiring such facilities to be used and preventing the construction of new facilities would increase the total economic costs of cargo movement.

Regulation and Rates

Although technological developments in intermodal transfer have resulted in greater potential efficiencies, optimum freight transport and interchange have been retarded by administrative constraints of regulatory agencies National transportation policy should encourage the efficient and economical flow of goods both within the United States and between points within the nation and the rest of the world.

Basis for Regulation

By preventing unfair competition among suppliers of transport services, regulation is intended to preclude the development of monopolies. Meyer et al., in assessing the extent of competition in the transport industries and the probable structure of those industries if regulatory restraints were removed, assert that, "regulation is essentially a substitute for competition in the protection of the public interest, and it has developed historically in the public service industries in which competition has demonstrated its inadequacy."[51] And, as Friedlaender notes

> Regulation is the exception rather
> than the rule in the United States.
> Competition is considered "workable"
> in that it leads to a reasonably

---

[51] John R. Meyer et al., *The Economics of Competition in the Transportation Industries*, Harvard University Press, 1959, p. 1.

efficient allocation of resources
and prevents a socially undesirable
exercise of economic power. Government regulation is usually justified
in an effort to promote economic
efficiency or to further some goal
concerning income distribution. It
generally has the following purposes:
(1) to prevent unreasonable prices
and earnings in situations where
technological and demand conditions
create natural monopolies; (2) to
prevent discrimination among groups
with unequal bargaining power; (3) to
maintain certain types of services
considered to be in the broad public
interest; and (4) to ensure sufficient
profits for the development and expansion of an industry in situations
where competition and large divergence
between average total and average
variable or marginal costs make it
profitable to cut rates to the floor
of variable costs and thus foster
rate wars and instability.[52]

The author points out that "economic efficiency and the
allocation of resources seem to be matters of less concern"
than either "prohibiting (of) the antisocial exercise of
monopoly power" or "promoting uneconomic but socially
desirable services."[53]

Regulatory Agencies

Both the Interstate Commerce Commission (ICC) and
the Federal Maritime Commission (FMC) were established
to meet the regulatory needs of various elements of the
transport system. Each was accorded a particular juris-
diction--domestic surface transport in the first case and
ocean transport in the other. Neither, however, has

---

[52] Ann F. Friedlaender, *The Dilemma of Freight Transport
Regulation*, Brookings Institution, Washington, 1969,
p. 7.

[53] *Ibid.*

proper authority to regulate freight movements of an intermodal character between land and ocean carriers. The ICC was created in 1887 to protect the shipper from the discrimination with which he was confronted in the latter half of the nineteenth century; the FMC was established in 1961 (replacing the earlier United States Shipping Board, the Shipping Board Bureau of the Department of Commerce, the United States Maritime Commission, and the Federal Maritime Board) to regulate "services, practices, and agreements of common carriers by water...engaged in the foreign commerce of the United States," to regulate "rates, fares, charges, classifications, tariffs, regulations, and practices of common carriers by water in the domestic offshore trades of the United States," and to investigate "discriminatory rates, charges, classifications and practices in waterborne foreign and domestic offshore commerce...."[54]

The legislation that originally created the ICC and the FMC was concerned with individual modes. Neither was concerned with the impact of that mode on other modes. Hence, each agency, in fulfilling its statutory objectives, conflicts with the other. Such conflicts may result in impasses in facilitating intermodal transport. For example, either regulatory agency can, in effect, suspend a through international intermodal rate by unilaterally suspending the portion of the rate that falls within its jurisdiction. Further, the jurisdiction of each agency over international trade is limited.

The ICC, for example, has jurisdiction over land and inland waterway rates including those for segments of international traffic originating or terminating within the United States. The FMC has no certification controls in either domestic or foreign waterborne commerce, and its rate powers in foreign trade are vaguely defined. In addition, both agencies are organized to handle quasi-judicial, conflict-adjusting functions. Such functions, while meeting routine litigation-oriented problems, result in the agencies' consideration of new developments in intermodal transport only in a haphazard, piecemeal fashion

---

[54] Federal Maritime Commission, Eleventh Annual Report, U.S. Government Printing Office, Washington, 1972, pp. 1-2.

generally to the detriment of those innovations that might
lead to the restructuring of rates and regulations themselves. The concern of regulatory agencies with perpetua-
tion of the status quo among ports has given rise to such
traditional but irrational ratemaking practices as port
equalizations, arbitraries, territorial rates, and other
devices that preclude the operation of market forces in
the routing of cargo.

The ICC, in mid-1969, sought to permit carriers
under its jurisdiction to file through international rates.
The purpose was to foster single-factor and combination
rates between inland carriers and ocean carriers engaged
in foreign commerce by permitting publication of through
routes and joint rates in single tariffs. Following FMC
protest, the ICC rescinded its order.

The effects of technological development are
directly influenced by regulation. Load-center ports may
serve regions that extend across national boundaries,
particularly around the North Atlantic and Great Lakes
ports, where cargo that would normally move through
American ports is transiting Halifax and Montreal. Thus,
individual U.S. ports must compete with Canadian ports
that are assisted by the National Harbors Board. The
primary reason for U.S. shippers and consignees to route
overseas traffic through Canadian ports is to take advantage of lower total transport charges. Economic and
regulatory differences between the two nations work to the
advantage of the Canadian carriers and ports, which not
only have lower costs but also have the freedom to adjust
rates and services to the requirements of individual
shippers. For example, the Canadian National Railway has
been offering full container service to such American
cities as Detroit and Chicago through the port of Halifax.
The advantage to Canada of major economic and regulatory
differences between it and the U.S. results from absorption
of inland transport costs by ocean carriers serving Canadian Atlantic ports, lower tariffs on volume shipments,
through bills of lading, and lower cargo-handling costs.
In Canada there is no regulatory body that exercises jurisdiction over ocean freight rates as does the FMC. The
Ministry of Transport can issue a "show cause" order if it
believes a freight rate to be too high or too low but has
exercised its authority only in connection with trucking.
Thus, free from constraint, the Canadian transport system
can provide true intermodal service at less cost to the
shipper.

The present awkward, inefficient, and highly unsatisfactory combination of route and rate arrangements in
international intermodal movements can only be resolved
by restructuring the regulatory process itself. Efforts
in the past to encourage interagency coordination have
generally failed because both the ICC and the FMC have
effectively guarded their respective jurisdictions while
publicly calling for greater cooperation.

One method of resolving joint international intermodal rate controversies would be the creation of joint
boards to which private parties or the transport agencies
might refer matters of superjurisdictional concern. Such
boards, similar to one involving the Interstate Commerce
Commission and the Civil Aeronautics Board, were called
for in President Kennedy's Transportation Message in 1962,
but no action has yet been taken to establish one between
the FMC and the ICC. Another possibility is the establishment of a separate agency solely for the purpose of exercising exclusive regulation of international movements.[55]
Operation of such an agency would create problems of
coordination, duplication, and possible waste. It appears
the merging of existing regulatory agencies into a single
agency would provide the most workable administrative means
for the integrated regulation of transport services and
rates. Legislation creating such an agency should specify
cost of service as the principal basis for ratemaking.

Basis for Ratemaking

In the late nineteenth century, and, indeed, well
into the twentieth century, the railroads, enjoying a
virtual monopoly of land transport, established their rates
according to the principal of charging "what the market
would bear." No consideration was given to the cost of
providing the service. The value-of-service principal was
accepted by the railroads, the Interstate Commerce Commission, and, since there was no alternative, the shippers.
With the introduction of truck transport in the 1920s, the
railroads lost their position as sole transporters of
commodities on land. Despite the growth of trucking during

---

[55] Maritime Transportation Research Board, *Legal Impediment
to International Intermodal Transportation*, National
Academy of Sciences, Washington, 1971, p. 67.

the next several decades, with significant capture of the
more highly rated cargo, the railroads consistently refused
to alter their rate structure, and the value-of-service
concept was perpetuated.[56]

More recently, whenever the railroads sought to
reduce rates on particular movements, the ICC, aware of
its responsibility for setting motor carrier and water
carrier rates, ruled that such reductions could not drop
below levels at which trucks and barges could compete with
railroads for traffic. This policy of "umbrella" ratemaking "generated excess capacity and resulted in both
railroads and trucks handling (the) kinds of traffic for
which the other was better suited."[57] However, the ICC
adhered to the railroads' value-of-service rate structure.
The railroads were unable to adjust rates to meet the
increasingly serious competition from trucks because the
truck lines published rates that closely approximated
railroad rates (depending on their ability to offer both
quick and flexible service), which could not be undercut
because of the rate umbrella.

Finally, in 1958, with the condition of American
railroads deteriorating by the month, the Secretary of
Commerce, in a letter to Senator George A. Smathers, Chairman of the Surface Transportation Subcommittee of the
Committee on Interstate and Foreign Commerce, urged the
Congress to enact legislation that would authorize "the
ICC to consider in setting minimum rates the effects of a
rate on competition or on a competitor only where its
effect might be substantially to lessen competition or to
tend to create a monopoly, or where the rate was established
for the purpose of eliminating or injuring a competitor.[58]
After prolonged debate over the wording of the bill, Congress
enacted the following as an amendment to Section 15a (the

[56] John T. Starr, Jr., *The Evolution of Unit Train Operations in the United States: 1960-1969*, The University
of Chicago, Department of Geography Research Paper
No. 158, 1974, p. 53.

[57] George W. Hilton, *The Transportation Act of 1958: A
Decade of Experience*, Indiana University Press, 1969,
p. 24.

[58] *Ibid*, p. 32.

rule of ratemaking) of the Interstate Commerce Act:

> In a proceeding involving competition
> between carriers of different modes
> of transportation...the Commission,
> in determining whether a rate is lower
> than a reasonable minimum rate, shall
> consider the facts and circumstances
> attending the movement of traffic by
> the carrier or the carrier to which
> the rate is applicable. Rates of a
> carrier shall not be held up to a
> particular level to protect the traffic
> of any other mode of transportation....[59]

With the passage of the Transportation Act of 1958,
legal status was given to the concept of cost-of-service
ratemaking. If the broad objective identified earlier is
to be realized--if the free flow of goods is to take place
most efficiently--then the traffic should be allowed to
flow by whichever routing and mode minimizes economic and
financial costs. The regulatory process should not
interfere unduly with such movements. The cost-of-service
basis for ratemaking would ensure, through the operation
of economic forces, that each port receives that share
of the total waterborne traffic it can handle at the least
cost to the nation.

Port Financing

Heavy capital investments by ports for modern cargo
handling facilities have created new demands for port
financing. Ports are confronted with major questions regarding large investments in new facilities and in the
modification of existing ones. Forecasts made by port
agencies indicate that an average level of expenditure of
nearly $300 million per year will be needed during the
remainder of the 1970s to enable the ports to serve the
growing import and export trade of the United States.[60]
The most serious problem facing port authorities is obtaining capital funds for development and expansion, because
new shipping and cargo handling systems are more capital-
intensive than the older conventional systems.

---

[59] *Transportation Act of 1958,* Public Law 85-625.

[60] *North Atlantic Port Development Expenditure Survey,* p. 4

In addition, the growing number of recently enacted
federal laws and regulations embracing port cargo security,
environmental preservation, and waterfront workers' safety
require port agencies to expend substantial sums. Other
costs arise from lengthy delays created by numerous federal,
state, and local agencies, each requiring different certificates, licenses, permits, and approvals for port,
navigation, and water resources projects.

The delays connected with the conception, authorization, and final approval of harbor improvement projects
are substantial in both time and money. For example, in
a speech delivered to attendees of the National Symposium
on Marine Transportation Management, a spokesman for the
Corps of Engineers stated that the average length of time
for dredging projects is approximately 18 years. In a
paper delivered by the Executive Director of the Port of
Oakland (February 27, 1974) it was indicated that the
project to dredge the shipping channel to Oakland's Inner
Harbor was started in 1955 and "it has taken nearly 20
years of studies, reports, hearings, permit applications,
and finally authorization before the work can be started."
Further, mention was made of another channel dredging
project that was expected to take 14 years from initiation
to the time of beginning work.

A last example pertains to the Port of San Diego.
The April 28, 1975 edition to Traffic World reported that
the dredging of San Diego Bay, a project initiated in the
1960s would finally begin in mid-1975. The estimated cost
of the project increased from $9.7 million when first
considered to about $17 million.[61]

Current Sources of Funds

Capital funds for port development, beyond those
relatively modest amounts generated by current port
operations, are generally obtained from long-term borrow-
ing, such as the issuance of general obligation or revenue
bonds or some form of direct or indirect subsidy at the
state or local level.

------

[61] Further examples of added costs because of federal
legislation are documented in Public Port Financing
in the U.S. Maritime Administration, pp. 20-27.

As a means of raising capital, the port authority can issue general obligation bonds, which are usually tax supported. The state, county, or municipality, when actin as the legislative parent of the port authority, as issuer of general obligation bonds, is required to provide collateral security by pledging its full faith and credit. Since this pledge is generally supported by the taxing authority of the political entity, the issuance of such bonds may be preceded by a referendum to determine the consensus of the community. Although this type of bond financing places a burden on the local taxpayer, its acceptance or rejection is based on the will of the community concerning the overall economic benefits of the new facility to be financed.

General obligation bonds are considered attractive because of their relative safety for the investor. Because they have the pledged support of a tax-collecting governmental entity, they carry a relatively low rate of interest which is exempt from federal income taxes. Approximately 32 per cent of the total port financing since the end of World War II has been by the issuance of general obligation bonds.

If port facilities can be leased or operated by the port at a level that will generate revenues sufficient to pay the principal and interest on a bond issue, the port may use revenue bonds as a means of financing. Operating income either from the facility or from some alternative revenue sources are pledged as security for the bonds. Since revenue bonds have a higher risk factor than general obligation bonds, interest rates are higher.

In addition to revenues that may be obtained through the issuance of bonds, state and local port development may be provided by various forms of direct and indirect subsidy. Such subsidies include the following:

   •••Direct appropriations by legislative bodies;

   •••Property tax assessment;

   •••State reservation of harbor areas and shorelines, which are tendered in trust to municipalities for harbor improvements;

   •••Perpetual bridge and tunnel tolls;

•••Revenues from mineral resource exploi-
tation, such as petroleum;

•••Contributed services (legal, accounting,
planning, engineering, security, etc.);

•••Exemption of port-owned property from
state and local real and personal
property taxes;

•••Donations of surplus public properties
or transfer at less than full fair market
value; and

•••Sharing in rental receipts from harbor area
leases of state-owned properties.

Current Federal Assistance Programs

Although most port development activities in the
nation have been established primarily through local
efforts, several federal agencies have also been involved
to a limited degree. While the programs of these agencies
have had varying impact on ports, they have not been designed primarily as port financial aid programs. The
programs of the Army Corps of Engineers (Department of
Defense), the Coast Guard (Department of Transportation),
and the Maritime Administration and Economic Development
Administration (Department of Commerce) are discussed
here. The main thrust and direction of these programs is
toward some other purposes: channel improvements and
maintenance, navigational aids, merchant marine promotion,
and unemployment relief. These programs and the other
federal assistance programs involving various modes of
transportation are discussed in greater detail in Appendix
C.

Army Corps of Engineers

The Army Corps of Engineers performs both military
and civil works functions. One of the Corps' principal
civil works activities is the construction and maintenance
of channels, harbors, and waterways for navigation, flood
control, and shore protection. The Corps is also responsible for the administration of federal laws relating to the
protection and preservation of the navigable waters of the
United States. In 1974 about 20 per cent of the Corps'
expenditures, or about $35 million, was for new construction

of deep-draft channels and harbors; estimates for 1975
indicate expenditures of about $75 million for this purpose
In addition, the Corps is responsible for analyzing the
economic feasibility of proposed projects under its jurisdiction and reporting to Congress. [62]

Coast Guard

The Coast Guard constructs, maintains, and operates
aids to navigation in all deep-draft ports and waterways
of the nation. In recent years this program has been expanded through research efforts to include the development
of sophisticated vessel traffic control systems. Total
Coast Guard expenditures related to deep-draft navigation
are about $25 million annually.

Maritime Administration

The Maritime Administration administers a number of
programs related to water transport. Port-related expenditures by the Maritime Administration were formerly
limited to salary and expenses of staff members working in
port promotion. Recently, the Maritime Administration has
become more heavily involved in port research and development and has also responded vigorously to the port industry
interest in pollution abatement and regional planning.
Current expenditures approximate $2 million annually,
divided fairly evenly between staff salaries and costs
for research and development.

Economic Development Administration (EDA)

The Economic Development Administration is concerned
with the creation of long-term employment opportunities in
economically distressed areas. For qualified projects, EDA
makes direct grants up to 50 per cent of total costs,
combined direct and supplementary grants up to 80 per cent
of total costs, long-term loans up to 100 per cent of total
costs, and guarantees of loans for working capital up to
90 per cent of loan amount. For port development projects,
EDA, with assistance and technical advice from the Maritime
Administration, has expended more than $100 million.

---

[62] Appendix D is an exposition of the 18 major steps of
the reporting procedure of the Corps of Engineers.

Emerging Federally Mandated Costs

Federal requirements affecting the construction and operation of marine terminal facilities encompass cargo security, environmental protection, and occupational health and safety.

As the latest in a long series of legislative measures, the Congress now has under consideration the Department of Transportation Security and Safety Bill. This bill would empower the Secretary of Transportation to establish nationwide regulations for the security of goods in transit, including transfer through and storage at port terminals. In addition, the Department of Transportation, in conjunction with industry groups, is issuing cargo advisory standards for seals, locking devices, and storage of high value cargo. Compliance with these standards will entail significant expenditures by ports.

Ports in recent years have felt the increasing impact of laws that impose restrictions on development of the coastal zones. States are being encouraged to ensure wise use of the land and water resources of their coastal zones, giving attention to ecological, cultural, historic, and esthetic values as well as to economic development. Environmental effects have now become part of our decision-making processes along with social, economic, and political considerations.

Congressional actions, such as the National Environmental Protection Act of 1969, the Coastal Zone Management Act of 1972, the Marine Protection, Research, and Sanctuaries Act of 1972, and the 1972 amendments to the Water Pollution Control Act seriously affect ports. Of particular concern are regulations that require the preparation of environmental impact statements for any new construction, expansion, or dredging; these statements are both time-consuming and costly. The port industry is apprehensive that the cost of new facilities to meet the environmental requirements will be substantial when the full impact of recent legislation is felt.

The National Occupational Safety and Health Act of 1973 authorizes the federal government to set mandatory occupational safety and health standards applicable to any business affecting interstate commerce, with responsibility for the standards resting with the Occupational Safety and

Health Administration (Department of Labor). Safety and health standards cover railroads, airlines, trucking, warehousing, and material-handling industries, including ports. Those standards that affect ports pertain to the handling of materials, indoor general storage, mechanical handling equipment (such as cranes, trucks, and yard equipment), fire extinguishing devices, including sprinkler systems, and general amenities for port labor (such as lighting, rest rooms, lunch rooms, and parking areas). Thus far, concerted efforts by the port industry to obtain waivers or modifications in some of the more stringent regulations have met with little success.

Rationale for Federal Port Assistance

The federal interest in port development was created with the ratification of the Constitution. Under the Constitution, the 13 colonies gave up their power to tax goods moving across their borders, and Congress assumed the power "to regulate commerce with foreign nations, and among the several states...."[63] The Constitution also provided for nondiscrimination among states, stating that "no preference shall be given by any regulation of commerce or revenue to the ports of one State over those of another...."[64] These provisions of the Constitution were further implemented by various laws that authorized and appropriated funds for federal construction, operation, and maintenance of channels, anchorages, harbors, break-waters, waterways, locks, and dams, all directed toward the encouragement of foreign and domestic commerce. Since 1789, the federal government has invested over $1.5 billion for channels, ports, and harbors. At the same time the federal government was given the responsibility of providing for the movement of commerce, it also took the power to collect customs, duties, and similar levies on imports. Total customs collections since the formation of the nation have exceeded $45 billion.

In addition, the federal government has been responsible for the safety of ships, the people on them, and the cargo they carry. As ships have become larger and the

---

[63] *Constitution of the United States of America,* Art. 1, Sect. 8, Para. 3.

[64] *Ibid,* Art. 1, Sect. 9, Para. 6.

volume and variety of hazardous cargoes they carry also
has grown, the federal government, through the Coast Guard,
has assumed more responsibility for safety in ports.
Hazardous cargoes can also be hazardous polluting substances,
thus posing a serious environmental problem. Increased
federal involvement in port safety can enhance environmental protection as well as prevent or minimize costly
ship collisions, groundings and other casualties.

It appears that total new capital expenditures for
port development (excluding all maintenance) during the
next few years will be more than $375 million annually,
consisting of approximately $300 million per year for the
construction of publicly owned marine terminals and $75
million per year for the construction of new deep-draft
channels, anchorages, and harbor works. In addition, the
federal government will spend approximately $150 million
per year for the construction of traditional and experi-
mental aids to navigation, removal of obstructions, and
maintenance dredging.[65] In addition, there is need for an
extensive data collection and analysis effort on the movement of commerce to and from the ports of the nation, and
for research and development in vessel traffic control,
the engineering of channels and harbor works, and similar
basic investigations that are beyond the capability of any
individual port or group of ports. It is considered that
an additional $5 million per year should be allocated for
such national research and development efforts to ensure
the continued technological development of the ports of
the United States.

In the past, financing of commercial marine terminal
construction has been almost exclusively the responsibility
of local port agencies. These agencies, principally
located in the major coastal cities of the nation, are
encountering financial difficulties common to all large
urban centers. With increasing demands on local tax revenues for education, medical care, housing, welfare, and

---

[65] Data from the Corps of Engineers show that, for 1974,
approximately $174.9 million was spent by the agency
for dredging and maintenance. Of this amount, $139
million, or 80 per cent was for maintenance dredging
and $35.7 million for new work. Estimates for 1975
indicate total expenditures of about $191.5 million,
of which $117 million is for maintenance dredging (60
per cent) and $74.3 million will be for new work. These
expenditures pertain to deep-draft channels and harbors.

other public services, funding for port development receiv a low priority, particularly where ports are supported by legislative appropriations. Thus, it appears unlikely that local sources will be able or willing to finance needed port development during the next decade.

Moreover, investment in port facilities is becoming increasingly unattractive to private investors, who have been the traditional source of capital for port developmen through purchase of bonds. A scarcity of money, competiti for funds for industrial development, pollution control, and other public needs, combined with the industry's relatively low rate of return, make it difficult for most ports to compete for investment funds from the private sector. Results of a recent survey indicate that even those ports that are making a net profit on operations are finding it difficult to show anything but a marginal rate of return. Despite the transition of general cargo ports from labor-intensive to capital-intensive, dramatic increases in ship berth productivity, and improved interface with other modes of transportation, the cost recovery of the nation's ports continues to be relatively noncompensatory.[66]

Environmental and Economic Considerations

As a natural consequence of market failure, non-market solutions for environmental management have emerged These include public acquisition of title to coastal resources, wider use of zoning, and other land-use control subsidies to help industry to reduce waste discharge.[67] Unfortunately, these approaches are often implemented in ways that are ineffective, inefficient, piecemeal, and inflexible. They impose additional jurisdictional layers that make the decision-making process less responsible to those affected. A particularly important nonmarket solutic is the adversarial process in court and agency hearings.

[66] U.S. Department of Commerce, Maritime Administration, *Public Port Financing in the United States*, Washington, June 1974, p. 19.

[67] Knetsch, J.L., *"Economics and Management of Coastal Zone Resources,"* in Nute, J.C., and Slepp, J.M. (eds.); Coastal Zone Resource Management, Praeger Publisher, N.Y. 1971.

Although these make the decision-making process accessible to the public, they are costly, time-consuming, and inefficient devices for management.[68]

There is clearly a need for alternative ways to find acceptable balances between environmental and economic considerations in port development. Ideally, collective action is needed to involve all affected groups in evaluating alternative actions, the impacts of which have been fully explored.

In practice, collective action organizations do exist. They range from conservation associations to political bodies at the local, state, and federal level. Unfortunately, some of these organizations have become advocates and do not provide the decisions that are needed.

Ducsik proposed general guidelines by which governments should make the necessary decisions.[69] These guidelines appear to be useful for port planning and development. He considers two fundamental questions:

1. What is the particular institutional setting (political and economic) within which certain problems, in this case port development, should be solved?

2. How should resource allocation decisions be made within the appropriate institutional setting?

The proper political setting for port development and environmental decisions appears to be mainly local. However, in compliance with the Principles and Standards of the Water Resources Council, and the Coastal Zone Management Act, appropriate regional and national considerations must be involved. Economically, an adjusted market system is preferable to purely preemptive actions outside the market system, such as moratoriums, master plans, and prohibitive regulations. Such an approach preserves the market advantages of free and decentralized decision-making, a concept which is in contradiction to a strong body of

---

[68] Baram, M.S., "The Legal and Regulatory Frameworks for Thermal Discharge from Nuclear Power Plants, *Environmental Affairs*, Vol. II, No. 3, 1972, pp. 505-532.

[69] Ducsik, op. cit.

opinion favoring centralized planning and control of the
decision-making process for coastal zone development,
rather than control by the market place. Once the appropriate institutional setting is defined, the problems of
how to allocate resources, how to adjust the market system,
and what actions to take if the market cannot be adjusted
properly remain. The multi-objective planning approach
of the Water Resources Council appears to be useful in
developing an effective decision-making process. The
primary approach is the accounting in monetary terms, if
possible, or in nonmonetary terms for all beneficial and
adverse effects of alternative actions on both economic
and environmental objectives. Even though such accountings
may be difficult and complex, this does not invalidate the
process as an effective approach to balancing economic
and environmental considerations in port development. It
is essential that all future port planning be carried out
in conformance with the Water Resources Council "Principles
and Standards for Planning of Water and Related Land Resources."

CHAPTER VI

SUMMARY AND CONCLUSIONS

The future port requirements of the United States are subject to an almost infinite variety of conditions and forces, many of which are nonquantifiable and unpredictable. Maritime traffic is affected not only by changes in the technology of land and water transportation but also by economic, political, and social conditions within the United States and throughout the world. In addition, national security considerations will have an impact on the traffic through a port, particularly in time of emergency.

The uncertainty of the forces affecting demand for port services presents a dilemma for decision-makers dealing with port development, a dilemma similar to that faced by planners in general. Long-term plans to cope with the population explosion, urban renewal, congestion in the central city, mass transit, suburban expansion and industrial sprawl, and other social problems must all be evaluated, ranked in priority order, and reconciled to a finite supply of funds, with no assurance that the conditions the plan is designed to alleviate will exist when the plan is fulfilled. Ports increasingly demand substantial long-term capital investments in channel improvements, land acquisition, landward transportation facilities, terminals, and mechanical equipment. Plans must be developed to fulfill these needs and must be reconciled with future demand for port services. Since many of the tangible as well as institutional elements of port operations may become rapidly obsolete and may require replacement, modification, or abandonment within a relatively short time, port planners, too, face the possibility of committing large investments for schemes that do not materialize. Compounding the problem is the unavailability of a sound

and comprehensive data base for making informed judgments
about port development needs.

Port Planning

A basic conclusion of the Panel on Future Port
Requirements of the United States is that centralization
of planning for U.S. ports is neither desirable nor
practicable. It appears not feasible to determine in a
centralized approach, either for the short-run or for the
long-term, the optimum amount or character of port development that will be required for the nation as a whole,
for individual coastal ranges, or for local areas.

Unlike ports in other nations, those in the United
States are characterized both by a fragmentation of
responsibility and by seemingly overlapping responsibilitie
Harbor improvements, for example, including the dredging
of channels, are a federal responsibility. The provision
and operation of port terminals and associated infrastructure, however, are generally nonfederal responsibilities.
They involve state, regional, county, and local agencies
as well as private industries and carriers. Many ports
consist of a multiplicity of operating and controlling
organizations, with varying degrees of coordination. Very
commonly, a lack of coordination, particularly with respect
to planning, exists.

Managers of individual ports as part of their planning process must, among other things, consider their
port's competitive relationships with each other, their
port's relationship to competitive hinterlands, and the
impacts of port actions on competitive ports. Alternative
methods of satisfying the demands of prospective and presen
traffic and other aspects of the economic geography of
associated regions must be taken into account, possibly
leading to decisions precluding additional development.
In addition, the effect of changes on the labor force and
the economic base of the city or region in which the port
is located must be considered.

For purposes of this report, "planning" is defined
as a process that includes three stages, portions of which
may be concurrent. The first stage is research and analysi
including generation, collection, collation, and interpre-
tation of data. The second stage, plan preparation, is
concerned with physical, organizational, and financial

matters, and the interrelationships among specific plans. The third stage is plan effectuation, which includes public and community relations, intergovernmental and interagency coordination, public participation, and continuous monitoring of feedback as programs are implemented.

The panel concluded that coordination among the ports in the first of these three stages, research and analysis, can and should be greatly improved, with the federal government taking a major role in this process. The federal role in the other two stages, in part related to legislation, should be subordinate to the nonfederal decision-making process.

Although the panel believes that port planning at the national level is neither practicable nor desirable, there are many instances in which regional port planning and development are essential. A prototype exists in the form of the Port Authority of New York and New Jersey, the first of several interstate port organizations formed to plan and develop a regional port. Even in the New York region, however, complete coordination of port planning and development has not been fully successful, as evidenced by the fragmentation of authority between New York and New Jersey, and the City of New York and also the establishment of additional private terminals in the bi-state port area. Ports near each other can achieve greater effectiveness by some degree of coordination when, for example, they share a common metropolitan location or coexist on a single harbor or waterway.

Redundancy

Another concern of the panel was the issue of possibly redundant port facilities. Since modern ports are increasingly capital-intensive, the commitment of large amounts of funds and the devotion of extensive waterfront and backup land areas to port facilities and operations involve important questions of public policy for the allocation of scarce capital and land resources. Waterfront land is especially scarce in many port areas, where other types of metropolitan land uses compete for these strategic waterfront locations. Also, demands for other public investments, either in physical infrastructure or for services such as education and welfare, may compete with ports for funding.[70]

---

[70] See Chapter 2, pages 14-15, and Chapter 5, page 121 for a discussion on competition for funds.

The panel has concluded that it cannot quantitative
determine the existence of redundancy. Redundancy implies
excess capacity, and it is impossible to provide an adequate measure for the capacity of a port. There are many
reasons for this measurement problem: One is that the
nature of cargo ships and productivity of facilities will
vary greatly through time. Cargoes are not uniform.
Peaking--the concentration of demand during limited period
of time--occurs in port operations as in all other aspects
of transportation. It is economical and, in some instance
physically impossible to provide for the maximum peaks.
At the same time, it is undesirable that undue waiting tim
leading to costly delays to vessels and cargo, occur
because of failure to provide for periodic peaks. Such
delays, if common, could result in traffic being diverted
to competing ports or, in some instances, not moving at
all.

Excess capacity, in one sense, does not exist even
though a port or terminal may have 100 per cent utilizatio
of its capacity for only short periods of time, if ever.
Consideration of peak activities, other than for very
infrequent occasions, is an important element of port
planning. Capacity must be supplied in order to provide
adequate service to the shipping public as well as to
anticipate possible national emergencies, when even the
largest ports may be crowded.

Another important reason, in the judgment of the
panel, for providing capacity in excess of normal demand
is to create competition among the various ports and port
services to the advantage of the shipping public. That
is, the public can be reasonably assured not only of
continued availability of port services in the event of
accidents or other closures or reductions but also of
competitive rates and services. Thus, the shipper receives
a series of options that would not be available unless
interport competition continued.

Investment in Port Securities

Public ports provide facilities through the use of
exclusive land leases or by building for a specific tenant.
Capital for such facilities is usually raised through
issuance of revenue or general obligation bonds of the
public port authority. As a rule, public general cargo
facilities either incur financial deficits or do no better
than break even. Although several do manage to produce

a modest financial surplus, most public ports require and receive some form of public financial support.

For some ports, revenue bond financing is becoming more difficult, because port revenues are not sufficient to amortize bonds. In others, where general obligation bonds are the traditional financing vehicle, competition for local tax dollars with other public projects is intense. Because local governments must direct their resources to fields of great social and political pressure, such as urban redevelopment, transit, recreation, and environmental protection, port development often receives a lower priority.[71]

Repayment of the principal and interest on general obligation bonds is done either from general revenues or through assessment of a special tax or levy on taxpayers. Some states require the port agency to return part of its surplus revenues to the state. These funds are either used to pay off the principal or debt service or they are placed in a special construction fund to help finance future port improvements.

From the port's point of view, there are several disadvantages to financing by general obligation bonds. Although the port is the direct beneficiary, the controlling government body assumes indebtedness. Such financial obligation on the part of the port, therefore, makes it subject to greater control and regulation by the parent organization. Many ports do not favor such controls because political controls are not always conducive to effective management and operation. A general observation in recent years is that new capital-intensive facilities can be fully self-supporting in only a few ports.

Because the public, which typically must approve general obligation bonds, might place a higher priority on parks, hospitals, or schools, the port's fate can depend on the vagaries of an electorate indifferent to the economic impact of the port on the community. Similarly, as local citizens have become very conscious of the need for a cleaner environment, the port has often been denied expansion opportunities on the grounds that increased traffic, liquid bulk in particular, would have a deleterious effect on the environment.

---

[71]Refer to Chapter V, pages 115-117, for a discussion on sources of funding.

Finally, another disadvantage of general obligation bonds is the ceiling placed on such indebtedness by the character of the parent organization or the bond market investors. Generally, this ceiling is based on the state's or city's assets, taxing authority, overlapping debt, and business potential. Once this ceiling is reached, further funding is denied, regardless of how financially attractive the proposed improvements may be.

Aside from these disadvantages, general obligation bonds are considered attractive because of their relative safety for the investor. Since these bonds are supported by the state, county, city, or port authority, they carry a lower rate of interest and are not subject to federal income taxes. Such financing also permits the port to use its general revenues for other expenditures that would not be eligible under the provisions of general obligation bonds.

Ports have traditionally resisted any federal financial assistance except for federal funding of channel and harbor improvements. This reluctance stemmed partly from a lack of cohesive national policy regarding the role and status of ports and partly from a fear by the ports themselves that Federal aid might result in federal control and would restrict the competitive nature of the port industry. In short, the port industry believed that acceptance of federal financial support might be the beginning of nationalization of the industry.

Environment and Safety Regulations

Superimposed on all needs and prospective capital outlays for current and future port development in the United States are recently enacted federal, state, and local laws and regulations embracing waterfront workers' safety, environmental preservation, and cargo security. These new regulations require port agencies to expend substantial sums for compliance; such regulations are often burdensome and lead to unnecessary and costly delays because each of a multitude of different federal, state, and local agencies requires different certificates, licenses, permits, and approvals for port, navigation facility, and water resources development projects.

The federal government has established mandatory occupational and health standards that apply to any activity affecting interstate commerce. The states can

enact similar standards, which must be at least as high as
the federal ones, subject to approval of the Secretary of
Labor. With respect to port safety, meeting such standards
requires significant expenditures, and the port industry
has unsuccessfully sought to obtain relaxation of some of
the more stringent regulations. The industry believes
that it has responded readily where use of extra precau-
tions or safety measures has been warranted but feels that
existing state and city regulations, as well as industry
standards, are sufficient to ensure the safety and health
of port workers.

Regulations that require environmental impact statements for any new construction, expansion, or dredging are
of particular concern to ports. These statements are
time-consuming and costly. They may take several years
to prepare and must clear several federal agencies. Some
ports are not equipped with personnel or resources to
undertake a comprehensive environmental impact statement.
They must, therefore, rely on consultants or state water
and air quality control boards to perform the task. Compounding their problems are confusing, ambiguous, and
conflicting federal and state guidelines as well as overlapping jurisdictions of government agencies. A detrimental
effect of such delays is the possibility of a shift in the
economic need if the facility is not build within a
reasonable time. A shipping line seeking to locate at a
port will not wait 2 or 3 years for the environmental
impact statement to be completed preceding actual construction of the facility. Instead, it might elect to bypass
that port in favor or one with existing facilities. The
economic loss to the port being bypassed no doubt would
be significant.[72]

Traffic Diversion

A complaint commonly heard in the United States is
that Canadian ports are able to divert substantial volumes
of U.S. cargo. This is particularly true of the North
Atlantic and Great Lakes ports, where cargo that would
normally move through U.S. ports is moving through Halifax,
Montreal, and St. Johns. Canadian ports are supported
directly by the national government through the National
Harbors Board. Thus, individual U.S. ports must compete

[72]Refer to Chapter 5, pages 114-115, for a discussion on
on the impact of legislation on ports.

with government-supported Canadian ports; for example, the Canadian National Railway has been offering full container service between such American cities as Detroit and Chicago directly to the port of Halifax. The foreign-flag steamship lines that serve Halifax have been absorbing the segment of the rail rate between Montreal and Halifax, a distance of over 800 miles. Thus, the shipper in the Midwest pays only the rail costs from origin to Montreal while his cargo moves all the way to seaboard.

U.S. shippers and consignees route overseas traffic through Canadian ports in nonstrike years to take advantage of lower door-to-door rates. Economic and regulatory differences between the two countries work to the advantage of the Canadian carriers and ports. They not only have lower costs but also have the freedom to use them in adjusting rates and services to the requirements of individual shippers. In addition, ocean carriers serving Canadian Atlantic ports can absorb inland transportation costs, can receive lower tariffs on volume shipments, can issue through bills of lading, and have lower cargo-handling costs. Regarding the latter advantage of Canadian ports, for instance, collective bargaining provisions permit an 8-man longshore gang size at Halifax; at New York, a gang is substantially larger, on the order of 18 men. An additional advantage that Canadian railways have over the U.S. railroads is the option to enter into "agreed charges" with shippers. This type of agreement is illegal in the United States.

Rate-making philosophies of the U.S. and Canadian governments differ fundamentally. Unlike the U.S. railroads, which are subject to ICC regulations, Canadian railways enjoy great flexibility in working with ocean carriers and are thus able to offer rates far more attractive than those offered in the United States. Their pricing flexibility is reflected in the favorable volume rates that they are able to offer in comparison to U.S. railroads. Rate flexibility has also allowed Canadian railways to capture container movements. Furthermore, there is no Canadian regulatory body that exercises jurisdiction over ocean freight rates from Canadian ports as the Federal Maritime Commission exercises authority over ocean rates through U.S. ports. Thus, free from the constraints of regulatory bodies such as the ICC and FMC, the Canadian transport system is more geared to true intermodal service at considerably less cost. This freedom from constraints results in a stronger position for Canadian ports, enabling them to divert cargo from U.S. ports.

Load-Center Concept

Containerization and the demands that container operations place on vessels, terminals, and ports have led to the concept of the load center. The concept is that of a small number of ports--one or two in each port region-- serving as the major terminal centers for all container cargo of the port region. Large, fast container vessels would call only at the load centers. Cargo for other ports in the region (range) would move by smaller feeder container vessels or by rail or truck. Inland points would be served by trains, trucks, or barge--depending on the distance, the volume of cargo, and the available internal transportation.

Load centers have occurred and will continue to occur nationally as a result of economies of scale in port and terminal operations and in vessel utilization. Container vessels are expensive, and undue port time reduces their annual throughput potential. Container terminals are expensive, and the utilization of berths, cranes, and other equipment should be as high as possible, commensurate with the avoidance of congestion.

Some ports have used the regulatory process in an attempt to maintain direct call service by established operators. The fight to preserve markets has resulted in some underutilization of capital investment because the port must have adequate facilities if it petitions for service maintenance and, perhaps, an excessive number of calls by container vessels.

Operators who can only attract a small market share in major load centers may be attracted to secondary ports. In this way, such ports can capture cargo from the load centers without competing directly. Such tactics are only effective on major trade routes with adequate cargo gene-ration at many ports, such as the North Atlantic-Europe routes.

Mini-Bridge

Although "land bridge" movements between the Far East and Europe across the United States have been infre-quent (they have become quite common across Canada), numerous "mini-bridge" operations exist. For instance, goods for Europe are now hauled overland from hinterlands normally tributary to Gulf Coast ports to the port of Charleston, South Carolina, rather than to nearer ports

that formerly handled the cargo. As many as 10 days are
saved by this diversion. Gulf Coast ports have sought to
have such service halted, arguing that its facilities are
the rightful recipients of the traffic. Several of the
ports in the North Atlantic range and the ILA have also
sought to prevent diversion of traffic to West Coast ports.
In the opinion of the panel, if the free flow of goods is
to take place most efficiently, then traffic should be
allowed to flow through whichever port offers the minimum
cost to the shipper. The regulatory process should not
interfere with such movements.

Offshore Terminals

Offshore terminals are an alternative to the provision of new extremely deep channels to port facilities.
Several federally funded studies have been completed that
thoroughly discuss the alternatives, types, and potential
locations of offshore terminals for use by deep-draft
tankers. Recent federal legislation (Deepwater Ports Act
of 1974) provides for federal licensing of the location,
construction, and operation of the deepwater port facilities. The current emphasis is on the adequate development
of a sufficient number of deep-draft offshore oil transfer
facilities to permit achieving economies of scale in the
long-distance transport of oil by use of very large crude
carriers (VLCCs).

In most cases, the projected offshore deepwater
terminal facilities should not adversely affect existing
ports. Rather, there is likely to be increased activity
in existing ports in support of the operation of any
offshore deepwater facility. Some port officials, however,
believe that onshore ports can be developed to service
supertankers, and they view the projected development of
offshore ports as not in their best interest. Each
potential offshore port location must be viewed individually
with respect to effects on existing ports. Alternative
sites, including expansion of existing port capacity,
should be examined from the viewpoint of both economic and
environmental impact.

Labor

The changing technology of cargo handling, exempli-
fied by unitization (in particular containerization), has
led to a change from the labor-intensive method of handling
break bulk cargo to the capital-intensive systems using

containers, barges and lighters, and roll-on-roll-off
(RoRo) ships. The impact on longshore labor has been great
and has resulted in dislocation of waterfront labor in
many ports. Advances in cargo handling techniques affect
overall demand and require shifts from unskilled to
skilled types of labor. The need then is one of retaining
and accommodating a shrinking employment base. The problem
of unemployment, too, is very real. The number of workers
required to handle containerships is small, and the productivity is much higher than with conventional ships.
The number of workers in the ancillary freight terminals
loading and unloading containers will probably rise, but
not in sufficient amount to compensate for the labor displaced from the holds of ships. Therefore, it will be
necessary to institute training for the upgrading of workers
who will need new skills and to develop a plan for maintaining a stable labor supply.[73]

Port Development Funding

The difficulties that the port industry is increasingly encountering portend a potentially serious financial
crisis. Prices of all elements of port planning, development, operation, and maintenance have increased drastically
in recent years. The financial problem is compounded
because some communities attach lower priorities to port
development than to other public services. This is
especially true of those communities in which ports are
supported with legislative appropriations, where they must
compete with education, hospitals, housing, recreation,
and highway projects for available funds. The result is
that ports are placed very low on the public priority list,
and port development financing is difficult to obtain.
Other pressing needs of the urban centers have gained
priority over local port development programs; consequently,
port agencies are facing intense competition for local
funding of expanded facilities.

If the ports are to continue to play the vital
economic role they have played to this time, they will
probably require some additional sources of funding.

---

[73] Refer to Chapter 2, pages 26-27, and Chapter 3, pages
63-70, for a detailed discussion of port labor.

Containerization and other unitized forms of cargo-handling
have changed a labor-intensive industry to one of capital-
intensiveness. This change has required significantly
greater capital investment in new terminal equipment and
supporting services to increase port productivity and lower
unit costs. As the benefits of port activity are both
regional and national in scope, it could be argued that
the responsibility for port development may be regional or
national, at least in part, as well as state and local.
Some segments of the port industry believe that, because
the nation as a whole enjoys some of the benefits of port
development, it is logical that it share in the cost of
port development. However, there are also important elements of the port industry that do not accept the premise
of federal cost-sharing except for certain specific port
expenditures.

The port industry, as a matter of record, has
accepted financial assistance from the federal government.
The biggest program used by the ports is the Economic
Development Administration (EDA) program of public works
and technical assistance grants and loans for communities
with high unemployment rates or depressed economic conditions. Even though the EDA program is not aimed specifically at the port industry, over $100 million of financial
assistance for construction and planning purposes has been
obtained since 1965. Thus, a precedent does exist for
federal financing of U.S. ports.

The present system of local financing of port
development has served well both the port industry and the
commerce of the United States. In some cases needs have
not been met, primarily because response has been blocked
by environmentally inspired court actions or delayed because of an intricate maze of federal and state requirements. At present, however, many ports are faced with
economic constraints that will not allow the construction
of needed and planned facilities. With the national policy
of revenue sharing in effect, it appears that the ports,
which are a positive economic factor in the growth of the
United States, should not be excluded from financial aid
programs. But, given the present method of relatively free
competition among ports, it is axiomatic that any federal
financial assistance must be given on a uniform and non-
discriminatory basis.

Objective

Goals of Port Policy

Questions relating to appropriate size, location, and type of facilities and the environmental impact of these facilities are critical when expansion of older ports and construction of new ports is considered. Responses to these questions must be made within the framework of general goals that determine the reason for developing a port or new facilities. Some will view a port as primarily serving to benefit the trade and commerce of a particular city or region, while others will view a port as a means for ensuring a coordinated and flexible transportation system for the country as a whole. Thus, individual goals will have different implications for the future development of a given port or port area.

There are several possible goals that will help to determine port policy. First, there is a need for an economically efficient transportation system in the United States. Port facilities are the important link between water and inland transport and must be of sufficient capacity to handle traffic flows carried by different modes. Decisions on the number and type of port facilities are connected to the location, size, operating characteristics, cost of the entire transportation system, and levels of service of alternate modes.

A second general goal is provision of sufficient port capacity to satisfy national security considerations. In times of emergency, the ability to move large amounts of military equipment, and sometimes personnel, is essential. Also, it is important that, unless such emergencies are of an extremely severe and extended nature, regular commodity flows not be disrupted significantly.

A third broad goal of future U.S. port policy is to give preference to the economic development of depressed regions. This is especially true if a new port is being proposed. A port can act like a magnet, attracting industrial development for the surrounding area. Industry will tend to locate close to a port if the savings in transportation charges to and from the port are greater than any increased costs in the movement of goods to hinterland markets.

Finally, a fourth goal of U.S. port policy is the maintenance of environmental quality. Port expansion and/or construction could result in explicit and implicit environmental costs that exceed all transportation cost savings and other benefits derived from such expansion. Economic theory then would dictate the quantification of environmental costs and benefits along with all other costs and benefits if a port project's impact is to be evaluated properly.[74]

The goals of U.S. port policy must be established by all interested parties. There will of necessity be trade-offs, the extent of which must be determined by the appropriate decision-making body. These decisions must be made in the context of a national interest that is increasingly centered on societal and environmental needs. The federal government, with a high degree of cooperation between local governments, regional planning groups, and private interests, is involved in planning urban renewal and conservation programs that deal with rehabilitation and conversion of existing waterfront lands and facilities. In many cases, there will be a direct effect on future port development programs sponsored by public and private interests in the port industry. Therefore, it is most important that transportation plans and goals be coordinate and clearly understood by all parties involved in the decision-making process of port development.

Conclusions

The panel has arrived at the following conclusions with respect to U.S. ports:

1. Ports are in the national interest of the United States.
   (Port's Role in the Economy, page 6).

2. Ports should remain competitive and free to develop within a local, state, or regional frame of reference without any federal comprehensive plan.
   (Institutional Aspects of Port Development, page 34).

---

[74] Refer to Chapter 3, pages 59-63, for a discussion of environmental and economic considerations.

3. The benefits of the port industry redound to the welfare of the nation; since the country as a whole enjoys the benefit of port development, it is only logical that the federal government participate in some of the expenses of port development. (Port Economics, page 38).

4. Public participation in financing port development, maintenance, and operation may be justified in proportion to public benefits, both economic and social, since ports are public utilities whose benefits are not always or necessarily reflected in a profit and loss accounting by the port agency. (Port Economics, page 38).

5. Existing national transportation regulations fail to reflect adequately the cost of producing transport services and lead to inefficient use of transport facilities, misallocation of traffic, and unsound financial conditions in the transportation industry. (Basis for Ratemaking, page 112).

6. Changes in rate structures and transportation technology have led to the growth of load-centers, thus creating "de facto" regional ports by enlarging hinterlands and bringing distant ports into competition with each other. (Containerization, page 22).

7. The proper role of the federal government in port planning should be confined to guidance and coordination. (Ownership and Control, page 35).

8. Port planning should be undertaken primarily at the local or regional level and should be consistent with the Water Resources Council's "Principles and Standards for Planning of Water and Related Land Resources." (Environmental and Economic Considerations, page 122).

9. Substantial expansion and improvement of collection, assembly, collation, and publication of data are required.
    (Chapter IV).

10. Data collection, processing, and dissemination would be greatly facilitated if the current gathering and publication activities were consolidated into a single federal agency.
    (Chapter IV).

11. Quantitative analyses of the effects of alternative transportation policies must be part of the local and national transportation decision-making process.
    (Chapter IV).

12. New research methods and better cost and trade flow data are needed to aid the development of a coordinationated, intermodal transportation policy.
    (Chapter IV).

13. Port efficiency cannot be judged by the availability of some apparently underutilized port facilities since some over-capacity is desirable for competitive flexibility and normally recurring peak loads.
    (Port Capacity, page 106).

14. Environmental issues do and will continue to play a major role in shaping port development.
    (Evaluation of Ecological Impact, page 52).

15. The market system cannot be the only decision-making mechanism in coastal zone management because it is difficult if not impossible to specify the acceptable economic costs for the conservation and preservation of desirable coastal environmental conditions and human values.
    (Economic Considerations, page 60).

16. The market system, operating in a local decision-making political setting, often fails to allocate resources properly and is therefore by itself an ineffective mechanism for balancing economic and environmental considerations in port development. (Economic Considerations, page 60).

17. Statewide coastal programs may emerge from the Coastal Zone Management Act that will have significant effects on port development, thus requiring that port agencies be active in developing such programs. (Legal Considerations and the Environment, page 53).

18. Delays in the issuance of required permits and the awarding and completion of contracts for dredging and other port projects increase development costs and reduce the possibility of economic advantage that might accrue from the investment. (Port Financing, page 114).

19. The federal government should continue to install and operate traffic systems, similar to the U.S. Coast Guard's Vessel Traffic Service, to monitor and control ship movements in congested ports and channels with high accident potential. This will help to reduce ship casualties, improve navigation in coastal waters, and enhance the protection of the environment. (Current Federal Assistance Program, page 117).

20. Port planning must be undertaken with full awareness that the port is not operating in a vacuum and with the understanding of the interplay between the port and the institutional, environmental, and economic structures of the area in which it is located. (Environmental and Economic Considerations, page 122).

CHAPTER VII

RECOMMENDATIONS

The Panel on Future Port Requirements of the United
States concentrated on the identification and classification
of the immediate problems and future needs of ports in the
United States and the development of a mechanism for providing port agencies with the necessary tools for solving
these problems and meeting these needs. The panel believes
that decision makers at local levels can and must bear the
responsibility to respond to changing demands for port
services caused by advances in technology and changes in
traffic volume and that their actions will in fact change
the port structure of the country. The panel further
believes that the nation's port development would be adversely affected if any single agency or group (including
the panel itself) were to establish the port requirements
of the United States in specific terms of number, location,
and type.

The panel has examined issues of national concern
within a local, state, regional, and national framework,
with special consideration of the federal interest and role
in port development and operations. Technical, socioeco-
nomic, and policy trends currently influencing the ports
of the nation have been identified. The effects of these
trends on the port and the impact of the port on (a) land
use, (b) the economic base of cities and regions, (c) the
labor force, (d) the social and physical aspects of cities
and metropolitan areas, and (e) the environment of the
coastal area form the basis for the panel's conclusions,
recommendations, and approaches to current and future
challenges.

The panel has agreed that its suggestions and
recommendations are concerned with a time period of no

more than one generation, or roughly between 1976 and the year 2000. Several of the recommendations deal with the near-term and can be instituted almost immediately, whereas others involve gradual changes in policy and implementation. Because new port development will necessitate the commitment of continuing financial investment for extensive periods and will set in motion a chain of consequences affecting port regions, coastal zones, and hinterlands, the effects of exogenous variables over long periods cannot be confidently projected. Consequently, the chosen time frame represents a compromise between the need to look beyond the immediate and the difficulty (if not the impossibility) of making valid predictions for longer periods.

The recommendations on the following pages pertain to the major topics of port planning, development, operation rate regulation, environmental concerns, labor, and finance. The recommendations represent the unanimous opinion of the voting members of the panel.

Port Financing

To provide for financing of port development:

*The federal government should partici-
pate in the financing of a portion of
the total capital costs for port development by establishing a Federal Aid
to Ports Program.*

The panel has concluded that the funds necessary to
meet the requirements for port development can no longer
be obtained solely from traditional sources. Since the
entire nation derives benefits from ports, a specific allocation of federal funds for capital expenditures for port
development should be authorized and appropriated.

The federal government should participate in port
financing on a partnership principle, whereby basic
decisions are made by local port agencies and are reviewed
for conformity to accepted standards of feasibility, safety,
and environmental protection by the federal funding agency.
Any system of federal participation in port financing should
recognize that the strength of the port industry is derived
from local autonomy and freedom to operate competitively,
and therefore local decision-making should be fostered. It
is further proposed that a single federal agency be assigned
responsibility for the funding program.

The Federal Aid to Ports Program should authorize
the use of federal funds as direct grants for port development. The act should provide for a formula whereby
the total funds appropriated (after deduction of an amount
for national data collection and research) would be allocated to all coastal states for use in subsequent grants
in connection with port development projects. Coastal
states would include all those so defined in previous acts
relating to coastal zone management. The allocation formula
would be based on various parameters that reflect port
needs and their contributions to the national economy.

Allocation of funds would provide money on a state
by state basis. It is proposed that grants be made only
after port agencies prepare and submit a justification
report for any project on which federal participation is
requested. The justification report would include the

considerations established in the "Principles and Standards for Planning for Water and Related Land Resources" developed by the Water Resources Council as well as other requirements for environmental impact analyses, safety standards under OSHA, and similar federal requirements. When the locally prepared justification report is approved by appropriate state and local agencies and found to demonstrate the economic, social, and environmental desirability of a project, the agency would obligate federal funds to the project on a matching basis. Actual payment of the federal funds would, as in other federal programs, occur after the expenditures by the local port agency.

Eligible projects would be limited to capital investments for construction or improvement of marine terminals, channels, anchorages, breakwaters, and other harbor works. Also included are such ancillary improvements as sewage treatment plants, security facilities, and recreational facilities. Privately owned industrial terminals, such as oil and ore docks, would be excluded from the program. Detailed studies are required to determine the appropriate federal share, which might range from nothing to 100 per cent, for various types of projects. The federal government should continue to bear 100 per cent of the costs for the maintenance and operation of channels, harbor works, and aids to navigation as traditionally performed by the Coast Guard and Corps of Engineers. Based on precedents in other federal-aid programs, such as for highways and airports, the following federal shares of participation are presented as suggestions for further study:

New channels, anchorages, and breakwaters	90 per cent
Federally mandated costs	70 per cent
Marine terminals	50 per cent
Public amenities	10 per cent

The port and new channel development costs identified in Chapter V totaled more than $375 million per year. On the basis of the suggested levels of federal participation listed above, between $200 million and $250 million per

year should be appropriated for implementation of the
proposed Federal Aid to Ports Program.[75] This amount
should be reviewed frequently so that it fully reflects
the changing needs of the port industry, the effect of
inflation on capital expenditures for port development,
and the increasing benefits to the United States of the
nation's deep-draft port facilities.

In recommending a Federal Aid to Ports Program, the
panel recognized that local taxation is currently the basis
for most port financing, either directly or indirectly.
As discussed previously, the panel has concluded that the
local tax base in most areas will not be readily available
to ports for financing all their capital costs in the
future, and that needed port development may therefore
suffer.

With restricted availability of the local tax base
for port financing, alternative methods of financing future
development must be devised. Ports can either finance
their continued development through a local-federal partnership (such as recommended herein) or can take on, in
effect, the attributes of private industry and finance
their development from their own revenues, without reliance
on local taxation. The 1974 Maritime Administration Report,
"Public Port Financing in the United States," indicated
that 70% of ports' capital funds were provided from sources
outside net revenues. Implementation of the private
industry alternative would thus require a major overhaul
in the rate practices of ports in the United States,
resulting in significant increases in their charges. Some
increases in port charges are implicit in the other
recommendations made in this report, specifically the
recommendation that cost be the principal basis for ratemaking. If all ports in the nation were to adjust their
rate structures to provide for a net return of 10% on
their investments, the total annual income made available
for capital investment would probably be only a fraction
of the $375 million annual investment required for port
development. Moreover, because the market in the United
States for municipal bonds is depressed, it is doubtful
that a 10% return on investment would be sufficient cover-
age to attract buyers for bonds backed only by port revenues,
even at high interest rates. The Maritime Administration
report referred to above indicates that a typical port
obtains a net return of only 4% on its investment, before

---

[75] This money does not include the traditional expenditures
of $150 million for aids to navigation, removal of
obstructions, and maintenance dredging.

any debt service. Therefore, public ports operating as a private industry will not generate sufficient revenues or provide an adequate financing base to attain the level of capital investment needed within the next few years for port development.

It has been pointed out that a Federal Aid to Ports Program might indeed lead to additional federal controls and there are many who do object to such controls. Federal control is currently exercised through authority over channel and harbor works in ports throughout the nation and requirements that ports meet safety and environmental standards. Under the private industry alternative, ports could be treated increasingly as public utilities with increasing control over rates and capital investment programs. The panel believes that a properly established Federal Aid to Ports Program would therefore not result in greater federal control than now exercised and that through the insertion of the states into the allocation and grant process, continued local control over decision making would be insured.

Cmbm

Port Planning and Development

To enable the ports of the United
States to develop efficiently:

1. *Centralized port planning for the United
   States port system should be avoided
   because it is neither feasible nor desirable.*

2. *The federal role should be expanded beyond
   the present emphasis on dredging and
   routine functions dealing with public
   health, immigration, and other control
   activities to include financial assistance
   for port planning, development, operation,
   and maintenance.*

3. *The number of federal agencies concerned
   with ports should be reduced and, wherever
   possible, the federal authority and
   responsibility for port affairs should
   be consolidated.*

4. *The federal government should discontinue
   channel maintenance when the cost of
   maintenance exceeds transportation benefits derived from the channel.*

5. *The federal government should take the
   leading role in port research and in the
   collecting, analysis, and dissemination
   of planning data, such as (1) inland and
   overseas origin and destination data by
   commodities and ports, (2) determination
   of hinterlands by commodities, port ranges,
   and individual ports, (3) modes of inland
   transportation, and (4) the effects of
   technological change on ports.*

6. *The Corps of Engineers should conduct
   regional as well as specific cost-benefit
   analyses to be certain that benefits are
   not overestimated when evaluating port
   improvement projects.*

7. *The mechanisms for securing authorization from the many government agencies for development within the coastal zone, including environmental impact statements, should be simplified to expedite port development.*

Decision-making authority for the planning and implementation of port construction, growth, and direction presently rests with local or state governing authorities. The impetus for growth of ports directed by such authoriti results from their positive and substantial economic impac and ability to attract port-related industry. The presenc of a port has been a sufficiently attractive economic factor to warrant direct and indirect local financial support. Any consideration of shifting this authority from local or state government to a national level would meet with resistance from port authorities, labor, and carriers alike. Master port planning for the entire Unite States appears to be politically unrealistic and economically unacceptable in a free, competitive society function ing under the constraints of the marketplace.

The current policy whereby the federal government provides free channels and the local port authorities act as landlords for private terminals operators has worke very well from a service standpoint. Adequate facilities for the rapid handling of all kinds of waterborne commerce have been built. The port system has not been a minimum-cost system for either the federal government or local port authorities because interport competition has fostere a certain amount of apparently redundant capacity to provi for normal peaks and options to shippers and carriers. Some argue that central government planning or guidance would prevent redundant facilities and forestall the waste of financial resources in such poor investments. This argument disregards the economic utility of some overcapacity and the acceptance by those who finance port development of the philosophy of risk-taking. In addition, becaus of the diverse and dynamic nature of port activities, it is not really possible to measure with confidence any redundancy, nor, for the same reason, is it possible to measure future port requirements quantitatively.

Port planners require substantial amounts of accurate and timely data to determine market trends and costs and to form sound fiscal and policy guidance. The federal government also needs information to perform cost-benefit analyses to evaluate harbor improvement projects under consideration by the Corps of Engineers. In the past, federal planners had considered each harbor as a separate planning entity with little, if any, evaluation of the competitive forces existing among harbors or ports in a given region. Although analyses usually were made of the comparative costs of supplying a harbor's trade territory by utilizing an adjacent harbor as the receiving or shipping point, evaluations were not made of the possible expansion or contraction of trade territories that could result from improvement of one harbor vis-a-vis another. Evaluation of projects on an independedt basis resulted in double-counting of benefits. This led, in some cases, to a bias in favor of overinvestment in harbor improvements, either because the region over which maximization of benefits occurred was incorrectly defined or the impact of projects under construction for different harbors was ignored. Thus, the benefits anticipated as the result of expenditures on port X could have been eroded in part or completely by expenditures on ports Y and Z. If this erosion had been considered, a different and perhaps smaller total level of expenditures may have been justified.

Regulation and Rates

> To achieve true intermodalism and to
> gain efficiency in traffic flow through
> ports:

> 1. *Interstate and foreign commerce of the
>   United States should be subjected to
>   an absolute minimum of federal regulation.*

> 2. *A single federal regulatory agency
>   should be established to regulate inter-
>   state commerce and the foreign commerce
>   of the United States.*

> 3. *The principal basis for ratemaking that
>   will ensure economic efficiency in the
>   movement of goods should be cost of
>   service.*

Changes in rate structures can affect ports even
more than those imposed by the need to accommodate containerization. The concepts of intermodalism and the
load center have greatly increased the areas of some port
hinterlands, thereby increasing the distances between
competing ports. In many cases a regional port becomes
less vulnerable to cargo diversions due to changes in
rate structures, because the high costs of container
facilities have tended to "fix" regional shipping to a
set pattern utilizing load-center ports. However, a
regional port becomes more vulnerable to cargo diversion
when viewing the nation's market as a whole, because its
hinterland is so much larger that a ratemaking policy
intended for a local situation may affect a load-center
port a thousand miles away, or on another coast.

Containerized and break bulk general cargo movements
to and from port hinterlands depend on rail, highway, and
inland waterway modes of transportation. As international
trade accelerates and cargo handling becomes more mechanized
intermodalism becomes a major factor in goods movement.
The division of federal regulatory jurisdiction at the
seaport no longer makes sense because of increased efficiency in the physical handling of cargo. Regulatory
changes, either inland or offshore, affect overall cargo
flow. When federal regulatory agencies were originally
created the domestic transportation system was viewed as

nationwide. This concept should now be applied by the U.S. government in its perception of international trade in order to obtain maximum benefits from a free interchange of goods. Just as the nation can no longer afford isolationism as a political or economic alternative, neither can it allow international trade to remain under several separate regulatory jurisdictions developed during earlier phases of the nation's transportation history.

Environmental Concerns

To provide for environmental quality
and land use planning:

1. *Problems of coastal zone management and
   land use affecting port location, design,
   operation, and maintenance should be
   resolved at local and regional levels,
   subject to federal guidelines such as
   the Water Resources Council's "Principles
   and Standards for Planning of Water
   Related Land Resources" and international
   agreements.*

2. *Comprehensive local, metropolitan, state,
   and regional land-use planning should be
   a continuing process to ensure allocation
   of sufficient land of appropriate character
   for government development and for port-
   oriented industries, as well as for other
   use.*

3. *A procedure should be developed to determine the value of the social benefits
   accruing from the conservation and preservation of desirable environmental
   conditions, so that decisions between
   conservation and development may be made
   more equitably.*

Coastal zone management programs are an attempt to
develop effective mechanisms for making social policy and
solving social problems in the complex setting of the
coastal zone. A socio-political process is needed to
balance environmental and economic considerations related
to port development. The problem is an economic one, but
the nature of the resources involved are inherently difficult, if not impossible, to include in the present market
system. Environmental resources of the coastal zone must
be brought into the economic system, whereby the real
costs of both resource alteration and improved environmental quality can be determined and incurred by those seeking specific objectives.

One alternative to current procedure is a pricing mechanism that might prove effective for pollution control. If benefits and costs could be measured and if those users who receive the benefits and pay the costs can be identified, then government could levy effluent charges or sell a fixed number of licenses to pollute. Under a system of levies, graduated to cause an increasing marginal cost of pollution, funds could be obtained to maintain a given level of environmental quality. Under a system of a fixed number of marketable licenses to pollute, those individuals and groups who feel strongly about environmental protection could purchase the licenses, through auction, and prevent any lowering of the environmental quality of a given area. Inherent in this approach, similar to a scenic easement, is the possibility that individuals or groups will not have access to financial means adequate to compete with established businesses or port authorities. Therefore, an auction system would have to recognize relative differences in financial resources and provide a means to balance any disparities. In either case, such plans would incorporate the costs of using scarce environmental resources into the costs of port development. One difficulty with this approach is the fixing of effluent charges: whose values count in the setting of charges? In addition, certain benefits and costs will always remain unquantifiable. Further study is needed in the vital subject of pricing environmental values and developing methods for allocating costs to uses of the coastal zone.

Port Labor

>To meet the changing needs of port labor:

>1.   *Issues of labor-management relations should be resolved through the normal processes of collective bargaining, with minimal governmental participation.*

>2.   *Policies to accommodate the surplus labor force and to discourage an excessive number of persons from entering the port labor force should be developed to ameliorate the effects of drastic reductions in requirements for waterfront labor, even in the face of traffic increases at some ports.*

When advances in technology reduce the labor demand of a port, there is a move to reduce the number of workers. This reduction in numbers can be accomplished by reduced hiring rates, institution of early retirement programs, and offering bonuses to those who leave voluntarily. When the increase in productivity caused by new technology has created a supply of labor beyond that which can be lessened through these methods, the problem becomes more serious. Either the extra workers must be carried until attrition reduces the labor force sufficiently or there must be direct layoffs. Any worker who may be laid off due to the inability of the port to sustain high volumes of traffic needs retraining for more promising fields or advice about regions of the country in which his particular skills remain in demand. If a situation involves such large numbers of workers that the economy of the surrounding area becomes depressed, then specific programs by government agencies may be required to attract new industry and to develop what latent resources, including human resources, the area may possess.

To a large extent, the problems of labor surplus caused by new technology in the shipping industry are similar to those caused by technical progress in other industries. A primary goal is retraining surplus workers. This retraining may be part of a general public manpower use program. In any retraining program an effort should be made to build on the specific skills of the port worker, to adapt them for work in other areas. Only as a last resort should the skills be abandoned for total retraining.

APPENDIXES

APPENDIX A
FEDERAL PORT STUDIES

In March, 1968, the Council on Marine Resources and Engineering Development (the Marine Science Council) issued its second report, (see Enclosure I) which annouced "a multi-agency research effort...to study requirements of a national system of ports with particular attention to regional aspects".[1] The result of this effort was the Conceptual Plan for Harbor and Port Development Studies proposed principally by the U.S. Army Corps of Engineers. The plan had the following objectives:

... determination of the optimum number, type and spacing of deep-draft harbors which will be required for prospective foreign and domestic waterborne commerce and

... development of practical economic solutions to problems imposed by rapidly changing vessel and cargo handling technology including identification and evaluation of technically feasible alternatives to conventional harbor and channel modifications, with minimum disruption of the natural environment.[2]

---

[1] *Marine Science Affairs - A Year of Plans and Progress*, the second report of the President to the Congress on Marine Resources and Engineering Development, U.S. Government Printing Office, Washington, March, 1968, pp. 87.

[2] National Council for Marine Resources and Engineering Development, *Conceptual Plan for Harbor and Port Development Studies*, Interdepartmental Ad Hoc Task Force for the Committee on Multiple Use of the Coastal Zone, November, 1968, p. 2.

In July, 1968, the Corps of Engineers issued a report, <u>Port Development and Redevelopment -- A Problem and An Opportunity</u>. An excerpt entitled "An Outline for Progress" is contained in Enclosure 2. This report concluded that:

> Comprehensive surveys are needed to determine the optimum number and spacing of ports and the harbor and specialized terminal facilities required to accommodate changing vessel and cargo handling technology. The surveys cannot be confined to harbor or port development only. They must involve detailed analyses of trends in industrial growth and location, commodity movements and fleet composition, identification of implications, by regions, of projected economic activity, traffic movement and vessel size; analysis of port cargo handling and associated facilities, including all foreseeable technology required to accommodate prospective traffic; plus evaluation and recommendations for financial participation by states, local political entities, and commercial and industrial interests.[3]

In January, 1969, the third report of the National Council on Marine Resources and Engineering Development, <u>Marine Science Affairs, A Year of Broadened Participation</u>, reiterated the need for an inter-agency port study to assist in meeting the goals of the Marine Sciences Act by:

> ... Preparing for development and redevelopment of our ports and harbors which are too often characterized

---

[3] This report was included in the Report of the Panel on Management and Development of the Coastal Zone, Commission on Marine Science, Engineering and Resources, U.S. Government Printing Office, Washington, February, 1969, pp. III-61 to III-73.

by obsolescent facilities and waterfront slums. It will be necessary
to incorporate new technology into a
national port system that will serve
ocean shipping of the future, very
likely to be characterized by much
deeper draft bulk carriers, containerization, and express and feeder services.
A conceptual framework is being developed
to provide the basis for a major study
of future port requirements to be conducted in cooperation with all interested parties.[4]

Finally, also in January, 1969, the Commission on
Marine Science, Engineering and Resources issued its report, entitled, Our Nation and the Sea. The Commission
recommended that "a major inter-agency study of the
Nation's port and waterways system be initiated under the
leadership of the Department of Transportation with the
assistance of other interested agencies".[5] This proposal
was based on the report of the Commission's Panel on the
Management and Development of the Coastal Zone, which
made the following recommendations to the parent commission:

... A National Port Survey should be conducted by the Department of Transportation in cooperation with the Department of Army, Commerce, and Housing
and Urban Development to define the
Nation's requirements in terms of major
ports, offshore terminals, and other
facilities for maritime commerce. On
the basis of this National Port Survey,
a rational scheme for port and harbor
development can be established against
which the real needs of this country
can be measured.

---

[4] *Marine Science Affairs - A Year of Broadened Participation,* the third report of the President to the
Congress on Marine Resources and Engineering Development, U.S. Government Printing Office, Washington,
January, 1969, p. 9.

[5] Commission on Marine Science, Engineering and Resources,
Our Nation and the Sea, U.S. Government Printing Office,
Washington, January, 1969, p. 66.

... The National Port Survey should examine
closely the Federal-local cost sharing
relationships to determine whether the
local government should be a stronger
participant in the development of its
port facilities.[6]

Position of the Port Industry: 1968-1973

The Port inudstry was thought by many of its representatives to be competitive, capable of determining its
ability to meet commercial and military shipping requirements. With the exception of modest support for
economically-distressed port cities provided by the Economic Development Administration (EDA), ports generally
have been considered able to obtain their own financing
for operation and development.

To counter the possibility of Federal control and
direction of United States ports considered inherent in
the Federal study proposals, the AAPA at its November 14,
1968, convention in Curacao resolved to:

oppose any effort of the Federal government to control or tend to control port
and terminal planning and development
at the nation's ports (including their
land transportation facilities) or to
allocate or mandate port activity as
to type, classification, scope or
location; and that the American Association of Port Authorities strongly
supports the right to the public ports
of the United States to self-develop-
ment in a climate of free competition;
and that the American Association of
Port Authorities insists on its right
to and the need for its full participation in any Federal examination
or study of the ports of this nation.
(Resolution E-12)

---

[6] Report of the Panel on Management and Development of
the Coastal Zone, Commission on Marine Science, Engineering and Resources, U.S. Government Printing
Office, Washington, February, 1969, p. III-4.

The AAPA fought hard and was successful in preventing any study implying Federal comprehensive port planning or a national port policy for the United States. In its condemnation of Federal planning studies, the AAPA reaffirmed its opposition to Federal involvement in port financing, except for channel dredging and maintenance. This opposition has been modified over the past several years.

At the Miami meeting in 1972, the AAPA rescinded its resolution opposing federal aid. In 1973, at its San Diego meeting, the AAPA went one step further by adopting two resolutions calling for federal aid. These declarations urged: a) federal funding assistance in connection with federal programs or policies that impose additional financial burdens on ports (Resolution E-17), and b) federal financial assistance for port capital improvement projects and a study to determine suitable sources and the equitable distribution of such assistance (Resolution E-18). This policy change was prompted by the increasingly greater competition for public funds by state and local agencies, the high cost of capital improvement, and stiffened environmental and safety requirements that increased costs without yielding additional revenues, thereby creating financial difficulties for many ports. These resolutions were reaffirmed at the AAPA's meeting in San Juan in 1974 with the added proviso that appropriate committees of the Congress, as well as governmental agencies, should be involved in any future study.

The Congress has acted to consider the possibility of federal financial assistance. In January, 1975 a bill with the following preamble (HR 4964) was referred to the House Merchant Marine and Fisheries Committee:

> To amend the Merchant Marine Act, 1920,
> to establish a grant program to enable
> public ports to comply with certain
> Federal standards, to direct the Sec-
> retary of Commerce to undertake a com-
> prehensive study of the present and
> future needs of public ports in the
> United States, and for other purposes.

Enclosure 3 is a copy of the Bill in its entirety.

APPENDIX A   (Enclosure 1)

Harbor and Port Development
excerpt from
Marine Science Affairs - A Year of Plans and Progress
March 1968 - Page 87

3. Harbor and Port Development. A multi-agency
research effort has been initiated to study requirements
of a national system of ports with particular attention
to regional aspects. As a first step, preliminary
planning and establishment of multi-agency working arrangements are being emphasized during FY 1968, and
initial fact-finding is to be conducted in FY 1969 at a
$100,000 level of effort by the Corps of Engineers. It
should also yield requirements for engineering development which will contribute to port efficiency in the
short run, as well as to the design of ports for the
future. The Department of Transportation and the Corps
of Engineers have primary concern in this research
program in its broadest aspects. The Maritime Administration will contribute technical engineering knowledge
in cargo handling, shipping requirements, and related
areas. Other Departments will participate in projecting
shipping loads. The Department of Housing and Urban
Development will consider relations between port development and urban expansion and redevelopment.
      This multi-agency effort will include a study of
port needs and the costs and impact of the kind of improvements that modern shipping technology indicates as
potentially desirable.
      As currently envisioned, the study will include
analyses of trends in commodity movements and fleet composition, and implications by region of projected traffic
movement and vessel size; requirements for port and related facilities to accommodate prospective traffic
effectively; alternative technological means for accommodating future transport systems; and appropriate
financial participation by non-Federal entities, including
States and local subdivisions.
      Port authorities and other State-local interests will

APPENDIX A (Enclosure 1)

be asked to participate in advisory capacities as well as
to provide basic information.

APPENDIX A   (Enclosure 2)

An Outline for Progress
excerpt from
Commission on Marine Science, Engineering and Resources

Panel on Management and Development

of the Coastal Zone

February 1969, Page III - 72

VIII. AN OUTLINE FOR PROGRESS
For a very sizeable number of U.S. cities, the water-front and harbor area was originally the economic key to the development of the community and the related interior lands. When the cities were young, the waterfronts were living, dynamic areas which provided employment and recreation, market places and parks, warehouses and consumer outlets, and contact with nature at the water's edge. Today many of these waterfronts are neither living nor dynamic, and nature has been crowded out or poisoned.

As pointed out, existing port areas are becoming obsolete because of rapid changes occurring and foreseen in transportation technology. Abandoned piers, warehouses and hulks clutter many of our waterfronts, contributing to harbor areas being a focus for decay and unsightliness.

These undesirable remnants, as well as the existing but technically inadequate terminal facilities, require replacement to permit more efficient servicing of larger, more productive ships.

The problem is highly complex. It transcends the ports themselves and includes the inland transportation networks, plus the recognition that the pattern of needs for seaports may be quite different in the future. It includes consideration of port and harbor operations on highly complicated ecological networks. It includes determination of pollution control in harbor areas and waterways. And it must consider the need for urban renewal and recognize growing requirements for recreation facilities in congested urban areas.

New, more productive transportation technologies will permit more efficient use of waterfront space. A greater flow of trade and transportation can take place using less area, thus releasing valuable waterfront property for housing, open space, or recreation purposes. New

APPENDIX A (Enclosure 2)

technology can be applied to reduce the polluting of harbors and estuaries.

Any concentrated effort at port and urban waterfront development and redevelopment must involve several groups and will require a high degree of cooperation between local governments, regional planning groups, private interests, and the Federal agencies. An effective program can be visualized as having three major and closely related components:

---comprehensive surveys of regional port-transportation requirements

---development of action plans for port, harbor and waterfront area renovation

---integration of transportation and waterfront renewal planning with programs for conservation of estuarine resources

Comprehensive surveys are needed to determine the optimum number and spacing of ports and the harbor and specialized terminal facilities required to accommodate changing vessel and cargo handling technology. The surveys cannot be confined to harbor or port development only. They must involve detailed analyses of trends in industrial growth and location, commodity movements and fleet composition; identification of implications, by regions, of projected economic activity, traffic movement and vessel size; analysis of port cargo handling and associated facilities, including all foreseeable technology required to accommodate prospective traffic; plus evaluation and recommendations for financial participation by states, local political entities, and commercial and industrial interests.

The studies should explore all technological alternatives of traditional harbor deepening, including installation of offshore transfer facilities or use of lightering vessels. Such alternatives may greatly reduce both the financial and ecological costs of accommodating supercarriers.

As short and long-range transportation requirements become identified for harbor and port areas, companion plans can be developed for rehabilitation of land areas adjacent to harbors, including consolidation and relocation of cargo handling and industrial facilities. The potential for offshore handling of petroleum commodities, coupled with the sharply rising use of containers, should provide many opportunities for land clearance and

APPENDIX A (Enclosure 2)

rehabilitation.

This is not to argue that waterfront operations must be sheltered from public view. To the contrary, where the waterfront use is for port facilities, the drama of docking and loading and unloading ships has a special fascination for both the local audience and tourists.

Such operations could be made readily accessible to the public from observation galleries which could inlcude dock-side restaurants and educational exhibits. Whatever use is made of waterfronts is enhanced if access is easy and attractive. Where waterfronts are devoted to transportation, the street or rail arteries could avoid the water's edge or be designed with tunnels, decks, depressed grades, or other techniques that can contribute to ease of public access to the area.

APPENDIX A   (Enclosure 3)

94TH CONGRESS
1ST SESSION

H. R. 4964

IN THE HOUSE OF REPRESENTATIVES

MARCH 14, 1975

Mrs. SULLIVAN (for herself, Mr. DINGELL, Mr. DOWNING, Mr. ROBERT W. DANIEL, JR., Mr. MURPHY of New York, Mr. JONES of North Carolina, Mr. ANDERSON of California, Mr. DE LA GARZA, Mr. METCALFE, Mr. BREAUX, Mr. ROONEY, Mr. STUDDS, Mr. BOWEN, Mr. EILBERG, Mr. DE LUGO, Mr. ZEFERETTI, Mr. OBERSTAR, Mr. AUCOIN, and Mr. FORSYTHE) introduced the following bill; which was referred to the Committee on Merchant Marine and Fisheries

A BILL

To amend the Merchant Marine Act, 1920, to establish a grant program to enable public ports to comply with certain Federal standards, to direct the Secretary of Commerce to undertake a comprehensive study of the present and future needs of public ports in the United States, and for other purposes.

1   *Be it enacted by the Senate and House of Representa-*

2   *tives of the United States of America in Congress assembled,*

3   That the Merchant Marine Act, 1920 (46 U.S.C. 861 et

4   seq.) is amended by inserting immediately after section 8

5   thereof the following new section:

I

1   "SEC. 8A. (a) (1) Any State, local government, or

2 interstate agency or other public port authority may apply to

3 the Secretary of Commerce (hereafter referred to in this

4 section as the 'Secretary') for financial assistance under this

5 subsection to assist such agency in making such improve-

6 ments as may be required to any port operated by it in

7 order to bring such port into compliance with any require-

8 ments relating to environmental protection, the public health

9 and safety, or port or cargo security which may be imposed

10 by Federal law. For purposes of this subsection, the term

11 'improvements' includes, but is not limited to, the construc-

12 tion, repair, or rehabilitation of port structures and areas,

13 the training of employees, and the hiring of additional

14 employees.

15   " (2) Application for financial assistance under this sub-

16 section shall be made in such manner and form as the Sec-

17 retary shall prescribe.

18   " (3) (A) Financial assistance under this subsection

19 shall be in the form of grants of money.

20   " (B) If the Secretary finds that an applicant for finan-

21 cial assistance under this subsection is required to make any

22 improvements described in paragraph (1) of this subsection,

23 the Secretary may grant to the applicant all or a part of the

24 money applied for. Any grant made pursuant to this sub-

25 section shall be subject to such terms and conditions as the

1 Secretary deems appropriate to insure that the moneys so

2 granted are used for the purposes intended.

3 "(C) Any agency or authority which receives a grant

4 under this subsection shall make available to the Secretary

5 or to the Comptroller General of the United States, or any

6 of their authorized representatives, for purposes of audit and

7 examination, any books, documents, papers, and records that

8 are pertinent to the moneys received by such agency or

9 authority under such grant.

10 "(D) No grant or aggregate of grants made under this

11 subsection to any State, local, or interstate agency or public

12 port authority may exceed $1,000,000.

13 "(b) (1) The Secretary shall undertake a compre-

14 hensive study to determine the immediate and long-range

15 requirements of public ports in the United States (A) for

16 expansion and modernization in order to meet adequately

17 the economic and defense needs of the United States, and

18 (B) to meet such standards as may be imposed by law for

19 purposes of environmental protection and port safety and

20 security. Such study shall also include a comprehensive eval-

21 uation and analysis of the amount and kinds of funding which

22 public ports have available to them for purposes of imple-

23 menting current and projected expansion, modernization, and

24 other improvements. If the Secretary finds that public ports

25 do not, or will not, have adequate funding capability for such

1 implementation, he shall include in the study his recommen-
2 dations for achieving such a capability; except that if the
3 Secretary makes any recommendation for Federal participa-
4 tion in achieving such a capability, such recommendation may
5 not propose any action which would disrupt the existing
6 competitive relationship among public ports or in any man-
7 ner discriminate between such ports.

8 "(2) In carrying out the study required under para-
9 graph (1) of this subsection, the Secretary shall solicit the
10 views of appropriate Federal, State, interstate, and local
11 agencies, as well as of representatives of shipping, cargo
12 handling, land transportation, and other interested indus-
13 tries. To the extent necessary, the Secretary shall consider
14 the requirements of public ports on a regional basis in order
15 that problems common to public ports in any region may be
16 given particular attention.

17 "(3) The Secretary shall report to Congress the final
18 results of such study not later than one year after the effec-
19 tive date of this section, and shall from time to time make
20 such interim reports to Congress on the study as the Secre-
21 tary deems appropriate. The final report shall, and any
22 interim report may, contain such recommendations, including
23 suggested legislation, as the Secretary deems appropriate
24 with respect to Federal actions, if any, which should be
25 undertaken to assist public ports.

1   "(c) (1) There is authorized to be appropriated the

2 sum of $30,000,000 for fiscal year 1975 and each fiscal year

3 thereafter for purposes of carrying out subsection (a) of this

4 section.

5   "(2) There is authorized to be appropriated the sum of

6 $1,000,000 for each of the fiscal years 1975 and 1976 for

7 purposes of carrying out subsection (b) of this section.".

APPENDIX B

COMMODITY FORECASTS

Data contained in this appendix summarize forecasts
from existing studies for the following selected commodities: crude petroleum, petroleum products, aluminum
ores, grains, iron ore, phosphate rock, iron and steel
scrap, and general cargo. In some instances, forecasts
by port range and nation of origin or destination are
included to illustrate the type of data required for port
planning. Projections for hinterland movements are not
available. The forecasts were derived from the following
studies, prepared for either the Maritime Administration
or the U.S. Corps of Engineers:

*Oceanborne Shipping: Demand and Technology
Forecast,* by Litton Systems, Inc., June 1968.

*Forecast of U.S. Oceanborne Foreign Trade in
Dry Bulk Commodities,* by Booz-Allen Applied
Research, Inc., March 1969.

*Projections of Principal U.S. Dry Bulk
Commodity Seaborne Imports and Exports for
1975 and 1995,* by Stanford Research Institute,
February 1969.

*U.S. Deepwater Port Study Commodity Studies
and Projections,* by Robert Nathan Associates,
August 1972.

*Forecast of World Trade in Containerizable
Commodities: 1975 and 1980,* by Manalytics,
Inc., June 1971.

Offshore Terminal System Concepts, by Soros
Associates, Inc., September 1972.

Crude Petroleum

Figure B-1 shows historical data (from U.S. Army Corps of Engineers, *Waterborne Commerce of the United States*). The forecast data include only projections for the continental United States. Figure B-2 shows comparisons of forecasts for crude petroleum from the Middle East, one of the many foreign exporting areas, to the U.S. North Atlantic range. Table B-1 provides origin and destination data for the forecasts. Table B-2 shows projections of supply and demand.

Petroleum Products

Figure B-3 shows forecasts of total U.S. imports of petroleum products, which are predominantly residual fuel oils from the Caribbean and South American areas. Table B-3 gives additional origin and destination data for the forecasts.

Aluminum Ores

Figure B-4 shows forecasts of total U.S. imports of aluminum ores, which includes bauxite and alumina. Figure B-5 shows forecasts showing one U.S. port area with one of its many foreign sources of tonnage. Table B-4 gives additional origins and destinations of forecast ore requirements.

Grains

Forecast data for grain exports are shown in Figure B-6 for wheat, Figure B-7 for feed grains, and Figure B-8 for soybeans. Tables B-5 and B-6 give origin and destination data.

Iron Ore

Figure B-9 compares forecasts for total U.S. iron ore imports. Nathan projections include all Canadian imports, while Stanford Research does not include imports from Canada destined for Great Lakes ports, and Soros included no Canadian ores. All tonnages are actual, except for Stanford Research and Booz Allen, which show tonnages by iron content. Table B-7 gives additional origin and destination data for the forecast iron ore imports.

Phosphate Rock

Figure B-10 compares forecasts for total U.S. exports of phosphate rock. Table B-8 gives additional origin and destination data for phosphate rock.

Iron and Steel Scrap

Figure B-11 shows forecasts data for total U.S. exports of iron and steel scrap. Table B-9 gives additional origins and destinations of the forecast iron and steel scrap movements.

General Cargo

General cargo traffic forecasts, segregated between containerized and break bulk traffic, are shown as Figure B-12, but historical data are not available. Forecast data are from the Litton study, the Manalytics study, and from preliminary forecasts prepared by the Maritime Administration. The Manalytics forecast data are reported in 20-foot container equivalents and are not directly comparable to the other two studies, which are in tonnage. In an effort to show comparable data these container equivalents have been converted to tonnage. The report does not indicate the factors used for converting container equivalents to weight data, but it does state that data were derived from actual loading experience in established container systems, and where such experience was not available, from density characteristics. The report also indicates that actual experience in 1969 for shipments from Western Europe to the U.S. Atlantic Coast was 8.7 tons per 20-foot container. Therefore, we have assumed for purposes of comparison an average load of 8.7 tons per container. Tables B-10 and B-11 give additional origin and destination data.

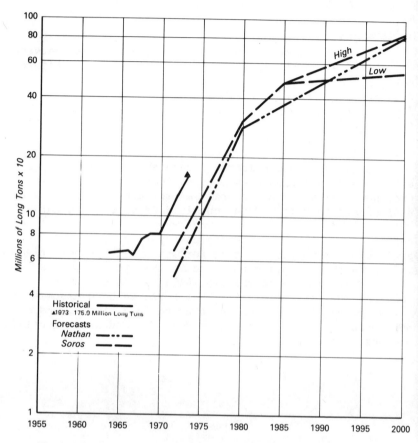

Historical data from U. S. Army, Corps of Engineers reports and includes all seaborne traffic. Traffic forecasts do not include Canadian imports through Portland, Maine, or U. S. imports from Canada.

FIGURE B-1

Forecasts of Crude Petroleum Seaborne Imports

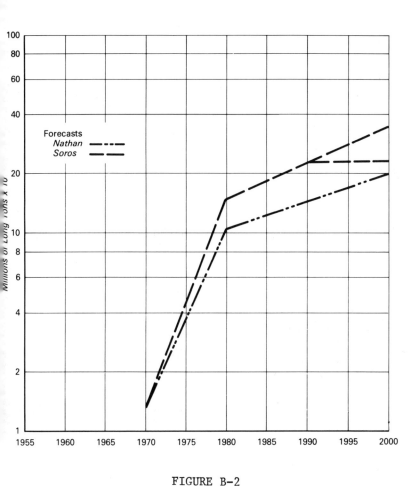

FIGURE B-2

Forecasts of Crude Petroleum from Middle
East to U.S. North Atlantic

TABLE B-1

CRUDE PETROLEUM OCEANBORNE IMPORTS

(Millions of Barrels Per Year — Millions of Long Tons Per Year)

Foreign Source	North Atlantic*		South Atlantic		Gulf		Pacific		Total	
	MBY	MLTY	MBY	MLTY	MBY	MLTY	MBY	MLTY	MBY	MLT
1969										
Persian Gulf	42.00	5.63	0.10	0.013	-	-	19.52	2.62	61.62	8.
West Africa	18.33	2.46	0.05	0.007	-	-	-	-	18.38	2.
North Africa	63.60	8.54	0.15	0.020	-	-	0.25	0.03	64.00	8.
Venezuela	104.00	13.93	0.12	0.016	-	-	7.60	1.02	111.72	14.
Latin America	14.29	1.91	0.01	0.002	-	-	8.53	1.14	22.83	3.
Far East	-	-	-	-	-	-	32.27	4.32	32.27	4.
Total	242.22	32.47	0.43	0.058	0.0	0.0	68.17	9.13	310.82	41.
1980										
Persian Gulf	1,132.00	151.30	25.00	3.35	60.00	8.06	253.00	33.90	1,470.00	196.
West Africa	37.00	4.96	-	-	-	-	-	-	37.00	4.
North Africa	336.00	45.00	-	-	18.00	2.40	-	-	354.00	47.
Venezuela	55.00	7.37	20.00	2.68	35.00	4.69	-	-	110.00	14.
Latin America	93.00	12.47	-	-	-	-	90.00	12.07	183.00	24.
Far East	-	-	-	-	-	-	110.00	14.75	110.00	14.
Total	1,653.00	221.10	45.00	6.03	113.00	15.15	453.00	60.72	2,264.00	303.
1985										
Persian Gulf	1,640.00	219.90	50.00	6.70	184.00	24.33	476.00	63.80	2,350.00	314.
West Africa	50.00	6.70	-	-	-	-	-	-	50.00	6.
North Africa	487.00	64.90	28.00	3.75	85.00	11.70	-	-	600.00	80.
Venezuela	55.00	7.37	25.00	3.35	40.00	5.36	-	-	120.00	16.
Latin America	100.00	13.40	-	-	-	-	100.00	13.40	200.00	26.
Far East	-	-	-	-	-	-	110.00	14.75	110.00	14.
Total	2,332.00	312.27	103.00	13.80	309.00	41.39	686.00	91.95	3,430.00	459.
2000 (Low Estimate)										
Persian Gulf	1,665.00	223.20	80.00	10.70	465.00	61.90	540.00	72.40	2,750.00	368.
West Africa	70.00	9.39	-	-	-	-	-	-	70.00	9.
North Africa	495.00	65.90	80.00	10.70	95.00	13.20	-	-	670.00	89.
Venezuela	50.00	6.70	40.00	5.36	40.00	5.36	-	-	130.00	17.
Latin America	130.00	17.42	-	-	-	-	130.00	17.42	260.00	34.
Far East	-	-	-	-	-	-	130.00	17.42	130.00	17.
Low Total	2,410.00	322.61	200.00	26.76	600.00	80.46	800.00	107.24	4,010.00	537.
2000 (High Estimate)										
Persian Gulf	2,680.00	359.00	80.00	10.70	590.00	79.10	830.00	111.10	4,180.00	559.
West Africa	100.00	13.40	-	-	-	-	-	-	100.00	13.4
North Africa	590.00	79.10	160.00	21.40	260.00	34.80	-	-	1,010.00	135.3
Venezuela	70.00	9.38	60.00	8.05	60.00	8.05	-	-	190.00	25.4
Latin America	200.00	26.80	-	-	-	-	190.00	25.42	390.00	52.2
Far East	-	-	-	-	-	-	190.00	25.42	190.00	25.4
High Total	3,640.00	487.68	300.00	40.15	910.00	121.95	1,210.00	161.94	6,060.00	811.7

* Excluding Portland, Maine

From: Bur. of Mines (1969); N.P.C. (1980-1985); Soros Assoc. (2000) as quoted in "Offshore Terminal System Concepts", by Soros Assoc., Table I-3

TABLE B-2
PETROLEUM DEMAND/SUPPLY PROJECTIONS – U.S. TOTAL

(In Thousands of Barrels Daily)

Demand/ supply	1970				1980				2000			
		Products				Products				Products		
	Crude	Residual	Other	Total	Crude	Residual	Other	Total	Crude	Residual	Other	Total
Demand	11,412 a/	2,204	12,512	14,716	18,700 a/	4,100	18,600	22,700	32,700 a/	4,100	30,900	35,000
Production	10,171	705	12,311	13,016 b/	11,800	1,100	17,600	18,700 b/	13,000	1,800	30,900	32,700 b/
Surplus or (deficit)	(1,241)	(1,499)	(201)	(1,700)	(6,900)	(3,000)	(1,000)	(4,000)	(19,700)	(2,300)	--	(2,300)
Exports	14	54	190	244	--	--	--	--	--	--	--	--
Imports from:												
Canada	672	--	--	--	1,900	--	--	--	2,500	--	--	--
L.A.– Carib	291	--	--	--	--	3,000	900	3,900	--	2,300	--	2,300
M.E.– Africa	291	--	--	--	4,900	--	--	--	15,400	--	--	--
Far East	70	--	--	--	100	--	100	100	1,800	--	--	--
Total	1,324	1,528	452	1,980	6,900	3,000	1,000	4,000	19,700	2,300	--	2,300
In million short tons/yr	74.3	85.8	25.4	111.2	387.5	168.5	56.2	224.6	1,106.2	129.2	--	129.2

a/   Runs to stills of crude and natural gasoline.
b/   Refinery output plus natural gas liquids (NGL) blended and produced at refinery.

Source: 1970 -- U.S. Department of the Interior, Bureau of Mines, Mineral Industry Surveys, "Monthly Petroleum Statement," December 1970, prepared by the Division of Fossil Fuels, March 23, 1970. 1980 and 2000 --RRNA. As quoted in "U.S. Deepwater Port Study Commodity Studies and Projections" by Robert R. Nathan Assoc., Table 13, p. 73

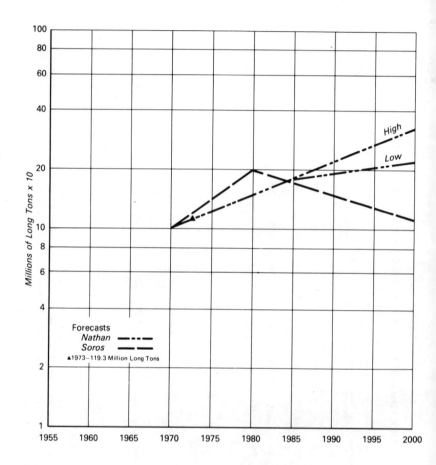

FIGURE B-3

Forecasts of Petroleum Products Seaborne Imports

TABLE B-3

OCEANBORNE IMPORTS
RESIDUAL FUEL OIL
(Millions of Barrels Per Year—Millions of Long Tons Per Year)

OTHER PRODUCTS U.S. TOTALS

Foreign Source	North Atlantic		South Atlantic		Gulf		Pacific		Total		Total for U.S.	
	MBY	MLTY	MBY	MLTY	MBY	MLTY	MBY	MLTY	MBY	MLTY	MBY	MLTY
1969												
Caribbean*	332.00	48.70	47.60	7.00	9.80	1.50	7.70	1.10	397.17	58.25	151.45	20.30
Europe	46.10	6.80	6.60	1.00	2.40	0.30	.	.	55.16	8.10	7.02	0.94
Latin America	.	.	.	.	.	.	.	.	.	.	.	.
Others	5.70	0.83	0.80	0.12	0.20	0.03	0.10	0.02	6.80	1.00	5.34	0.71
Total	383.80	56.33	55.00	8.12	12.40	1.83	7.80	1.12	459.13	67.35	163.81	21.95
1980												
Caribbean*	418.00	61.30	60.00	8.75	13.50	2.00	8.50	1.25	500.00	73.30	167.00	22.40
Europe	.	.	.	.	.	.	.	.	.	.	.	.
Latin America	268.00	39.30	39.00	5.65	8.50	1.25	5.50	0.80	321.00	47.00	107.00	14.25
Others	.	.	.	.	.	.	.	.	.	.	.	.
Total	686.00	100.60	99.00	14.40	22.00	3.25	14.00	2.05	821.00	120.30	274.00	36.65
1985												
Caribbean*	418.00	61.30	60.00	8.75	13.50	2.00	8.50	1.25	500.00	73.30	167.00	22.40
Europe	.	.	.	.	.	.	.	.	.	.	.	.
Latin America	383.00	56.20	55.00	8.05	12.50	1.80	7.50	1.15	459.00	67.20	151.50	20.20
Others	.	.	.	.	.	.	.	.	.	.	.	.
Total	801.00	117.50	115.00	16.80	26.00	3.80	16.00	2.40	959.00	140.50	318.50	42.60
2000 (Low Estimate)												
Caribbean*	460.00	67.40	66.00	9.60	15.00	2.15	9.00	1.35	550.00	80.50	185.00	24.80
Europe	.	.	.	.	.	.	.	.	.	.	.	.
Latin America	460.00	67.40	66.00	9.60	15.00	2.15	9.00	1.35	550.00	80.50	185.00	24.80
Others	60.00	9.20	9.00	1.30	3.00	0.30	2.00	0.20	74.00	11.00	21.00	2.80
Total	980.00	144.00	141.00	20.50	33.00	4.60	20.00	2.90	1,174.00	172.00	391.00	52.40
2000 (High Estimate)												
Caribbean*	670.00	98.00	96.00	14.00	21.00	3.20	13.00	2.00	800.00	117.20	265.00	35.50
Europe	.	.	.	.	.	.	.	.	.	.	.	.
Latin America	670.00	98.00	96.00	14.00	21.00	3.20	13.00	2.00	800.00	117.20	265.00	35.50
Others	84.00	12.20	12.00	1.75	2.50	0.40	1.50	0.25	100.00	14.60	33.00	4.50
Total	1,424.00	208.20	204.00	29.75	44.50	6.80	27.50	4.25	1,700.00	249.00	536.00	75.50

*Including Mexico, Venezuela and Columbia

From: Dept. of Commerce (1969); N.P.C. (1980-1985)
Soros Associates (2000) as quoted in "Offshore Terminal System Concepts" by Soros Assoc., Table 1-5

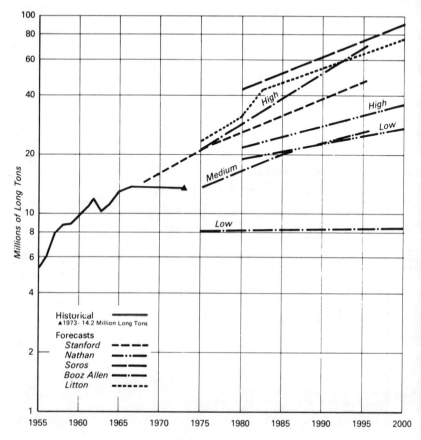

Historical data from Bureau of Census and Bureau of Mines as quoted in "Projection of Principal U. S. Dry Bulk Commodity Seaborne Imports and Exports for 1975 and 1995 " by Stanford Research Institute.

FIGURE B-4

Forecasts of Bauxite and Alumina Seaborne Imports

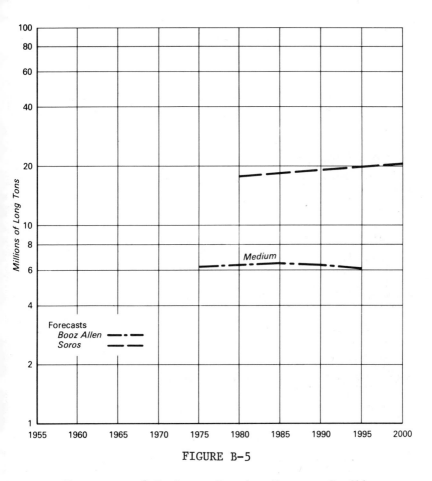

FIGURE B-5

Forecasts of Seaborne Bauxite Imports Caribbean
Area to U.S. Gulf Area

TABLE B-4

TRADE FORECAST OF
U.S. OCEANBORNE BAUXITE
AND ALUMINA IMPORTS

(Millions of Long Tons)

	1970	1975	1980	1985	1990	1995
Total U.S. Oceanborne Imports	15.52	21.95	29.35	38.47	51.45	70.50
	12.19	14.56	17.13	20.40	22.85	25.76
	9.91	8.19	8.19	8.19	8.19	8.19
Total Bauxite Imports	12.62	13.25	13.90	14.40	14.90	15.40
	9.32	9.24	9.43	9.80	9.52	9.04
	8.21	7.11	7.11	7.11	7.11	7.11
Jamaica	4.88	4.84	4.94	5.13	4.98	4.73
Haiti and Dominican Republic	1.74	1.73	1.76	1.83	1.79	1.69
Surinam and Guyana	2.70	2.67	2.73	2.84	2.75	2.62
Other	—	—	—	—	—	—
Total Alumina Imports	2.90	8.70	15.45	24.07	36.55	55.10
	2.87	5.32	7.70	10.60	13.33	16.72
	1.70	1.08	1.08	1.08	1.08	1.08
Australia	1.00	1.80	2.90	4.26	5.44	6.94
Japan	—	—	—	—	—	—
Guinea	0.06	0.30	0.60	1.00	1.60	2.60
Jamaica	1.17	2.00	2.59	3.18	3.57	3.90
Surinam and Guyana	0.64	1.22	1.61	2.16	2.72	3.28

Source: Forecast of U.S. Oceanborne Foreign Trade in Dry Bulk Commodities by Booz Allen Applied Research, Table 47, p. 199-200

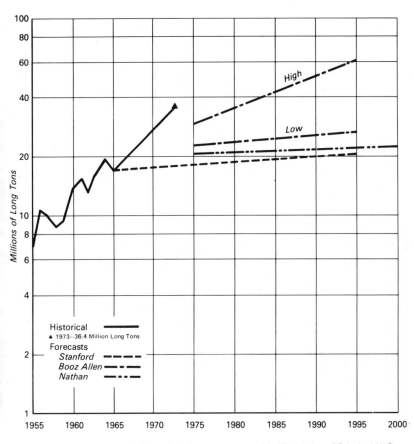

Historical data from U. S. Dept of Agriculture as quoted in "Projection of Principal U. S. Dry Bulk Commodity Seaborne Imports and Exports for 1975 and 1995", Stanford Research Institute

FIGURE B-6

Forecasts of Wheat Seaborne Exports

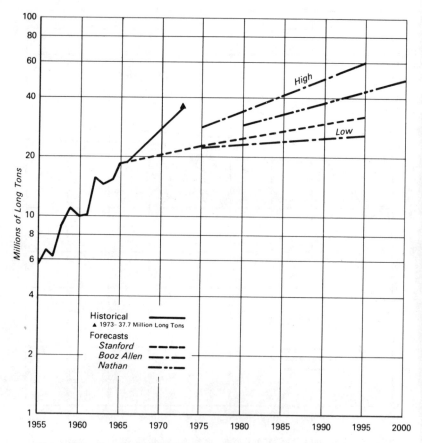

Historical data from U. S. Dept of Agriculture as quoted in "Projection of Principal U. S. Dry Bulk Commodity Seaborne Imports and Exports for 1975 and 1995", Stanford Research Institute

FIGURE B-7

Forecasts of Feed Grain Seaborne Exports

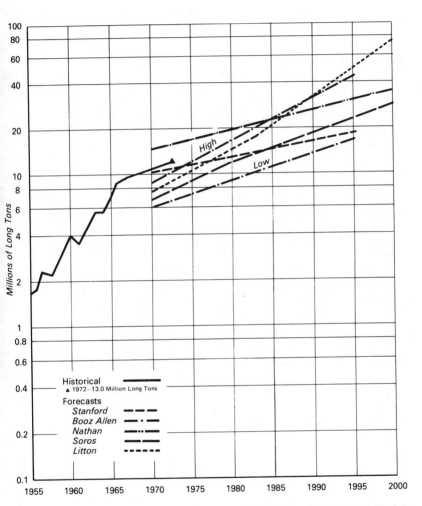

Historical data from U.S. Dept. of Agriculture as quoted in "Projection of Principal U.S. Dry Bulk Commodity Seaborne Imports and Exports for 1975 and 1995," Stanford Research Institute.

FIGURE B-8

Forecasts of Soybean Seaborne Exports

TABLE B-5

TRADE FORECAST OF
U. S. OCEANBORNE WHEAT EXPORTS
(Millions of Long Tons)

	1970	1975	1980	1985	1990	1995
	24.69	29.42	35.05	41.76	49.76	59.29
Total U.S. Oceanborne Export	20.69	24.45	26.63	29.38	32.33	35.94
	20.60	22.78	23.59	24.43	25.39	26.19
Countries of Destination	Medium Forecast Destinations					
India	6.40	7.46	7.64	7.81	7.82	7.93
Japan	2.10	2.49	2.48	2.78	3.08	3.42
EEC*	1.53	1.54	1.57	1.59	1.60	1.62
Yugoslavia	0.16	—	—	—	—	—
Brazil	1.16	1.41	1.65	1.91	2.23	2.55
U.A.R.	—	—	—	—	—	—
U.K.	0.27	0.20	0.16	0.11	0.06	0.01
Pakistan	1.95	2.83	3.01	3.13	3.28	3.50
Algeria	0.14	0.16	0.18	0.21	0.22	0.26
S. Korea	0.68	0.83	1.00	1.20	1.42	1.67
Venezuela	0.23	0.29	0.34	0.40	0.47	0.55
Philippines	0.29	0.36	0.44	0.54	0.64	0.77
Taiwan	0.37	0.43	0.48	0.54	0.60	0.66
All Other	5.41	6.45	7.68	9.16	10.91	13.00

* The European Economic Community

Source: Forecast of U. S. Oceanborne Foreign Trade in Dry Bulk Commodities by Booz-Allen Applied Research, Inc., Table 9, p. 33-34

TABLE B-6

TRADE FORECAST OF
U. S. OCEANBORNE SOYBEAN EXPORTS
(Millions of Long Tons)

	1970	1975	1980	1985	1990	1995
	8.57	12.00	16.80	23.52	32.92	46.09
Total U.S. Oceanborne Exports	6.69	8.93	11.11	13.67	17.03	21.46
	6.02	7.45	9.93	11.25	14.00	17.18
Countries of Destination	Medium Forecast Destinations					
Netherlands	1.16	1.27	1.38	1.51	1.64	1.77
Belgium and Luxembourg	0.15	0.16	0.18	0.19	0.21	0.23
France	0.01	0.02	0.02	0.02	0.02	0.03
W. Germany	0.68	0.75	0.81	0.88	0.96	1.04
Italy	0.34	0.37	0.41	0.45	0.48	0.51
EEC	(2.34)	(2.57)	(2.80)	(3.05)	(3.31)	(3.58)
Japan	2.03	2.66	3.39	4.02	4.80	5.74
Spain	0.37	0.43	0.49	0.55	0.62	0.70
Denmark	0.43	0.48	0.52	0.57	0.61	0.66
All Other	1.52	2.79	3.91	5.48	7.69	10.78

Source: Forecast of U. S. Oceanborne Foreign Trade in Dry Bulk Commodities, by Booz-Allen Applied
Research, Inc., Table 15, p. 69-70

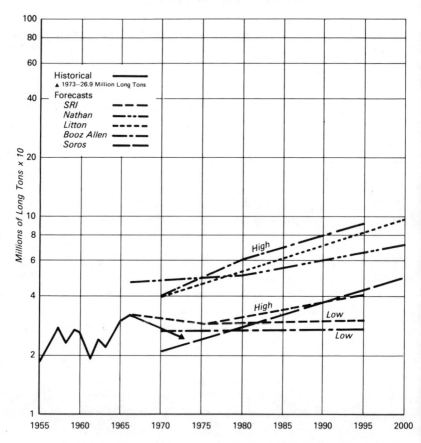

Historical data from Bureau of Census as quoted in "Projection of Principal U. S. Dry Bulk Commodity Seaborne Imports and Exports for 1975 and 1995", Stanford Research Institute

FIGURE B-9

Iron Ore Seaborne Imports

TABLE B-7

TRADE FORECAST OF
U. S. OCEANBORNE IRON ORE IMPORTS
(Millions of Long Tons)

	1970	1975	1980	1985	1990	1995
Total U. S. Oceanborne Imports*	31.60	33.90	35.40	37.80	39.50	41.90
Countries of Origin						
Canada	9.27	11.55	12.33	13.32	13.85	15.63
Venezuela	12.65	12.86	13.58	13.98	14.56	15.18
Peru	0.89	0.89	0.93	0.97	1.02	1.05
Chile	2.66	2.66	2.83	2.91	3.06	3.14
Brazil	2.22	2.22	2.35	2.43	2.55	2.62
Liberia	3.32	3.33	3.52	3.64	3.73	3.93
All Other	0.32	0.34	0.35	0.38	0.40	0.42

---

* Medium forecast data

Source: Forecast in U. S. Oceanborne Foreign Trade in Dry Bulk Commodities by Booz-Allen Applied Research, Inc., Table 39, p. 159-160

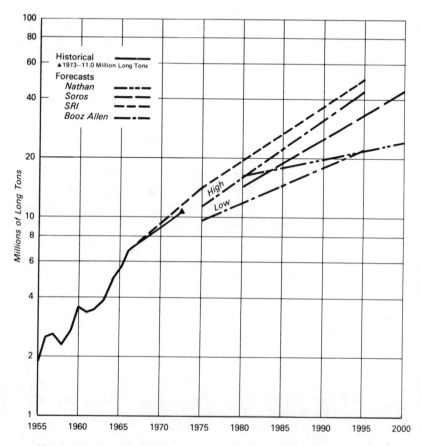

Historical data from Bureau of Census as quoted in "Projection of Principal U. S. Dry Bulk Commodity Seaborne Imports and Exports for 1975 and 1995", Stanford Research Institute

FIGURE B-10

Phosphate Rock Seaborne Exports

TABLE B-8

TRADE FORECAST OF
U. S. OCEANBORNE PHOSPHATE ROCK EXPORTS

(Millions of Long Tons)

		1970	1975	1980	1985	1990	1995
		7.900	11.100	15.600	21.900	30.800	43.100
Total U. S. Oceanborne Exports		7.900	10.400	13.500	16.800	20.800	25.200
		7.570	9.600	12.000	15.000	18.400	22.000
Countries of Destination		Medium Forecast Destinations					
Canada	North and						
Mexico	Central America	.575	.650	.900	1.100	1.300	1.600
Cuba							
Brazil	South America	.175	.250	.400	.600	.800	.900
Uruguay							
Sweden							
Denmark							
Britain							
Netherlands	Western Europe	3.300	3.700	4.600	5.600	6.200	6.700
W. Germany							
Spain							
Italy							
Korea							
Taiwan	Far East	1.900	2.700	3.600	4.300	5.500	7.000
Japan							
All Other		1.950	3.100	4.000	5.200	7.000	9.000

Source: U. S. Maritime Administration
Forecast of U. S. Oceanborne Foreign Trade in Dry Bulk Commodities by Booz-Allen Applied Research, Inc., Table 24, p. 101-102

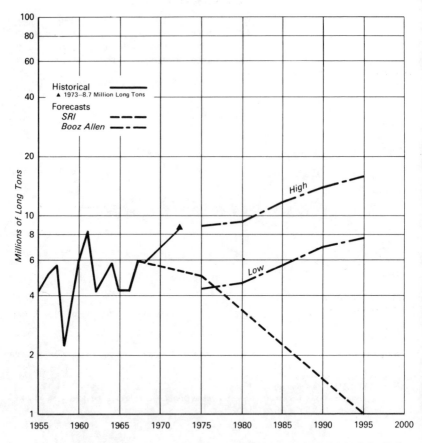

Historical data from Bureau of Census as quoted in "Projection of Principal U. S. Dry Bulk Commodity Seaborne Imports and Exports for 1975 and 1995", Stanford Research Institute

FIGURE B-11

Scrap Iron and Steel Seaborne Exports

TABLE B-9

**TRADE FORECAST OF
U. S. OCEANBORNE IRON
AND STEEL SCRAP EXPORTS**
(Millions of Long Tons)

	1970	1975	1980	1985	1990	1995
	8.3	8.9	9.6	11.6	14.1	15.9
Total U. S. Oceanborne Exports	5.8	6.2	6.7	8.1	9.8	11.1
.	4.0	4.3	4.6	5.6	6.8	7.7

Countries of Destination	Medium Forecast Destinations					
Japan						
Taiwan						
Korea						
Other Far East						
Far East Total	3.60	4.03	4.36	5.43	6.86	7.77
Italy						
Other EEC						
United Kingdom						
Other W. and C. Europe						
W. and C. Europe Total	1.04	0.93	0.67	0.65	0.49	0.56
Mexico						
Argentina						
Other Latin America						
Latin America Total	0.99	1.05	1.34	1.62	1.96	2.22
All Other	0.17	0.19	0.33	0.40	0.49	0.56

Source: Forecast of U. S. Oceanborne Foreign Trade in Dry Bulk Commodities by Booz-Allen Applied Research, Inc., Table 34, p. 137-138

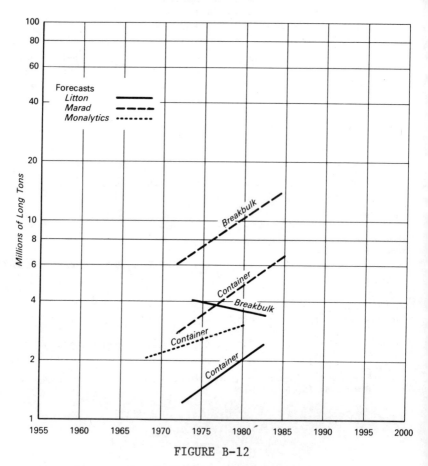

FIGURE B-12

Forecasts of General Cargo Seaborne Imports
and Exports Segregated between
Breakbulk and Container
Traffic

TABLE B-10

U.S. WATERBORNE IMPORTS, CONTAINERIZABLE COMMODITY FLOWS, 1968-1980

(Thousands of 20-Foot Container Equivalents)

	North Atlantic			U.S. SEABOARDS South Atlantic			Gulf		
	Actual	Estimated		Actual	Estimated		Actual	Estimated	
FOREIGN TRADE AREA	1968	1975	1980	1968	1975	1980	1968	1975	1980
Caribbean	15	19	23	3	4	7	4	5	6
East Coast, South America	45	54	67	2	3	4	27	34	41
West Coast, South America	50	60	74	2	2	3	16	21	25
West Coast Central America, Mexico	3	3	4	*	*	*	1	2	2
Gulf Coast Mexico	8	10	12	*	*	*	11	14	17
United Kingdom/Eire	63	76	94	4	5	8	6	8	9
Baltic, Scandinavia	48	58	71	2	3	4	6	8	10
Bayonne-Hamburg Range	141	171	211	18	26	40	30	39	47
Portugal/Spain	17	21	26	1	1	1	3	3	4
Azores/Mediterranean	78	94	115	8	11	17	9	12	14
West Coast of Africa	27	33	40	*	*	*	11	14	17
South and East Africa	21	25	31	1	1	2	9	12	14
Australia	25	30	38	7	10	15	1	2	2
India/Persia	30	37	45	24	34	54	18	23	28
Malaysia	20	24	30	1	2	3	7	10	11
Far East-South Area	56	67	83	9	14	21	9	12	14
Far East-North Area	123	149	184	14	21	32	25	33	39
TOTAL FOREIGN TRADE AREAS	769	930	1,149	95	136	214	194	250	302

*Less than 500 containers per year.

TABLE B-10 (cont'd)

U.S. SEABOARDS

FOREIGN TRADE AREA	Pacific			Great Lakes			Total U.S.		
	Actual	Estimated		Actual	Estimated		Actual	Estimated	
	1968	1975	1980	1968	1975	1980	1968	1975	1980
Caribbean	1	1	1	—	—	—	23	29	36
East Coast, South America	8	10	12	1	1	2	82	103	127
West Coast, South America	6	8	10	1	1	2	74	94	115
West Coast Central America, Mexico	5	6	7	1	—	—	9	11	13
Gulf Coast Mexico	—	—	—	*	*	*	19	24	30
United Kingdom/Eire	8	10	13	12	21	25	93	117	144
Baltic, Scandinavia	7	8	10	4	7	9	67	84	104
Bayonne-Hamburg Range	18	22	27	19	32	39	226	284	350
Portugal/Spain	3	3	4	2	3	4	25	31	38
Azores/Mediterranean	8	10	12	4	7	9	107	135	166
West Coast of Africa	2	3	3	1	2	3	42	52	64
South and East Africa	4	5	6	2	3	4	37	47	58
Australia	9	11	13	*	*	*	42	53	65
India/Persia	11	13	16	1	1	1	83	105	129
Malaysia	9	11	13	2	4	5	40	51	62
Far East-South Area	38	47	57	1	2	2	113	143	176
Far East-North Area	111	134	167	12	21	26	286	361	444
TOTAL FOREIGN TRADE AREAS	247	301	371	62	106	130	1,367	1,724	2,120

Source: Forecast of World Trade in Containerizable Commodities:
1975 and 1980 by Manalytics, Inc., Table 1, p. 2 & 3.

TABLE B-11

U.S. WATERBORNE EXPORTS, CONTAINERIZABLE COMMODITY FLOWS, 1968-1980

(Thousands of 20-Foot Container Equivalents)

	U.S. SEABOARDS								
	North Atlantic			South Atlantic			Gulf		
	Actual	Estimated		Actual	Estimated		Actual	Estimated	
FOREIGN TRADE AREA	1968	1975	1980	1968	1975	1980	1968	1975	1980
Caribbean	46	52	64	11	16	19	40	57	65
East Coast, South America	21	23	29	1	2	2	18	26	30
West Coast, South America	17	19	24	1	1	2	14	20	23
West Coast Central America, Mexico	3	4	5	*	*	*	5	7	8
Gulf Coast Mexico	3	3		*	*	*	4	5	6
United Kingdom/Eire	31	34	43	3	5	6	19	27	31
Baltic, Scandinavia	19	21	26	*	*	*	9	13	15
Bayonne-Hamburg Range	89	100	124	17	24	29	47	67	76
Portugal/Spain	5	6	7	*	*	*	2	3	4
Azores/Mediterranean	42	47	59	8	12	14	30	42	48
West Coast of Africa	9	10	13	1	2	3	13	18	21
South and East Africa	14	15	19	2	3	2	8	11	12
Australia	18	20	25	2	3	4	9	12	14
India/Persia	25	28	35	2	3	3	23	33	38
Malaysia	5	5	7	1	1	1	14	19	22
Far East-South Area	24	27	33	6	9	11	26	37	43
Far East-North Area	19	21	26	7	10	12	38	54	62
TOTAL FOREIGN TRADE AREAS	390	436	541	63	91	110	320	451	515

* Less than 500 containers per year.

TABLE B-11 (cont'd)

U.S. SEABOARDS

FOREIGN TRADE AREA	Pacific Actual 1968	Pacific Estimated 1975	Pacific Estimated 1980	Great Lakes Actual 1968	Great Lakes Estimated 1975	Great Lakes Estimated 1980	Total U.S. Actual 1968	Total U.S. Estimated 1975	Total U.S. Estimated 1980
Caribbean	5	7	9	1	1	1	104	131	158
East Coast, South America	3	4	5	2	2	2	45	57	69
West Coast, South America	6	8	10	1	1	1	39	49	59
West Coast Central America, Mexico	3	4	5	*	*	*	12	15	18
Gulf Coast Mexico	*	*	*	—	—	—	6	8	10
United Kingdom/Eire	10	13	16	5	5	5	68	86	103
Baltic, Scandinavia	8	10	13	2	2	2	38	49	58
Bayonne-Hamburg Range	25	33	42	11	12	13	189	240	288
Portugal/Spain	*	*	*	*	*	*	8	10	12
Azores/Mediterranean	7	9	12	5	5	6	92	117	140
West Coast of Africa	*	*	*	3	4	4	27	34	40
South and East Africa	2	2	3	1	1	1	26	33	40
Australia	10	13	16	1	1	1	39	50	60
India/Persia	11	14	18	7	8	8	68	86	104
Malaysia	8	11	14	*	*	*	28	35	42
Far East-South Area	31	41	52	1	2	2	90	113	136
Far East-North Area	53	69	88	3	4	4	120	152	182
TOTAL FOREIGN TRADE AREAS	182	239	303	45	49	50	999	1,266	1,519

Source: Forecast of World Trade in Containerizable Commodities: 1975 and 1980 by Manalytics, Inc., Table 2, p. 4 & 5.

APPENDIX C
U.S. FEDERAL AGENCIES AND THE
NATION'S PORTS

There are over 40 organizations in the Executive
Branch of the Federal Government with functional responsibilities directly or indirectly affecting the
operations or future development plans of ports in the
United States. Summaries of each agency's role as related to the port industry are presented within the
following categories:

A. Federal Inspection Agencies

B. Federal Port-Related Agencies

C. Federal Independent and Regulatory Agencies

A. Federal Inspection Agencies

Department of Health, Education & Welfare

Animal and Plant Health Inspection Service (APHIS)

The APHIS administers federal laws and regulations on animal and plant health and quarantine, meat and poultry inspection, humane treatment of animals, and the control and eradication of pests and diseases. Its inspectors are involved with every vessel entering port and may board after clearance by the Public Health Service.

The jurisdiction of plant quarantine inspectors-- whose function is certification of freedom from injurious pests and diseases of plant and plant products--extends not only to these cargoes, but to the vessel itself and to all other cargoes that, in themselves or their packaging, may contain unprocessed plant products or be carriers of plant pests. Ashore, they inspect export cargoes to certify them as free from such pests and diseases.

The port functions of APHIS meat and poultry inspectors include: 1) inspection, proper handling, and quarantine of imported animals and animal products; 2) inspection, humane treatment, and safe transport of animals for export; 3) examination and certification of animals and animal products for export, in accordance with both U.S. and the importing nation's requirements; and 4) certification of imported animals as purebred for Customs purposes. Generally, imported animals and animal products are inspected on the pier before they move to quarantine areas, and certification for export takes place close to the port of embarkation. Tests for wholesomeness of animal products also are conducted in port-located laboratories.

Public Health Service(USPHS)

The U.S. Public Health Service is charged with improving environmental health, with emphasis on preventing the introduction and spread of communicable disease. Some USPHS regulations deal with structural features of vessels. Issuance of the required Certificate of Sanitary Construction and the Deratization Exemption Certificate is based less on review of the vessel's plans than on inspections during construction, and each renewal requires a new inspection covering rat-proofing and sanitation features of the design. There are no direct fees for USPHS services.

The USPHS also maintains quarantine stations at U.S. ports of entry. Any vessel entering from a foreign port is subject to both quarantine and sanitary inspections. A USPHS quarantine officer boards the vessel on arrival.

He inspects its passengers and crew, to determine the
presence or risk of communicable disease; and inspects
the vessel, its cargo manifest, and other documents to
ascertain the sanitary history and condition of the
vessel. If health conditions aboard ship are found satisfactory and fumigation is not required, he issues a
certificate of pratique to the vessel's Master, permitting
him to land passengers and discharge cargo. The quarantine
inspector is the first to board the inbound vessel; no
other federal agency, including the Customs Service, will
complete its inspection until a valid certificate of
pratique has been issued.

Food and Drug Administration
The FDA enforces the Federal Food, Drug, and
Cosmetic Act, the Tea Importation Act, the Hazardous
Substances Labelling Act, and other such laws. Its main
responsibility is to assure that specified products moving
in interstate commerce comply with certain standards of
purity, lack of contamination, non-adulteration, and
proper labelling. Its port activities are an extension
of its domestic mission, since all imported goods, once
entered, can move freely in interstate commerce. The FDA
depends upon cooperation from the Customs Service, which
will not grant final release to any goods subject to FDA
purview until the FDA has cleared them. The FDA conducts
chemical and biological analyses at its own laboratories,
using samples drawn by FDA personnel at the pier, warehouse, or consignee's premises.

Department of Justice

Immigration and Naturalization Service (INS)
The INS is responsible for controlling the
arrival and departure of people, both citizens and aliens.
It may refuse entry to aliens, and after admission may
even secure their deportation. Its control is primarily
administered at the arrival point. An immigration inspector normally will board an inbound vessel either
instream, enroute to or at dockside, depending on the established procedure at each port, to check the identity
papers of passengers and crew. A passenger and crew manifest must be presented by the ship's Master and all pass-
ports with visas (green cards in the case of aliens) are
then examined individually. In the event a person is
found without proper identification or his name is in the
Lookout Book, he is refused admission to the U.S. and the
vessel which transported him is responsible for his return.

Department of Transportation

United States Coast Guard (USCG)

The U.S. Coast Guard is charged with implementing those laws that are concerned with safety of life at sea, in harbors, and on all the navigable waters of the United States and with safety of maritime property, including the safe carriage of cargoes. These laws, which probably constitute the most comprehensive compilation of maritime regulations in existence, affect the physical characteristics of U.S. merchant vessels as well as their operation.

Among its functions, the Coast Guard approves plans for construction, repair, and alteration of vessels; approves materials, equipment, and appliances used in the construction and operation of vessels; inspects vessels and their equipment and appliances, and issues certificates of inspection; issues permits for vessel operations that may be hazardous to life and property; administers load-line requirements; controls log books and provides for the registry, enrollment, and licensing of vessels; records vessel mortgages and sales; and issues certificates of admeasurement, which are the basis for computing and collecting tonnage taxes. It examines, and issues licenses and certificates to, U.S. merchant marine officers, seamen, and harbor pilots (and can suspend or revoke licenses and certificates); superintends the shipment and discharge (sign-on and sign-off), protection and welfare of merchant seamen; and examines, and issues licenses to, motorboat operators.

Through the Captain of the Port, the Coast Guard enforces rules and regulations governing the anchorage and movements of vessels; exercises supervision over the loading and unloading of explosives and other dangerous cargoes by vessels in harbors and adjacent waters; and discharges its responsibility for protection of the marine environment. (Environmental emphasis to date has been mainly on oil pollution; the Captain of the Port is responsible for implementing the oil spill recovery program.)

The Coast Guard collects merchant vessel statistics; maintains and operates all lights and other navigation aids in navigable channels of the United States; investigates marine casualties; and conducts air-sea patrols, vessel assistance, and rescue operations. It also enforces laws relating to immigration, quarantine, and miscellaneous maritime statutes for other Federal agencies and assists them in performing their assigned duties. In addition, the Coast Guard is charged with

safeguarding harbors, ports, and waterfront facilities
against destruction, loss, or injury from sabotage, acci-
dents, and other specified causes. The safety regulatory functions of the Coast Guard
are centered in the Office of Merchant Marine Safety,
comprising five divisions: Merchant Marine Technical,
Merchant Vessel Personnel, Merchant Vessel Inspection,
Merchant Vessel Documentation, and Hazardous Materials.
The Coast Guard maintains some 50 Marine Inspection Offices,
each under an Officer in Charge of Marine Inspection(OCMI).
The OCMI's inspect vessels for compliance with laws and
regulations and, in case of new construction and alterations, also conduct shipyard inspections and factory inspections of vessel materials and equipment. Primary
areas of Coast Guard concern include structure, subdivision
and stability, fire protection, lifesaving appliances,
navigational devices, and the carriage of bulk grain and
of dangerous cargoes. There are generally no direct fees
for Coast Guard inspections.

Department of the Treasury

U.S. Customs Service

The Customs Service administers a variety of
powers and duties vested in the Secretary of the Treasury.
Among its chief functions, it controls the entry and
clearance of vessels (and aircraft), and enforces a variety
of shipping laws. It collects duties, taxes, and fees on
imported goods; collects vessel tonnage taxes; and administers the Export Control Program, inspecting export
declarations and permits to ensure compliance with federal
licensing provisions covering "controlled materials". The
shipping laws it enforces include those regulating vessels
in U.S. coastal and fishing trades, and the use of foreign
vessels in U.S. territorial waters. It also licenses
customhouse brokers; handles the remission and mitigation
of fines, penalties, and forfeitures incurred under the
laws it administers; and compiles trade statistics for
the Bureau of Census, as well as for internal use. Its
authority and functions give the Customs Service a key
role among port inspection agencies, and it necessarily
works closely with the U.S. Public Health Service, the
Animal and Plant Health Inspection Service, the Food and
Drug Administration, and the Immigration and Naturalization
Service.

B. Federal Port Related Agencies

Department of Agriculture

Commodity Credit Corporation (CCC)
The CCC, an agency of the Department of Agriculture stabilizes and protects farm income and prices through a variety of programs. It facilitates the distribution of commodities acquired under its stabilization program throug domestic and export sales, transfers to other government agencies, and donations for domestic and foreigh welfare.

The CCC carries out its foreign assistance under Public Law 480, the Agricultural Trade Development and Assistance Act of 1954, also known as the Food for Peace Act. Though Title I and II of the Act, agricultural commodities are purchased from U.S. stocks and are exported for foreign currencies, famine relief and donations, and bartered for materials and services required abroad by other Federal agencies. The CCC also conducts a commercial program, the Export Credit Sales Program, whereby short-term dollar credit is extended for up to 36 months to encourage foreign nations to purchase U.S. agricultural commodities. The various activities of the CCC have fostered the movement of millions of tons of exports through many ports within the United States.

Department of Commerce

Bureau of Domestic Commerce (BDC)
The BDC provides analyses of current and developing industry and trade conditions; recommends policies and program objectives to stimulate balanced growth of U.S. industry; and serves as the principal office within the Department for examining issues of specific industries and business segments as these might affect the economic and technical growth of the economy.

BDC serves as the Department's principal medium of contact with the local business community for disseminating industry information, business opportunities, technological data, and other information products of the Department applicable to business. It obtains information on business industry and community conditions and trends in order to deal with key issues facing the economy.

Bureau of International Commerce (BIC)
The Bureau promotes the foreign commerce of the U.S. and assists business in its operations abroad in order to stimulate the expansion of U.S. exports.

BIC helps U.S. business sell its goods in international markets by providing commercial, economic, and

marketing information on the best export prospects and
methods of marketing goods, and by providing information
on prospective customers and agents. BIC also prepares
statistical analyses on trade between and among the United
States and other countries, and is a major source for
analyses of trade statistics of foreign countries.

In addition, BIC sponsors a nationwide program
to publicize and ensure the broadest possible use of
recently enacted legislation permitting U.S. firms to
establish Domestic International Sales Corporations (DISC),
which are entitled to defer tax on 50 per cent of export
income. BIC operates its overseas marketing programs by
maintaining trade centers in established foreign marketing
areas, staging U.S. commercial exhibitions at international
trade fairs and sending U.S. trade missions to develop
sales opportunities for U.S. firms.

Economic Development Administration (EDA)

The EDA provides long range economic development
and programming for areas with substantial and persistent
unemployment and underemployment and low family income.
It creates employment opportunities by developing or expanding existing facilities and resources in such areas
and regions.

The EDA program includes the following types of
financial aid: (1) grants for public works and development
facilities, (2) loans up to 100 percent to assist in financing public works, loans up to 65 percent for industrial and commercial expansion, and guarantees of up
to 90 percent of associated working capital loans; (3)
loans and grants to redevelopment areas and centers in
multi-county development districts; (4) technical and
planning assistance to multi-state regional planning commissions; and (5) technical assistance and research.

Maritime Administration (MARAD)

The Maritime Administration is charged with
fostering the development, promotion, and operation of a
U.S.-flag merchant marine adequate to meet the needs of
the domestic and foreign waterborne commerce and the
national defense of the United States. Its functions include determining the ocean services necessary for
developing and maintaining U.S. foreign waterborne commerce, and the vessel types required to provide such
services; administering the construction-differential and
operating-differential subsidy programs and other government aids to shipping; overseeing the construction and
operation of all vessels built or operated with government
aid; consulting with the Department of Defense concerning

subsidized ships, to ensure that defense features are incorporated in their design and construction, and making recommendations to the Department of the Navy for the payment of the cost of such defense features; supervising the construction of merchant-type ships built for federal agencies; maintaining the National Defense Reserve Fleet of government-owned ships; and training merchant marine officers, including operation of the U.S. Merchant Marine Academy. It conducts and supports R&D on ship design, construction, operation, maintenance, and repair; cargo handling systems and port facilities; and water transportation systems. MarAd's involvement in U.S. shipping is thus quite broad; in its promotional role, it represents the interests--and often acts as an advocate--of the shipbuilders, shipowners and operators, and related industry sectors; and, in exercising its prescribed functions it issues rules and regulations that affect each of these sectors.

To safeguard government interests, MarAd is concerned with all aspects of the initial design and detailed specifications of subsidized merchant ships and of merchant type ships built for federal agencies. It participates with the owner in plan review (and in review of changes under the construction contract), inspection tests, and sea trials. Except with respect to ships constructed directly for government account, MarAd comments have force only through the owner, who channels them to the shipbuilder. On occasion, owners may delegate to MarAd the authority to conduct owners' inspections. During a subsidized ship's operation, MarAd conducts the guarantee survey, as well as subsequent inspections during repair and overhaul. There are no fees for MarAd inspections.

National Oceanic and Atmospheric Administration (NOAA)

The mission of NOAA includes exploring and charting the oceans and translating physical and biological knowledge into systems capable of assessing the oceans' potential yield. Among its principal activities, NOAA reports the weather of the United States and its possessions and provides weather forecasts to the general public; issues tornado, hurricane, and flood warnings; and provides special services to aeronautical, maritime, agricultural, and other weather-sensitive activities. It administers the National Sea Grant Program, which provides financial grants to institutions for aquatic research, education, and advisory services, and, under the Coastal Zone Management Act of 1972, assists the states in planning

for the proper use of ecologically sensitive coastal lands
and waters.

Social and Economic Statistics Administration (SESA)

The Social and Economic Statistics Administration
brought together the Bureau of the Census and the former
Office of Business Economics to form a single organization
for carrying out statistical programs of the Department.
The Bureau of Census publishes statistical reports on a
variety of subjects including industry, business, foreign
commerce and trade and transportation. The Office of
Business Economics provides five basic economic measures
of the national economy, current analyses of the economic
situation, and analysis of the factors affecting regional
economic development.

Department of Defense

Office of the Secretary - Installation and Logistics

The Secretary is responsible for material requirements; production planning and scheduling; distribution movement and disposal of material, supplies, tools,
etc., transportation, and other logistical services; commercial and industrial activities and facilities including
military construction and real estate and real property,
including general purpose space. The Secretary also co-
ordinates and maintains liaison with appropriate agencies
outside the DOD on installations and logistic matters.

Military Sealift Command (MSC)

An agency of the Department of the Navy, the MSC
provides ocean transportation for personnel and cargo for
all components of the Department of Defense and, in some
cases, for other government agencies. It also operates
Special Project ships involved in missile tracking, cable
laying, oceanographic mapping and research, and hydro-
graphic research.

The MSC operates a mixed fleet of government-owned
ships and time-chartered commercial ships. Some of these
are manned by Navy crews; others, by Civilian Marine
Personnel, who are Civil Service employees and are represented by the same unions that represent industry sea-
going personnel. It also charters and books space on
privately operated commercial ships. It thus functions as
both shipowner and operator, and as a shipper.

Military Traffic Management Command (MTMC)

An agency of the Department of the Army, the MTMC
is responsible for military traffic management, land

transportation, and common-user ocean terminal service within the continental United States, and for worldwide traffic management of Department of Defense household goods movement and storage. It also provides transportati planning support and services. The MTMC thus combines the functions of a shipper, freight consolidator (domestic freight forwarder), marine terminal operator, stevedore, foreign freight forwarder, and customhouse broker.

Corps of Engineers

The Corps of Engineers, under the jurisdiction of the Department of the Army, administers all matters relating to construction, maintenance, and real estate necessary for the improvement of rivers, harbors, and waterways for navigation,[7] flood control, and shore protection; and administers the laws for the protection and preservation of U.S. navigable waters. Among its maritime-related activities, the Corps provides for anchorages and channels, removes obstructions to navigation, and conducts surveys of rivers, harbors, and other navigable waters. The Corps designs and operates a small number of vessels, including dredges and harbor craft.

Also, the Chief of Engineers submits annual reports to Congress describing the terminal and transfer facilities existing on every U.S. harbor or waterway under maintenance or improvement and stating whether they are considered adequate for existing commerce. Many of the actions recommended by the research arm of the Corps, the Institute of Water Resources, directly affect ports and navigable waterways. Works and improvments involving navigable waters must be approved by the Corps, and the Corps administers harbor lines (established by the Secretary of the Army) beyond which no pier or bulkhead may be extended nor deposits of spoil made without specific authorization.

The regulations of the Corps of Engineers are extensive but do not affect major features of merchant vessel design and construction. The Corps impinges on vessel operations primarily through its periodic issuance of *Notices to Mariners*, concerning harbor, channel, and waterway engineering operations, and other hazards to navigation.

---

[7] The Corps is responsible for the system of locks and dams on the inland waterways and Western Rivers System.

Department of Housing and Urban Development

Community Planning and Management
The Assistant Secretary for Community Planning
and Management is responsible for the following programs;
provides grant assistance to State and local governments
and multi-jurisdictional organizations to encourage
officials to improve planning and decision-making; encourage
community planning and management as a continuous process;
and assist State and local governments in dealing with
community development and growth for urban and rural areas.
The planning assistance spans the broad range of governmental activities, services, and investments for which
assisted governments are responsible.

Community Development
The Assistant Secretary for Community Development
is responsible for programs that provide; funding and
technical assistance to a selected number of cities
throughout the country for a comprehensive program to
deal with social, economic, and physical problems in slum
and blighted areas (Model Cities Program); loans and
grants available for urban renewal, rehabilitation projects, and for the acquisition and development of open
space land. Also, grants are provided for basic water and
sewer facilities and loans for public facilities.

Department of the Interior

Bureau of Sport Fisheries and Wildlife
The program of the Bureau consists of the production and distribution of hatchery fish, the operation
of a nationwide system of wildlife refuges, the regulation of migratory bird hunting, the management of fish
and wildlife populations and the improvement and protection of a quality environment for fish and wildlife.
The Bureau studies environmental impact statements and water use projects proposed by Federal or
private agencies for the probable effects of such projects
on fish and wildlife resources and recommends measures
for their conservation and development. Emphasis is
placed on conservation of estuaries and development of
comprehensive river basin plans which consider future
recreational needs based on fish and wildlife.

Geological Survey
The Geological Survey performs surveys, investigations, and research covering topography, geology and
the mineral and water resources of the U.S., classifies
land as to mineral character and water and power resources;
furnishes engineering supervision for power permits; and

enforces regulations applicable to oil, gas, and other mining leases, permits, licenses, development contracts and gas storage contracts.

The Survey also supervises the operation of private industry on mining and oil and gas leases on public domains, including the Outer Continental Shelf, to ensure maximum utilization and prevent waste of the mineral resources, and to limit environmental damage and pollution.

Office of Land Use and Water Planning

This Office is responsible for policy development and interagency coordination on use of public land and water resources, liaison with the Water Resources Council, and coordination of River Basin Commission activities.

Office of Oil and Gas (OOG)

The Office of Oil and Gas serves as a focal point for leadership and information on petroleum matters in the Federal Government, and the principal channel of communication between the Federal Government, the petroleum industry, the oil producing states, and the public. OOG includes the duties of the former Oil Import Administration which administered the importation of crude oil and other petroleum products.

The Office conducts a continuing study of the effects of oil and gas production, transportation, manufacturing, and consumption on the environment, and reviews for accuracy and completeness of Environmental Impact Statements which relate to oil and gas.

Department of Justice

Law Enforcement Assistance Administration (LEAA)

The purpose of LEAA is to assist State and local governments to reduce crime. The block-grant concept embodied in the legislation implies that more authority and power should be shifted to state and local levels of government in order to decentralize operations of the Federal government. Grants and loans are available for training, planning, and improving law enforcement at all levels of government.

Block planning funds are granted to each State to finance development of an annual comprehensive low enforcement plan. The plan is prepared by the State Planning Agency and reflects the needs of city and county, as well as State governments. LEAA planning grants provide agencies throughout the state with the resources to create program concepts and set up detailed plans for carrying out these programs.

Department of Labor

Labor-Management Services Administration (LMSA)

The LMSA provides assistance to collective bargaining negotiators and keeps the Secretary informed of developments in labor-management disputes of national importance. It administers the Labor Management Reporting and Disclosure Act which requires labor organizations to file financial reports and prescribes rules for the election of union officers, administration of trusteeships by labor organizations, rights of union members and the handling of union funds.

Employment Standards Administration

The Administration has responsibility for administering and directing employment standards programs dealing with: minimum wage and overtime standards; equal pay; age discrimination in employment; promotion of women's welfare; standards to improve employment conditions other than safety, non-discrimination, and affirmative action in government contracts and subcontracts and in federally assisted construction; and workman's compensation programs for Federal and certain private employers.

Occupational Safety and Health Administration (OSHA)

An agency of the Department of Labor, OSHA issues occupational safety and health standards, and related regulations; conducts investigations and inspections to ensure compliance; and issues citations for noncompliance. Its marine jurisdiction covers workers engaged in longshoring, ship repairing, and related employment. Many standards and codes, originally developed by consensus for voluntary industry use, have been incorporated by reference into OSHA's voluminous regulations, so that compliance has become legally enforceable. Thus, OSHA regulations affect almost every activity in shipyard and marine terminal operations.

Department of Transportation

Office of the Secretary - Policy, Plans, and International Affairs

Functions performed in this area, include the analysis, development and articulation of new and revised policies, plans and programs for domestic and international transportation; analysis of the social, economic, and environmental interplay between transport systems operations and established policies, regulations, and laws; transportation facilitation; international technological cooperation; technical assistance to developing countries; and a comprehensive transportation data and information system.

Federal Aviation Administration (FAA)

The FAA regulates air commerce to foster aviation safety; promotes civil aviation and a national system of airports; and develops and operates a common system of air traffic control and navigation.

The FAA administers airport planning and development programs that identify the type and cost of public airports required for a national airport system. Also, the FAA provides grants to assist public agencies in airport system planning, airport master planning, and public airport development.

Federal Highway Administration (FHA)

The Administration provides for: Federal and Federal-Air highway construction, national highway and vehicle safety, coordination of highways with other modes of transportation systems and facilities. The FHA is also concerned with the total operation and environment of the highway system.

The FHA administers the Federal Aid to Highways program of financial assistance to states for highway construction. The 42,500 mile National System of Interstate and Defense Highways is financed on a 90 percent Federal, 10 percent State basis, while the improvements of 872,000 miles of other Federal-aid primary and secondary roads and their urban extensions is financed on a 50-50 basis.

Federal Railroad Administration

The purpose of the Administration is to consolidate Government support of rail transportation activities, provide a unified and unifying national policy for rail transportation, conduct research and development activity in support of improved intercity ground transportation and the future requirements for rail transportation.

Urban Mass Transportation Administration (UMTA)

The missions of the Administration are: to assist in the development of improved mass transportation facilities, equipment, techniques, and methods; to encourage the planning and establishment of areawide urban mass transportation systems; and to provide assistance to State and local governments in financing such systems.

Grants and/or loans are made to assist communities in acquiring or improving capital equipment and facilities for urban mass transit systems. The maximum grant is two-thirds of net project cost (that part which cannot be financed from system revenues). To qualify, the urban area must prepare a program for a unified or officially coordinated urban transportation system as a part of the comprehensive planned development of the area.

Saint Lawrence Seaway Development Corporation

The Corporation is responsible for the construction, maintenance, and operation of that part of the seaway located in the U.S. territory; financing the U.S. share of the Seaway cost, and encouraging the development of traffic and maximum utilization of the Seaway.

Executive Office of the President

Council on Environmental Quality (CEQ)

The CEQ was established by the National Environmental Policy Act of 1969, to formulate and recommend national policies to promote the improvement of the quality of the environment. The CEQ also performs a continuing analysis of changes or trends in the national environment.

Council on International Economic Policy

The Council on International Economic Policy was created by the President's memorandum of January 19, 1971. It's purposes are to achieve consistency between domestic and foreign economic policy, provide top level focus for the full range of international economic policy issues, deal with international economic policy, consider the international economic aspects of foreign policy issues and maintain close coordination with basic foreign policy objectives.

C. Federal Independent or Regulatory Agencies

Environmental Protection Agency (EPA)

The goal of the EPA is to assure protection of the environment by the systematic abatement and control of pollution. It develops and enforces environmental quality standards, with emphasis on air and water quality. It is charged with making public its written comments on environmental impact statements, and with publishing its determinations where these hold that a proposal is unsatisfactory from the standpoint of public health or enviornmental quality. The EPA also conducts research, monitoring, and technical assistance in such areas as the safety and effectiveness of pesticides and advanced technology for solid waste disposal.

Export-Import Bank of the United States

The purpose of the Bank is to aid in financing and to facilitate exports and imports and the exchange of commodities between the U.S. or any of its Territories or insular possessions and any foreign country or its agencies

or nationals. It develops credit programs to meet specific
exporter needs in order to broaden the export opportunities
of U.S. industry.

Federal Communications Commission (FCC)

The FCC regulates interstate and foreign communications by wire and radio. It licenses and regulates a
number of "nonbroadcast" radio services, including aviation
and marine. Its marine jurisdiction includes both radio
channels and shipboard radio equipment, with certain ex-
emptions for government-owned and operated radio facilities; and it implements the compulsory provisions of laws
and treaties covering the use of radio for the safety of
life at sea.

Federal Maritime Commission (FMC)

The FMC regulates ocean carriers, maritime terminal
operators, and ocean freight forwarders engaged in the
foreign commerce and domestic offshore commerce of the
United States. The latter jurisdiction covers ocean
carriers providing service between the continental United
States and such non-contiguous states, territories, and
possessions as Hawaii, Alaska, Puerto Rico, Guam, Wake
and the Virgin Islands. Intercoastal shipping is regulated by the Interstate Commerce Commission.

It approves or disapproves agreements filed by common
carriers, including conference and interconference agreements, and cooperative working agreements among common
carriers, terminal operators, ocean freight forwarders,
and others subject to the shipping laws; reviews their
activities under these agreements for regulatory compliance;
regulates their practices; accepts or rejects tariff
filings (and, in the domestic offshore trades, may set
maximum or minimum rates, or suspend rates); prescribes
accounting rules; and licenses ocean freight forwarders.
It also issues or denies certificates of financial responsibility of ship owners and operators with respect to
passenger indemnity and liability for oil pollution clean-
up.

Interstate Commerce Commission (ICC)

The ICC regulates certain classes of surface carriers
engaged in interstate and foreign commerce, to the extent
the latter takes place within the United States. Among
its major functions, the ICC settles controversies over
rates and charges among competing and like modes of

transportation, shippers, and others;[8] grants operating
rights; rules on applications for mergers and consoli-
dations, acquisitions of control, and sale of carriers;
prescribes accounting rules; acts to prevent unlawful
discrimination, destructive competition, and rebating;
and awards reparations.

The ICC's maritime jurisdiction includes: 1) certain
classes of barge carriers on U.S. inland and coastal
waterways;[9] 2) coastwise and intercoastal shipping between
points in the continental United States;[10] 3) inland movement of barges carried aboard oceangoing "LASH" and "Seabee" ships; and 4) regulation of through routes and joint
rates established between common carriers by water (including those otherwise subject to Federal Maririme Commission jurisdiction) and ICC-regulated rail or motor
carriers. In addition, the ICC has authority over the
transportation of certain dangerous articles (e.g., explosives, radioactive materials, etiological agents), and
certain powers to establish what items fall within these
classifications. Under this authority, the ICC can issue
regulations for the safe transportation of such articles
within the United States by any carrier engaged in interstate or foreign commerce by land or water.

Occupational Safety and Health Review Commission

The Occupational Safety and Health Review Commission
is an independent agency established by the Occupational
Safety and Health Act of 1970. It was created to insure
just and equitable enforcement of those occupational
health and safety standards which are contested by employers, employees, and representatives of employees.

---

[8] With respect to inland and coastal water carriers, the
ICC can suspend new rates or charges; and it has considerable authority to fix rates and charges, their
maximum and minimum levels, and their divisions among
carriers.

[9] In general, unpackaged bulk commodities and liquid
cargoes in bulk are exempted from ICC regulation, as
are private carriers. Regulated common and contract
carriers account for less than half of inland waterways
traffic.

[10] Non-contiguous domestic shipping is regulated by the
Federal Maritime Commission, *infra*.

The Commission functions are strictly adjudicatory.

Panama Canal Company

The Company maintains and operates the Canal and conducts business operations incident thereto and to the civil government of the Canal Zone. It issues regulations governing the Canal's use and collects tolls from vessels transiting the Canal.

Tolls are based on each vessel's Panama Canal Tonnage, which is computed from--but differs from--both gross and net register tonnages (g.r.t. and n.r.t.). These are, respectively, crude measures of ship size (enclosed cubic capacity) and earning capacity (enclosed revenue-earning cubic capacity), and each is expressed in units of 100 cu. ft.

United States Tariff Commission

The Commission serves the Congress and the President as an advisory, fact finding agency on tariff, commercial policy, and foreign trade matters.

Water Resources Council

The Council maintains a continuing study of the adequacy of supplies of water necessary to meet the requirements in each water resource region in the U.S., the relation of regional or river basin plans and programs to the requirements of larger regions of the Nation and of the adequacy of administrative and statutory means for the coordination of the water and related land resources policies of several Federal agencies.

National Transportation Safety Board (NTSB)

The NTSB is an independent agency[11] whose main functions are accident cause determination and safety promotion in aviation and surface transportation. For the surface modes (rail, highway, pipeline, and marine), accident cause determination is usually delegated to the modal Administrations within the Department of Transportation; however, the NTSB reserves the right to investigate, determine cause, and report the facts of all surface

---

[11] Established simultaneously with the Department of Transportation (1966) as an autonomous agency placed administratively under that Department, the NTSB became a separate, independent agency on April 1, 1975. The functions described above come under the Marine Safety Division of the Board's Bureau of Surface Transportation Safety.

transportation accidents it declares to be major.

In the case of a marine casualty, the Coast Guard forms a Marine Board of Investigation, which is required to make findings of fact and may (and usually does) arrive at conclusions and recommendations. The Coast Guard's findings are then reviewed by the NTSB and incorporated into a Marine Casualty Report, which also includes the NTSB's synopsis, analysis, determination of probably cause, and appropriate recommendations. These recommendations may be addressed to the Coast Guard, to other government agencies (e.g., the Maritime Administration, the Federal Communications Commission), or to non-government organizations (e.g., the American Bureau of Shipping).

APPENDIX D

MAJOR STEPS FOR WATER RESOURCES PROJECTS REQUIRING SPECIFIC CONGRESSIONAL AUTHORIZATION [1]

PHASE I. STUDY AUTHORIZATION

Step 1. Initiation of Action by Local Interests: Local citizens who desire Federal assistance in improvements for navigation, beach erosion control, flood control, and related water resources purposes should contact their U. S. Senators and Representatives and request that provision of the desired facilities be considered by the Federal Government. Local interests may also request advice from representatives of the Corps of Engineers on the appropriate procedures, particularly on whether a study and project may be accomplished under one of the general continuing authorities for small projects.

Step 2. Consultation by Senator or Representatives with Public Works Committee:

a. If previous studies and reports on navigation, flood control, or related purposes have been made for the area in question, the Senator or Representative may request the Senate or House Committee on Public Works to adopt a resolution authorizing a review of previous reports to determine whether any modifications of the Chief of Engineers' recommendations in such reports would be advisable.

b. If no previous study and report has been made, the Senator or Representative may request the Committee to include authorization for a study in either an omnibus river and harbor and flood control bill or a separate bill.

c. In the case of beach erosion control, hurricane protection, and related purposes, the Senator or Representative may sponsor a bill authorizing a study or may request the Committee to adopt a resolution authorizing a study in accordance with Section 110 of the River and Harbor Act approved 23 October 1962.

---

[1] Department of Army, Corps of Engineers, *Water Resources Development*, Washington, D.C., July 1974.

Step 3. <u>Action by the Senate or House Public Works Committee</u>: Each Committee may seek advice from the Chief of Engineers on the desirability of authorizing a particular study. If the Committee to which a study request is referred is convinced of the need for the study, it will take appropriate action. In the case of a previous study report on navigation or flood control, such action is a resolution adopted by the Committee, calling upon the Board of Engineers for Rivers and Harbors to make a review and referred to the Chief of Engineers for action. In the case of a beach erosion problem, the resolution requests the Secretary of the Army to cause the study to be made. If the previous report involves the project for the alluvial valley of the Mississippi River and tributaries, the resolution calls for a review of that report by the Chief of Engineers rather than by the Board. Where no previous study has been made, the authorization for a study may be included in either an omnibus river and harbor flood control bill or a separate bill for consideration by Congress.

PHASE II. ACCOMPLISHMENT OF STUDY

Step 4. <u>Assignment and Funding of Study</u>: When Congress authorizes a study, the Chief of Engineers assigns it to an appropriate reporting officer, usually the Division Engineer in whose region the study area is located. The Division Engineer usually further assigns the study to the appropriate District Engineer. However, before a study can be undertaken, funds for that specific purpose must be appropriated by the Congress and there is generally a time lag of one or more years between study authorization and study funding. Such funding is an entirely separate action.

Step 5. <u>Conduct of Study by Division or District Engineer</u>:
    a. The conduct of a study and preparation of a report by a Division or District Engineer is a large undertaking requiring three to five years, occasionally longer, depending upon the size and complexity of the study. It involves analyses of the engineering, economic, environmental, and social aspects of potential alternative plans, or solutions. Coordination with interested Federal and non-Federal agencies and other groups and individuals is an integral part of the study process. Public involvement is encouraged, and public meetings are held as one means of fostering such involvement. The development and

circulation of a draft environmental impact statement is
part of this overall process.

b. Basically, a study seeks to identify and assess
the water and related resources problems and needs in the
area under study; define and analyze potential alternative
solutions, and their effects and feasibility; and select
the most feasible plan, or solution, if there is a feasible
one. This includes evaluating the various economic, environmental, and social effects and estimating the tangible
benefits, costs, and cost sharing. A favorable recommendation depends upon a project's overall effects, including
tangible benefits and costs, and upon the obtaining from
responsible non-Federal officials a written expression of
their intent to participate in the project.

c. Typically, a study begins with a preliminary study
to determine if there is sufficient reason to spend time
and money on a detailed study. Coordination and public
involvement begin early in this stage. This includes
an initial public meeting to discuss the study and seek
the views and desires of local people. Such meetings are
publicized and copies of an announcement are sent directly
to all those known to be interested. If the preliminary
study indicates that a feasible plan is possible, a more
detailed study is made. At this time a formulation stage
public meeting is held, during which the study results
thus far are presented. As the study nears completion
and the most feasible plan becomes more apparent, general
coordination is continued, the draft environmental impact
statement is developed and coordinated, a late stage public
meeting is usually held, and the report is written.

Step 6. Issuance of Report and Public Notice by Division
Engineer: Upon completion of the report of the District
Engineer, the Division Engineer having jurisdiction reviews the report and transmits it with his recommendations
and accompanying papers to the Board of Engineers for
Rivers and Harbors, except that reports on the alluvial
valley of the Mississippi River are transmitted to the
Mississippi River Commission instead of the Board. For
a study and report accomplished by a Division Engineer
instead of a District Engineer, the completed report is
similarly transmitted to the Board or the Commission. At
this time, the Division Engineer also issues a public
notice to all persons known to be interested, setting
forth the findings of the study and the report recommendations, and inviting those who wish to do so to furnish
further views to the Board or Commission. It is at this
time that the field report is considered complete

and official, and may be purchased at the cost of repro-
duction.

PHASE III.   STUDY REVIEW AND PROJECT AUTHORIZATION

Step 7. Review by the Board of Engineers for Rivers and
Harbors or the Mississippi River Commission: The Board
of Engineers for Rivers and Harbors, an independent review group with a staff in Washington, D. C., is required
by law to review all Corps of Engineers study reports
specifically authorized by Congress, except for those
which are under the jurisdiction of the Mississippi River
Commission. The Commission, which is located in Vicksburg,
Mississippi, reviews the reports under its jurisdiction.
The Board, or the Commission, may hold public meetings
before making its recommendations to the Chief of Engineers.
A reviewed report is transmitted, with recommendations,
to the Chief of Engineers.

Step 8. Preparation and Coordination of Proposed Report
of the Chief of Engineers: Following receipt of a report
and recommendations from the Board or the Commission, the
Chief of Engineers prepares his proposed report and for-
wards copies of the report with accompanying papers to
the Governors of the affected States and to other interested Federal agencies for formal review and comment.
The revised draft environmental impact statement is also
circulated for comment at this time. The Federal agencies
generally involved may include, but are not limited to,
the Departments of Agriculture, Transportation, Commerce,
Interior, and Health, Education and Welfare; the Federal
Power Commission; and the Environmental Protection Agency.
The States and Federal agencies are normally expected to
forward their comments to the Chief of Engineers within
90 days.

Step 9. Transmittal of Report to the Secretary of the
Army: After the Chief of Engineers receives and considers
the comments of the Governors of the affected States and
those of other interested Federal agencies, as well as
all comments on the revised draft environmental impact
statement, he prepares his final report and the final
environmental impact statement. He then submits the
report along with the statement and other pertinent papers
to the Secretary of the Army.

Step 10. Referral of the Report to the Office of Management and Budget: The Secretary of the Army submits a
draft of his letter of transmission to Congress, along

with the report of the Chief of Engineers and all pertinent papers, to the Director of the Office of Management
and Budget for a determination of the relationship of the
report to the program of the President.

Step 11. Transmittal of Report to Congress: Upon receipt
and consideration of the comments of the Office of Management and Budget, the Secretary of the Army transmits the
report of the Chief of Engineers, with all pertinent papers
and comments, to the Congress. This step completes the
action required of the Chief of Engineers and the Secretary of the Army in complying with the Congressional resolution or act authorizing the study. The final environmental impact statement is also filed with the Council
on Environmental Quality at this time and is available
to the public.

Step 12. Project Authorization by Congress: After the
report is forwarded to Congress by the Secretary of the
Army, it may be printed as a Senate or House Document,
which is referred to as the project document. The Committees on Public Works of the Senate and the House may
hold hearings on the report and consider those projects
recommended in the report for inclusion in an authorization bill. Authorization for construction of projects
is usually included in nation-wide omnibus river and harbor
and flood control bills. However, in 1974 this resulted
in a Water Resources Development Act which, for the first
time, authorized only certain advanced engineering and
design work on some of the projects contained in the Act.
These projects will require further Congressional authorization. Project authorization may also be by resolution
by both Public Works Committees rather than by an Act
when such a project has a Federal cost of less than $10
million. In all cases, however, Congress must appropriate
funds before advanced planning, design, and construction
can be undertaken; such funding is an entirely separate
action.

PHASE IV. ADVANCE PLANNING, DESIGN, AND CONSTRUCTION

Step 13. Project Scheduling and Reaffirmation of Local
Cooperation: Since budgets are limited, authorized projects are in competition with each other for funding.
When a District Engineer is considering the scheduling of
advanced planning, design, and construction of an authorized project, a pertinent factor is the availability of
the required local cooperation. When appropriate, the
District Engineer notifies responsible non-Federal officials

concerning the required local cooperation. If satisfactory assurances are not received regarding intent to furnish local cooperation, the project is considered inactive. In the specific case of local flood protection projects, such projects are deauthorized as provided by law if the assurances are not provided within five years after a formal written request is made. See Step 16 regarding the actual provision of local cooperation.

Step 14. Request for Project Funds: In order to undertake a project authorized by Congress, funds for advanced planning, design, and construction must be requested from Congress. All requests for such funds are made annually through the Office of Management and Budget. If found to conform with the President's budgetary policies, the requests are transmitted to the Congress as part of the President's Budget and later considered by the Appropriations Committees.

Step 15. Appropriation of Project Funds: After completion of hearings by the Appropriations Committees considering the Department of the Army Civil Works Appropriations, a bill is reported out of Committee and referred to the full Congress for passage. The enactment then goes to the President for signature. Authority and funds are thereby given to the Chief of Engineers to initiate advanced planning, design, and construction of the projects included in the Act. Generally, further appropriations are required in succeeding years until the project is completed.

Step 16. Preparation of Detailed Plans: Before construction of a project can start, advanced planning and detailed design must be accomplished by the District Engineer, with such assistance, review, and approval by the Division Engineer and the Chief of Engineers as are necessary. During this period, however, further Congressional authorization will be required for those projects for which only certain advanced engineering and design work was authorized, as mentioned in Step 12 above. The preparation of detailed plans averages several years, depending upon the type and size of project. Essentially, this process begins with a review and updating of the basic plan authorized and proceeds through progressively more detailed design to produce construction plans and specifications along with detailed cost estimates. A public meeting is also held in connection with the advanced planning. If the changes in the basic plan authorized are substantial, a draft environmental impact statement is also prepared and circulated for comment. A final statement is subsequently filed. Coordination with the affected States, other

Federal agencies, and other affected interests is also
maintained during advanced planning and design. At this
time, the formal agreements and local cooperation required
by law, of which local interests were notified in Step
13, must be provided by local interests and approved by
the Secretary of the Army.

Step 17. Award of Contract: Upon completion of detailed
construction plans and specifications for a project or a
separable portion of it, qualified contractors are invited
to bid on the construction of the proposed improvements.
A contract is then awarded to the eligible low bidder for
construction in accordance with the plans and specifications.

Step 18. Construction of Project: After award of a
contract, the successful bidder mobilizes his equipment
and personnel, and starts construction. The work is
accomplished under the technical direction of Corps of
Engineers personnel to insure that it conforms to the
contract requirements. Upon completion of a project,
which may involve more than one contract, a final sharing
of the cost is determined and the Corps of Engineers or
local interests assume operation and maintenance of the
project in accordance with authorized requirements. Construction averages three to four years but may take more
or less time, depending upon the type and size of project.

BIBLIOGRAPHY

American Petroleum Institute, Transportation by Water Committee, *15th Annual Tanker Conference: Discussion of Offshore Storage*, held at Seaview Country Club, Absecon, New Jersey, April 27-29, 1970.

Arthur D. Little, Inc., *Foreign Deep Water Port Developments: A Selective Overview of Economics Engineering and Environmental Factors, Vol. I of III*, prepared for Department of Army, Corps of Engineers, Washington, Dec. 1971.

Arthur D. Little, Inc., *Foreign Deep Water Port Developments: A Selective Overview of Economics, Engineering and Environmental Factors, Vol. II of III, Appendix A-C, Vol. III of III, Appendix D-I*, prepared for Department of Army, Corps of Engineers, Washington, Dec. 1971.

Arthur D. Little, Inc., *Port Management Problem Study*, prepared for Department of Commerce, National Bureau of Standards, Washington, July 15, 1968.

Arthur D. Little, Inc., *Potential Onshore Effects of Deepwater Oil Terminal-Related Industrial Development*, prepared for Council on Environmental Quality, Washington, Sept. 1973.

Balfe, Margaret, Heilmann, Ronald, Johnson, James, and Wendling, Wayne (under the direction of Eric Schenker), *Analysis of International Great Lakes Shipping and Hinterland, Special Report No. 23*, Center for Great Lakes Studies, The University of Wisconsin-Milwaukee, 1975.

Borland, Stewart, and Oliver, Martha, *Port Expansion in the Puget Sound Region 1970-2000*, University of Washington, Division of Marine Resources, Seattle, Oct. 1972.

Bragg, Daniel M., and Bradley, James R., *The Economic Impact of a Deepwater Terminal in Texas*, Texas A&M University, Nov. 1972.

Bragg, Daniel M., and Bradley, James R., *Work Plan for a Study of the Feasibility of an Offshore Terminal in the Texas Gulf Coast Region*, Texas A&M University, June 1971.

Booz, Allen Applied Research, Inc., *Forecast of U.S. Oceanborne Foreign Trade in Dry Bulk Commodities*, prepared for Department of Commerce, (MarAd), March 28, 1969.

Boyer, Walter C., *Concerning Containers in the Port of Baltimore*, Department of Transportation, State of Maryland, Aug. 1971.

Boyer, Walter C., *World Trade and the United States' Share*, Department of Transportation, State of Maryland, Aug. 1971.

Burke, William, "On the Waterfront," *Federal Reserve Bank of San Francisco Monthly Review*, Oct. 1972.

Carroll, Joseph L., et al., *Planning for Coastal Ports On A Systems Basis: Preliminary Methodological Design*, prepared for U.S. Army Corps of Engineers, Institute for Water Resources, Washington, May 1972.

Carter, Anne F., *Ship and Port Development 1967 through 1972*, Naval Weapons Development Department, China Lake, California, Dec. 1973.

Control Systems Research, Inc., *A Critical Analysis of the State of the Art in Containerization*, prepared for U.S. Army Mobility Equipment Research & Development Center, Ft. Belvoir, Va., Nov. 1970.

Council on Environmental Quality, "Preparation of Environment Quality, *Federal Register*, Vol. 38, No. 147, Part II, Aug. 1, 1973.

EBS Management Consultants, Inc., *The Freight Transportation Development Potential of the Port of Providence, Rhode Island,* prepared for Department of Commerce, Washington, March 1969.

Etter, Wayne E., and Graham, Robert C., *Financial Planning for the Texas Port System,* Texas A&M University, March 1974.

Evans, A.A., *Technical and Social Changes in the World Ports,* International Labour Office, Geneva, 1969.

Federal Maritime Commission, *Seminars on the Container Revolution,* U.S. Government Printing Office, Washington, June 1968.

Frankel, Ernest, *Port Design and Analysis Methodology, Vol. I, Technical Report, Vol. II, Appendixes,* M.I.T. Press, Dec. 1, 1974.

Fritzke, Herman E., *A Historical and Critical Review of the Factors Affecting the Development of United States Ports and Their Relationship to Public Policy,* U.S. Naval Postgraduate School, Monterey, California, 1965.

Gilman, Roger H., *Views of the Port Industry,* American Society of Civil Engineers National Meeting on Transportation Engineering, Washington, July 21-25, 1969.

Goldberg, J.P., "Longshoremen and the Modernization of Cargo Handling in the U.S.," *ILR,* March 1973.

Goss, R.O., *Studies in Maritime Economics,* Cambridge University Press, 1968.

Hite, James C., and Stepp, James M., *Coastal Zone Resource Management,* Praeger, New York, 1971.

Hoffmaster, B.N., and Neidengard, C.A., *Containerization 1968: International-Intermodal-Integrated,* Pan American Union, Sept. 1968.

International Longshoremen's and Warehousemen's Union, *Information and Union Comment on the 1960 Mechanization and Modernization Fund Agreement Between the Longshoremen of the Pacific Coast and the Steamship and Stevedoring Employers,* San Francisco, 1960.

Japan Container Association, *Containerization in Japan*, Tokyo, April 1971.

Labor-Management Maritime Committee, *The U.S. Merchant Marine Today: Sunrise or Sunset?*, AFL-CIO, Washington, 1970.

Litton Systems, Inc., *Oceanborne Shipping: Demand and Technology Forecast*, prepared for Department of Transportation, Washington, June 1968.

Louisiana State University, Center for Wetland Resources, *Louisiana Superport Studies, Report No. 1, Preliminary Recommendations and Data Analysis*, prepared for U.S. Department of Commerce, Office of Sea Grant, Washington, Aug. 1972.

Louisiana State University, Center for Wetland Resources, *Louisiana Superport Studies, Preliminary Assessment of the Environment Impact of a Superport on the Southeastern Coastal Area of Louisiana, Report No. 2*, prepared for Department of Commerce, Office of Sea Grant, Washington, Aug. 1972.

Louisiana Superport Task Force, *A Superport for Louisiana*, June 1972.

Manalytics, Inc., *The Impact of Maritime Containerization on the United States Transportation System, Vol. I, Executive Summary, Vol, II, Main Body*, prepared for Department of Commerce (MarAd), Washington, Feb. 1972.

Manalytics, Inc., *U.S.-Canadian Overseas Trade Diversion*, prepared for Federal Maritime Commission, Washington, March 1972.

Marine Science Affairs: A Year of Broaden Participation, Third Report of the President to the Congress on Marine Resources and Engineering Development, U.S. Government Printing Office, Washington, Jan. 1969.

Marine Science Affairs: A Year of Plans and Progress, Second Report of the President to the Congress on Marine Resources and Engineering Development, U.S. Government Printing Office, Washington, March 1968.

Maritime Research Center, *Maritime Transport Data for Marketing, Research and Development,* report on the international symposium held at Institute for Shipping Research, Bergen, Norway, Sept. 11-14, 1973.

Marsden, Howard J., *The Regional Approach to Port Development Planning,* speech given at the National Meeting on Transportation Engineering, American Society of Civil Engineers, Washington, July 22, 1969.

Mascenik, John M., *Deepwater Offshore Petroleum Terminals,* American Society of Civil Engineers National Transportation Meeting, Milwaukee, July 17-21, 1972.

Matson Research Corporation, *The Impact of Containerization on the U.S. Economy--Vol. I and II,* prepared for Department of Commerce (MarAd), Washington, Sept. 1970.

Mayer, Harold M., *Port,* from Encyclopedia Britannica, William Benton, 1971.

Morris, J.P., et al., *Federal Policy for United States Ports,* prepared for Department of Commerce, National Bureau of Standards, Washington, Aug. 25, 1964.

National Academy of Sciences, *Maritime Cargo Transportation Conference,* Vol. I and II, Washington, May 1964.

National Ports Council, *Survey of Non-Scheme Ports and Wharves,* London, Oct. 1972.

National Water Commission, *New Directions in U.S. Water Policy, Summary, Conclusions and Recommendations,* U.S. Government Printing Office, Washington, June 1973.

National Water Commission, *Water Policies for the Future,* final report to the President and to the Congress of the United States, U.S. Government Printing Office, Washington, June 1973.

Organisation for Economic Co-Operation and Development, Maritime Transport Committee, *Development and Problems of Seaborne Container Transport, 1970,* Paris, 1971.

Organisation for Economic Co-Operation and Development, Maritime Transport Committee, *Maritime Transport, 1972,* Paris, 1973.

Padelford, Norman, *Public Policy for the Seas*, M.I.T. Press, 1970.

Pacific Maritime Association and International Longshoremen's and Warehousemen's Union, *Memorandum of Agreement on Mechanization and Modernization*, San Fransicso, Oct. 1960.

Pan American Union, *Port Information Bibliographic and Institutional Sources*, prepared for Department of Commerce, (MarAd), Division of Ports & Systems, Washington, Sept. 19, 1968.

Planning Research Corporation, *Transoceanic Cargo Study: Forecasting Model and Data Base*, Vol. I, prepared for Department of Transportation, Washington, March 1971.

Planning Research Corporation, *Transoceanic Cargo Study: Distribution Costs and Productivity of Transoceanic Transport Technologies*, Vol. II, prepared for Department of Transportation, Washington, March 1971.

Planning Research Corporation, *Transoceanic Cargo Study, Computer Program Documentation: Demand Forecasting Model and Distribution Cost and Production Model*, Vol. III, Department of Transportation, Washington, March 1971.

Plumlee, Carl H., "Optimum Size Seaport," *Journal of the Waterways and Harbors Division*, ASCE, Vol. 92, No. WW3, Proc. Paper 4880, Aug. 1966, pp. 1-24.

Port Authority of New York and New Jersey, *Foreign Trade During 1972 At The Port of New York - New Jersey*, New York, 1973.

Port of Seattle Commission, *Seattle Maritime Commerce and Its Impact on the Economy of King County*, Seattle, 1971.

Port of Seattle Commission, *Seattle-Puget Sound Transportation Gateway of the Pacific Northwest*, Seattle, May, 1972.

Port Statistics, United National Conference on Trade and Development, Geneva, 1971.

Ports of the Pacific, Conference on Maritime Administration Role in Port Development, (transcript of proceedings), San Francisco, July 2, 1974.

Report of the 22nd International Navigation Congress, Section II, Ocean Navigation, 3 Vols., Permanent International Association, Brussels, Belgium, 1969.

Robert R. Nathan Associates, Inc., *Institutional Implications of U.S. Deepwater Port Development for Crude Oil Imports*, prepared for Department of Army, Institute for Water Resources, Washington, June 1973.

Robert R. Nathan Associates, Inc., *U.S. Deepwater Port Study: Commodity Studies and Projections, Vol. II of V*, prepared for Department of Army, Corps of Engineers, Institute for Water Resources, Washington, Aug. 1972.

Robert R. Nathan Associates, Inc., *U.S. Deepwater Port Study: Physical Coast and Port Characteristics, and Selected Deepwater Port Alternatives, Vol. III of V*, prepared for Department of Army, Corps of Engineers, Institue for Water Resources, Washington, Aug. 1972.

Robert R. Nathan Associates, Inc., *U.S. Deepwater Port Study: The Environment and Ecological Aspects of Deepwater Ports, Vol. IV of V*, prepared for Department of Army, Corps of Engineers, Institute of Water Resources, Washington, Aug. 1972.

Robert R. Nathan Associates, Inc., *U.S. Deepwater Port Study: Transport and Benefit-Cost Relationships, Vol. V of V*, prepared for Department of Army, Corps of Engineers, Institute of Water Resources, Washington, Aug. 1972.

Robert Reebie & Associates, Inc., *The Relationship of Land Transportation Economics to Great Lakes Traffic Volume*, prepared for Department of Commerce, (MarAd), Washington, Oct. 1971.

Savory, A. J., *Tanker and Bulk Carrier Terminals Proceedings*, prepared for Institution of Civil Engineers, William Clows & Sons, Ltd., London, Nov. 13, 1969.

Schenker, Eric, and Brockel, Harry C., *Port Planning and Development as Related to U.S. Ports and the U.S. Coastal Environment*, Cornell Maritime Press, Cambridge, Md. 1974.

Schenker, Eric, and Jechoulek, Karl, *Technical Progress and Planning At Ports and the Hinterland*, paper presented at the 8th Conference of the International Association of Ports and Harbors, Amsterdam - Rotterdam, May 6-12, 1973.

Schenker, Eric, *The Port of Milwaukee: An Economic Review*, University of Wisconsin Press, 1967.

Schenker, Eric, *Trends and Implications of Container Shipping*, reprint of paper presented at the Seventh International Association of Ports and Harbors Conference, Montreal, June 1971.

Schwimmer, Martin J., Amundsen, Paul, and Kesterman, Frank, *Management of Seaport*, National Maritime Research Center, Kings Point, 1972.

Science and Environment, Panel Reports of the Commission on Marine Science, Engineering and Resources, Vol. I, U.S. Government Printing Office, Washington, Feb. 9, 1969.

Scientific American, Cargo Handling, Oct. 1, 1968.

Soros Associates, Inc., *Feasibility of a North Atlantic Deep-Water Oil Terminal*, prepared for Department of Commerce, Washington, July 1972.

Soros Associates, Inc., *Offshore Terminal Systems Concepts, Executive Summary*, prepared for Department of Commerce (MarAd), Sept. 1972.

Soros Associates, Inc., *Offshore Terminal System Concepts, Part I, Evaluation of Requirements and Capabilities for Determination of the Needs of Offshore Terminals*, prepared for Department of Commerce (MarAd), Sept. 1972.

Soros Associates, Inc., *Offshore Terminal System Concepts, Part II, Connections Between Deep-Draft Terminals and Existing Facilities by Utilization of Feeder Vessels, Pipelines and/or Shore Facilities Relocation*, prepared for Department of Commerce (MarAd), Sept. 1972.

Soros Associates, Inc., *Offshore Terminal System Concepts, Part III, Formulation of Advanced Concepts for Offshore Terminals*, prepared for Department of Commerce (MarAd), Sept. 1972.

Surveyor, American Bureau of Shipping, New York, Nov. 1971.

Surveyor, American Bureau of Shipping, New York, Nov. 1972.

Port and Harbor Development System, Texas A&M University, Architecture Research Center, College Station, Aug. 1971.

Port and Harbor Development System-Phase 2, Planning Summary, Texas A&M University, Architecture Research Center, College Station, Oct. 1972.

Deepwater Terminals for Texas: An Overview and a Plan, Texas A&M University, Industrial Economics Research Division, College Station, March 1973.

Economic Development Study of the Texas Coastal Zone, Texas A&M University, Industrial Economics Research Division, prepared for Interagency Council on Natural Resources and the Environment, State of Texas, June 1972.

The Aerospace Corporation, *Port System Study for the Public Ports of Washington State and Portland, Oregon,* prepared for the Washington Public Ports Association, the Port of Portland, and the U.S. Maritime Administration, Seattle, March 1975.

The American Association of Port Authorities, Ship Channels and Harbors Committee, *Merchant Vessel Size in United States Offshore Trades by the Year 2000,* Washington, June 1969.

The American Association of Port Authorities, Ship Channels and Harbors Committee, *National Channel Capability Study Through the Year 2000,* Washington, Sept. 1970.

The Boeing Commercial Airplane Company, Cargo and Analysis and Development Unit, *U.S.-Europe Econometric Forecasts of Trade and Air Freight to 1980,* June 1973.

The West Coast Ports of North America, A lecture given by Commissioner Frank R. Kitchell, Sister Port Seminar, Kobe, Japan, June 1972.

United Nations, *Port Statistics,* United National Conference on Trade and Development, Geneva, 1971.

U.S. Bureau of Census, *Domestic and International Transportation of U.S. Foreign Trade: 1970*, U.S. Government Printing Office, Washington, 1972.

U.S. Congress. House. *Deepwater Ports*, joint hearings before the subcommittee on Water Resources and the subcommittee on Energy of the Committee on Public Works, 93rd Cong., 1st sess., U.S. Government Printing Office, Washington, 1973.

U.S. Congress. Senate. *Deepwater Port Act of 1973*, Part I, Part 2, Appendix, joint hearings before the special joint subcommittee on Deepwater Ports Legislation of the Committee on Commerce, Interior and Insular Affairs, and Public Works, 93rd Cong., 1st sess., U.S. Government Printing Office, Washington, 1974.

U.S. Congress. Senate. *Deep Water Port Issues*, hearings before the Committee on Interior and Insular Affairs, 92nd Cong., 2nd sess., U.S. Government Printing Office, Washington, 1972.

U.S. Congress. Senate. *Energy Transportation Security Act of 1974*, report of the Committee on Commerce, 93rd Cong., 2nd sess., U.S. Government Printing Office, Washington, 1974.

U.S. Congress. Senate. *Seminars on the Container Revolution*, prepared for the use of the Committee on Commerce by the Federal Maritime Commission, 90th Cong., 2nd sess., U.S. Government Printing Office, Washington, 1968.

U.S. Department of Army, Corps of Engineers, *Conceptual Plan for Harbor and Port Development Studies*, National Council for Marine Resources and Engineering Development, Washington, April 1968.

U.S. Department of Army, Corps of Engineers, *Gulf Coast Deep Water Port Facilities Texas, Louisiana, Mississippi, Alabama, and Florida*, Vols. 1-13, Lower Mississippi Valley Division, Vicksburg, June 1973.

U.S. Department of Army, Corps of Engineers, *Interim Report Atlantic Coast Deep Water Port Facilities Study*, Philadelphia District, North Atlantic Division, June 1973.

U.S. Department of Army, Corps of Engineers, *San Francisco Bay Area In-Depth Study*, San Francisco, March 1969.

U.S. Department of Army, Corps of Engineers, *San Francisco Bay Area In-Depth Study*, San Francisco, March 1971.

U.S. Department of Army, Corps of Engineers, *Water Spectrum*, Washington, 1971.

U.S. Department of Army, Corps of Engineers, *West Coast Deepwater Port Facilities Study*, Vols. 1-8, North and South Pacific Divisions, June 1973.

U.S. Department of Commerce, Maritime Administration, *Containerized Cargo on Selected Trade Routes, Calendar Year 1970*, U.S. Government Printing Office, Washington.

U.S. Department of Commerce, Maritime Administration, *Manual of Traffic Studies for Marine Container Terminals*, U.S. Government Printing Office, Washington, Oct. 1974.

U.S. Department of Commerce, Maritime Administration, *Mammoth Tankers, Deepwater Ports and the Environment Forum*, (Transcript of Proceedings), New York, May 18, 1972.

U.S. Department of Commerce, Maritime Administration, *North American Port Development Expenditure Survey*, U.S. Government Printing Office, Washington, March 1974.

U.S. Department of Commerce, Maritime Administration, *Public Port Financing in the United States*, Washington, June 1974.

U.S. Department of Commerce, Maritime Administration, *Port Information Sources*, Washington, Sept. 1972.

U.S. Department of Commerce, Maritime Administration, *Relationship of Land Transportation Economics to Great Lakes Traffic Volume*, Executive Summary, Washington, Oct. 1971.

U.S. Department of Commerce, Maritime Administration, *The Economics of Deepwater Terminals*, U.S. Government Printing Office, Washington.

U.S. Department of Commerce, Maritime Administration, *U.S. Ports' Foreign Trade: 1973*, Washington, July 1974.

U.S. Department of Commerce, National Bureau of Standards, *Systems Analysis of Inland Consolidation Centers for the U.S. Maritime Administration,* Washington, 1969.

Water Resources Council, "Water and Related Resources," *Federal Register,* Vol. 38, No. 174, Part III, Sept. 10, 1973.

Waugh, Richard G., Jr., *Problems Inherent in Ship Characteristics as They Affect Harbor Design,* paper presented at Northeast Regional Meeting of Society of Naval Architects and Marine Engineers, Baltimore, Oct. 21, 1971.

Wise, Harold F., et. al., *A Guide for Federal Approval of State Coastal Zone Management Programs* (working paper), prepared for Office of Coastal Environment, National Oceanic and Atmospheric Administration, U.S. Department of Commerce, Nov. 30, 1973.

SECURITY CLASSIFICATION OF THIS PAGE *(When Data Entered)*

REPORT DOCUMENTATION PAGE	READ INSTRUCTIONS BEFORE COMPLETING FORM	
1. REPORT NUMBER	2. GOVT ACCESSION NO.	3. RECIPIENT'S CATALOG NUMBER
4. TITLE *(and Subtitle)* PORT DEVELOPMENT IN THE UNITED STATES	5. TYPE OF REPORT & PERIOD COVERED Final	
	6. PERFORMING ORG. REPORT NUMBER	
7. AUTHOR*(s)* PANEL ON FUTURE PORT REQUIREMENTS IN THE UNITED STATES. Eric Schenker, Chairman Leonard Bassil, Project Manager	8. CONTRACT OR GRANT NUMBER*(s)* ONR N00014-75-C-0711	
9. PERFORMING ORGANIZATION NAME AND ADDRESS Maritime Transportation Research Board, National Academy of Sciences/National Research Council 2101 Constitution Ave., N.W., Wash., D.C. 20418	10. PROGRAM ELEMENT, PROJECT, TASK AREA & WORK UNIT NUMBERS NA	
11. CONTROLLING OFFICE NAME AND ADDRESS Office of Naval Research	12. REPORT DATE January 1976	
	13. NUMBER OF PAGES	
14. MONITORING AGENCY NAME & ADDRESS*(if different from Controlling Office)* NA	15. SECURITY CLASS. *(of this report)* Unclassified	
	15a. DECLASSIFICATION/DOWNGRADING SCHEDULE	

16. DISTRIBUTION STATEMENT *(of this Report)*

17. DISTRIBUTION STATEMENT *(of the abstract entered in Block 20, if different from Report)*

NA

18. SUPPLEMENTARY NOTES

Financial support provided by the Departments of Defense, Commerce, and Transportation.

19. KEY WORDS *(Continue on reverse side if necessary and identify by block number)*

Port, Port Planning, Port Finance, Port Operation, Coastal Zone, Coastal Environment, Harbors, Marine Terminal, Maritime Transportation, Load Center, Containerization, Longshore Labor, Port Policy, Port Development.

20. ABSTRACT *(Continue on reverse side if necessary and identify by block number)*

The problems and issues of national concern facing ports are examined in terms of the implications of technological change and public policies affecting port planning, development, and operation. Major areas of concern are classified in four categories: a) decision-making on federal, regional, state, and local levels; b) measures of national, regional, and local requirements; c) institutional constraints; and d) shoreline usage.

———————————————— over

DD FORM 1473 EDITION OF 1 NOV 65 IS OBSOLETE
1 JAN 73
S/N 0102-014-6601

Unclassified
SECURITY CLASSIFICATION OF THIS PAGE *(When Data Entered)*

20. Cont'd.

The ability of ports adapting to containerization, the need
to balance economic and environmental concerns, and the sale of
labor and management in port operations are discussed. The
report concludes with a recommendation and guidelines for a
federal aid to ports program, as well as recommendations relating
to port finance, development and planning, rates and regulations,
and environmental concerns.